Pioneer Doctors
of Coos County Oregon

OTHER TITLES BY WILLIAM A. "BILL" LANSING

The Mills That Built Coos Bay and The Men Who Made It Happen (2020)

Gone Fishin' Volume 2: It Takes a Watershed to Make a River (2018)

Gone Fishin' Volume 1: It Takes a River to Make a Fish (2018)

Horses, Chickens and Baseball, Memories Growing Up
(2009; reprinted 2018)

*Camps and Calluses: The Civilian Conservation Corps in
Southwestern Oregon (2014)*

Southwestern Oregon Community College (2011)

*Honoring Our Past, Lighting the Future: 1961–2011
Southwestern Oregon Community College (2011)*

*The Lansing Family Journey: A 360-year Genealogy of
the Lansing Family in America* (2009)

Remember When: Coos County, Oregon Schools 1850–1940 (2008)

*Can't You Hear the Whistle Blowin': Logs, Lignite and Locomotives in
Coos County, Oregon* (2007)

*Seeing the Forest for the Trees: Menasha Corporation and
Its 100-year History in Coos County* (2005)

Pioneer Doctors
of Coos County Oregon

William A. Lansing

Bridge View Publishing ✣ North Bend, Oregon

ISBN: 978-1-7348046-1-4

First Printing – September 2020

Content Editor: Karalynn Ott
Copyeditor: Jami Carpenter @ theredpengirl.com
Proofreader: Blair Holman
Cover and book design: Sue Campbell Book Design

Bridgeview Publishing, LLC
North Bend, Oregon

BillLansing.com

CONTENTS

PREFACE

I undertook research into the *Pioneer Doctors of Coos County* in order to capture the history of the trained medical doctors (and other "doctors"— since some never had a medical degree!) who found their way to Coos County in the early years of the area's development. A few came to settle for the long term, making a career out of serving the communities of our county and retiring after decades of practicing medical science; while others came and then, for numerous reasons, left the region after a few short years.

This book brings into focus those who stayed longer, with only passing references to those doctors who did not. To qualify as one of my "pioneer doctors," I set an arbitrary number of ten years minimum that each stayed in the county. It wasn't a hard and fast rule, however: some doctors stayed a shorter time, but were actively involved in the development of the area, so they were included. Others who did not make the main cut are mentioned in the Appendix.

It became quite a puzzle as to how to piece together the relevant facts from different sources about these early pioneer doctors. It wasn't easy, and I know that many holes remain. Even some of the best sources didn't always include the basics, like dates. Thus, many of the photos I include remain without an identifying date, and readers may occasionally see a question mark or a blank where a relevant date would typically be.

My main sources of information were local newspapers and medical journals that often carried brief articles about and ads for local physicians. (Doctors and lawyers advertised in local newspapers as early as the 1870s, but stopped about 1915. Dentists, however, continued to advertise their services up to 1920s.) How I wished they were alive today so that their real stories could be captured with in-person interviews. I'm sure they had many interesting tales to tell!

Hoping I could uncover some interesting tidbits about medicine in the old days, I interviewed a few of the "old-time doctors" (though they're "too young" to qualify as a pioneer doctor in the book) who still lived in our area. The stories about how they got into medicine or came to Coos County were interesting—but still, they knew little about the "pioneer doctors" as I defined them. And so, I did my best to stitch together an informative and interesting account of our pioneer docs with the sources I had.

One of the earliest references to the history of the Coos Bay area was written by S. S. Mann in 1879 and published by The Coast Mail Book and Job Printing Office in Marshfield. It contained personal sketches, accounts of eccentric characters and historical reminiscences of the people who first came to Coos Bay. The book contained nearly forty pages, and through the courtesy of its owner, Jack Flanagan, the *Coos Bay Times* published it as a serial. One of the men referenced was Dr. Abram N. Foley. We'll learn more about him a little later.[1,2]

As the book unfolded, it became apparent that the early physicians did not operate in a vacuum. Many started their careers as drug store owners and dispensers of patent drugs—a host of colorful remedies popular in the eighteenth and nineteenth centuries, with claims to cure many ailments—typically without regard to their effectiveness. Some doctors started small hospitals associated with their clinics, and some clinics evolved into stand-alone hospitals to serve their communities. Medical schools were created in the Western U.S. to better train the students of medicine; Oregon had two, and their histories are interesting and intertwined. Then there was the evolution of requirements for licensing physicians in the state. Oregon was slow to institute specific requirements for medical practitioners—and as a result, numerous charlatans and quacks migrated to the state before licensing was put in place. All these topics are included in support of the heart of the book: the personal facts and stories about the early physicians that served the people of Coos County, Oregon.

The book begins, however, with an overview of how early "doctors" migrated along with Oregon's homestead pioneers as they headed west from the East and Midwest, crossing the plains and the western mountain ranges. Some homesteaders came seeking gold in the upper reaches of the Rogue, the Sixes and the South Umpqua Rivers, while others came to the area for personal health reasons. Whatever their reasoning, many stayed and called Coos County their home. And no doubt, without the pioneering doctors alongside to tend to and mend them, many homesteaders might not have finished the journey, or lived long and prosperous enough lives to establish the county's communities.

INTRODUCTION

In the late nineteenth and early twentieth century, medicine in the settlements of the Pacific Northwest was in short supply, and treatment was often carried out far from a doctor's office. Under such medically bereft conditions, it typically fell to the women of rural households to serve as the everyday "doctors." They used simple remedies. Bleeding from a cut was checked with cobwebs, a treatment possibly learned from the local Native Americans. The women also often used a poultice made of wheat flour, when available, and salt. Whiskey was the universal medicine, used for everything from snake bites to rheumatism. For the latter condition, caretakers would soak sunflower seeds in whiskey for twelve hours, then feed them to their "patients." Onion syrup was the remedy for children with colds, and a poultice of salt pork chopped up with onions was applied to the child's neck.[3]

Settlers living on isolated farms, ranches, and in mining or logging camps regularly undertook long and sometimes arduous journeys in order to obtain medical treatment—or even simply to inform the "local" doctor of a medical condition back at their home or camp. A minor injury or a common complaint could quickly become an emergency, or even result in death, solely due to the lack of proximity to medical help.

If a settlement was lucky enough to have a doctor living within a day's journey, settlers often expected the doctor to come to them. (Nonetheless, as mentioned, someone still had to be sent to notify the doctor that help was needed—adding to the time frame to get help!) The doctors themselves then traveled long distances to attend to their patients, making their trips by any means necessary—be it on foot, on horseback, in wagons, buggies, ferries, canoes, and boats. Traveling might be a journey on nothing more than an unmarked trail in order to get to the ailing patient. Physicians would travel ridge trails like these by horse, and when an impediment such as a river needed to be crossed, the doctor would row a local farmer's boat across the water while his horse swam the current. The doctor's bag was designed to carry the tools of the trade and withstand travel in all sorts of weather. Unsurprisingly, these bags were made of durable oiled canvas or leather, and stood up to extended travel, whatever the season and terrain.

Rural doctors were general practitioners by necessity. The family doctor was well known in the community and was often considered the most valuable asset in the area. They delivered babies, set broken limbs, pulled teeth, and tended to all sorts of wounds and diseases. They were often called upon to deliver treatment to the farm animals too! They sat with dying patients during their last few hours or days to give comfort and care. They often created their own medications, as well as many of the instruments they used. They saw people into and out of this world, and in the meantime tried to keep them alive and healthy.

Rural settlers, however, often had nothing to offer as payment for medical services except the fruits of their labor. Thus doctors were commonly paid with items such as a cord of wood, produce, meat, eggs, potatoes, blankets, or many other items of value.

The doctor was also often considered a family friend, and he might know more than anyone about any given person or family in the region. When a town's doctor passed away, it was cause for great mourning.[4]

The following excerpt from the *Coos Bay Times*, March 5, 1909, details the hardship of the pioneer doctor's life.

DOCTOR'S LIFE SPAN [1909][5]
DISEASES TO WHICH THEY
ARE ESPECIALLY LIABLE

Doctors as a class are more subject to illness than their fellow-men, and their expectancy of life is less than that of most. An explanation of this, says the British Medical Journal, *is readily found in the anxieties caused by responsibilities which must weigh heavily on every man of right feeling; in the amount and trying nature of the work, the doctor has to do; in irregularity of meals and broken sleep; in exposure to weather and to infection and last, but not least, in the scanty remuneration which his labor too often brings him.*

The combined influence of all these causes is sufficient to undermine the strongest constitutions long before a man has reached the limit of threescore and ten. A comparison of tables compiled by statisticians in different countries gives doctors an average of fifty-seven years at death.

Doctors as a class are especially liable to certain diseases. Setting aside afflictions due to exposure and infection, the practice of medicine levies a disproportionate tribute from its professors in the form of diseases of the cardio-vascular and nervous system. Angina Pectoris has been called the doctor's disease; neurasthenia deserves to be ranked in the same category, and severer forms of neurosis are, as might be expected, common among men whose profession compels them to live at the highest tension both of brain and nerve force.

It is scarcely to be wondered at, therefore, that the narcotic habit is so common among doctors. After all, what shortens the doctor's life is overwork, mental and bodily strain manifesting itself at the point of least resistance.

Some of the early challenges faced by Oregon's pioneers were diseases such as diphtheria and typhoid fever. In the winter of 1889, an epidemic of influenza was rampant in our region; as was the case of the Spanish Flu that wracked the nation in 1918. Pneumonia and smallpox were always present, especially in children, and the drugs prescribed were very primitive. To combat these contagious diseases, city and county doctors were given the authority to quarantine houses where the disease was present. The local district attorney was given the task of policing the quarantine.

Few pioneer doctors in the Coos Bay area had formal training in the academic sense. Some had studied medicine under older doctors in the east; others even journeyed across the Atlantic from Europe, where they had studied under older established physicians, travelling around Cape Horn (or walking across the Isthmus of Panama and boarding a sailing schooner heading north), and landing in San Francisco. From there they caught sailing ships destined for Coos Bay. Some were simply druggists with a background in herbal medicines who claimed to be certified physicians, as, in the early days, no registration or license was needed to make such a claim.

During the 1860–1880s, unscrupulous people posing as physicians often took advantage of the settlers. Some would, for example, make frequent trips to a patient's home in one day, and prescribe drugs that were made in the pharmacy owned by the prescribing doctor. Each of these visits ran up the cost of medicine to the growing population. In 1874, the Oregon State Medical Society was founded in an effort to organize the better trained doctors of the state—to protect themselves and the often-ignorant public from the unprincipled. We'll learn more about them as the book unfolds.[3]

As mentioned, the universal pain reliever was whiskey, often administered in copious quantities. In 1842 a Georgia physician named Crawford Williamson Long became the first doctor to use ether as a general anesthetic during surgery. Then in 1846, ether was used by William Thomas Green Morton, a dentist in Boston. It was thought to be the first time ether was used as an anesthetic by a dentist. Dr. Morton was able to extract a tooth from a patient without pain. The word "anesthesia" was coined by Dr. Oliver Wendell Holmes following Morton's experiment after the Greek word "anaisthesis" meaning insensibility or loss of sensation. By the time of the American Civil War, though, most surgeons preferred to use chloroform over ether, as it was faster acting and far less explosive.[6]

Some General Background on Coos County's Early Settlements and Doctors

In the spring of 1853, nineteen men from the upper Rogue Valley at Jacksonville, Oregon, organized the Coos Bay Commercial Company to explore, settle, and develop the Coos Bay region, to "civilize" the Native American population, and to bring attention to the potential of the area for expansion. They founded Empire City on the west arm of the bay as the city of their vision. William H. Harris and Perry B. Marple were their leaders. Included with Harris and Marple were three medical practitioners: Dr. Foster, Dr. Shields, and Dr. Overbeck. The first three families, including that of Dr. Andrew B. Overbeck (1820–1872), arrived in October 1853 to find a town consisting of a few log cabins and a hotel built of logs. Dr. Overbeck came from Jacksonville, lured to the coast by the romance of helping to build a new town, but he later returned to Jacksonville.[7,8]

With the discovery of gold on the beaches north of the Coquille River and near the town of Randolph, Doctors V. M. Coffin and J. H. Foster came west and settled in Empire City. Another name prominent in the area was Dr. Abram N. Foley, who took out a Donation Land Claim at Empire. Regarding Foley's medical qualifications, the following account is of interest:

> Doctor Foley was probably never blessed with a diploma. He could manage to read slowly and laboriously, had a habit of talking in broad Pike county [Missouri] dialect with his expressive 'thar' and 'whar.' He had a few medical books and would often say to an anxious patient, 'you can see for yourself' [pointing at some relevant page in his books]. He thought he had made an entirely new discovery in medical science, a bitter, turnip-like root found around Coos Bay, which he called 'old-man-in-the-ground' was deemed by him to be a universal panacea, which he kept constantly on hand for all diseases. He had a wise venerable look and was elected to some responsible offices.[2,3]

The Coquille valley was colonized in 1859 by a party of Germans led by Dr. Henry E. Hermann (1810–1869), who had set out from Baltimore, Maryland—and hence the group settlement became known as the "Baltimore Colony." Dr. Hermann was educated in Germany and graduated from the University of Marburg. Upon landing in Baltimore, Dr. Hermann built up a large medical practice in the city. He was not a well man, however, and as his health began to fail, he travelled west to the Coquille River valley seeking a less hectic life style. So taken was he with the region that he traveled back to Baltimore, formed a group, and made the trip back to the Coquille. We will learn more about Dr. Hermann later in the book.[3]

Dr. Coffin was also an early settler at Empire City, arriving when gold was first discovered in the upper reaches of nearby rivers. Other early arrivals in Empire were Dr. Thomas McKay and Dr. J. G. Cook. Dr. McKay had studied medicine at the University of Virginia as well as in Philadelphia, receiving his medical degree in 1864. Following a stint in a Confederate hospital during the Civil War, Dr. McKay came west and settled in Marshfield in 1875. At one point, he was in charge of the U.S. Maritime Hospital located in that town. Dr. Cook came to Empire around 1874 and practiced medicine in the area until his death on November 11, 1904.[7,9,10]

Throughout Coos County's early history, other doctors arrived in the area. Dr. Evans, a graduate of the Cooper Medical College of San Francisco (1858–1959, aka Stanford in 1908) arrived in Coos Bay in 1891, and Dr. J. Burt Moore from the University of Pennsylvania Medical School had a brief practice in the area in the same year. Other physicians who settled in the town of Coquille City were Drs. Sponagle, Vance, and Stockman. The latter visited patients by riding about in a two-wheeled horse-drawn cart, the wheels of which were made by him, hand-hewn out of a large solid Douglas fir log.

The first physician to arrive in Bandon, Oregon, was Dr. J. M. Starr in 1883. A few years later, Dr. James H. Kime opened a practice in Bandon after graduating from the University of Oregon Medical School in Portland in 1890; he then moved on to California in 1897. However, while Dr. Kime was in Bandon, his son, Dr. Albert W. Kime, studied medicine under his father's watchful eye and entered the University of Oregon Medical School in Portland; he graduated in 1897 and opened a practice in Cottage Grove, Oregon, a small community in the Willamette Valley.[3]

Dr. D. M. Brower practiced in Myrtle Point, Oregon, from 1889–1898 before moving to Ashland, Oregon. Brower reported one case that demonstrated the ingenuity that these early pioneer doctors had to create:

... The case involved a man who had severely broken three ribs and lived in a remote part of Dr. Brower's territory. There was no adhesive tape in his surgical kit. It was the middle of the night, with snow falling in the mountains, so no one could get to Myrtle Point for the needed supplies. After trying pine pitch as a substitute without success, the doctor asked if there was any black wax in the house. There were three balls upstairs. These were melted and spread on three strips of cloth with holes. The cloth was cut to the proper length and width and when the wax cooled enough to be applied, the improvised tape brought immediate relief. Three weeks later, the patient rode to town on horseback, the plasters were removed and the ribs were pronounced sound ...[3]

The point is, there were many early doctors and dentists who came to Coos County, Oregon—and they did so for a variety of reasons. Some simply were seeking adventure after completing their medical training. Some simply *said* they were "doctors" and yet after practicing their art, they often provided the small communities in our area with at least some degree of medical assistance. Many started as druggists making their own patented medicines behind the counter for one customer while preparing to set a fractured arm for another. Others—in particular the Keizer family—produced several physicians over generations, and they helped our area grow.

Oregon was slow to license doctors and consequently became somewhat of a haven for hucksters peddling their drugs as a cure-all for everything. Advertising bogus cures was unregulated until President Theodore Roosevelt and the U.S. Congress intervened and passed food and drug laws that improved the safety of consumables—and put a stop to false advertising.

The first medical school west of St. Louis was started in San Francisco in 1858, where a few of the early Coos County physicians received their training. Eight years after the Cooper College in San Francisco began, Oregon had its own medical college, in 1867 on the Willamette University campus in Salem. It was called the Willamette Medical College. The school bounced back and forth between the Salem campus and a rudimentary campus in Portland, Oregon—in an old grocery store.

For the next twenty-odd years, the Willamette College had difficulty producing adequately trained doctors, so in 1887, a group of established physicians in Portland started their own medical school connected with the Good Samaritan Hospital. It was called the Oregon Medical School and was associated with the University of Oregon in Eugene. Many of our Coos County doctors received their medical training from one or the other of these two schools.

As the two medical colleges vied for students and funding, the quality of physicians produced drew extensive criticism from the American Medical Association, as they found performance by the graduates lacking. Something had to be done, and in 1913, the two medical schools in Oregon merged. We now take great pride in noting the terrific quality of medical care provided by the Oregon Health and Science University atop Marquam Hill in Portland. While its birth can be connected to sixteen physicians from both early schools, the property where OHSU was built came from a donation from the Oregon Railway and Navigation Company, who had designs to build a rail line around the hill. The property on Marquam Hill continued to grow when C. S. Jackson, publisher of the *Oregon Journal* donated 88 acres adjacent to the railroad grant.

Many of the early doctors who ventured into Coos County took on other activities in the communities. Some were county coroners, some became city councilors, while others were successfully elected mayor of their towns. They were all challenged to provide medical care to the families living outside the towns. One record even documented a doctor who ended up swimming across Isthmus Slough to reach a mother giving birth to her first child!

As I researched the material for this book, I came away with a sense of admiration for how these pioneer doctors helped build what we now call home. My thanks to them for making it possible.

Above ad from the *Coast Mail*, January 17, 1880.
In 1880, Dr. C. B. Golden (1812–1889) settled in
Marshfield, where he practiced medicine and operated
a drug store until his death in 1889. He received his
medical training at the Medical College of Cincinnati,
graduating in 1868. Golden Falls, located 20 miles
northeast of Coos Bay, was named after Dr. C. B.
Golden, first Grand Chancellor of the Knights of Pythias
of Oregon, and one of the first visitors to the falls.

Ads from *Coquille City Herald:*
(Dr. Steele): September 1, 1885;
(Dr. Cook) January 2, 1890
(Dr. Brower) November 12, 1889;
(Dr. Wheeler) November 20 1894;

PART I

Early Medical Schools, Training and Tools

MEDICAL SCHOOLS IN OREGON

Before we delve into the main body of the book—the personal stories and histories of Coos County's pioneer doctors—it seemed to make sense that we learn a bit about how medical training in Oregon first came to be.

Early Medical Treatment, Training and Schools Elsewhere

Of course, trained medics in Oregon followed their initial arrival and establishment on the East Coast. The first doctor to set foot in the American colonies came ashore in 1610 for the London Company in Virginia. The first physician in New England, Dr. Samuel Fuller, arrived soon thereafter—in 1620 on the Mayflower. These and other early medical practitioners had received their medical training in Europe. Early efforts to train new doctors in the colonies essentially involved apprenticeships of two to five years under the tutelage of a resident doctor. These students attended patients with the doctor and learned by watching until they were ready to launch out on their own.

The first official medical school in America was started in Philadelphia in 1765. As the westward migration began in earnest after the Treaty of Paris (which ended the American Revolutionary War) in 1783, the medical profession crept along with the pioneers as they crossed the plains.

The Willamette Medical Department/Waller Hall. Photo courtesy of Willamette University.

While physicians of all sorts and persuasions have existed for eons, major turning points in the practice of medicine seemed to happen as the result of treating the wounded during and after a war, or simply through experimental processes handed down from Native American customs or European practices. One of the first technological advancements was the stethoscope that was used in training medical students in 1829. It was nothing more than a piece of wood with a hole drilled in the center that transferred the sound of a beating heart![11]

However, it wasn't until 1858 that the first medical college was established in the Western United States. It was founded that year in San Francisco by Elias Samuel Cooper, but his death in 1862 threw leadership of the new college into turmoil. Cooper's cousin, Levi Cooper Lane, took over the effort and reinvigorated the new college of medicine. It was called Cooper Medical College. In 1908, Stanford University acquired Cooper College and the medical departments of both universities merged.

Oregon's First Medical School

As noted earlier, the early doctors who headed westward brought along a plethora of remedies to cure the sick. Some worked, while others simply had positive psychological effects—if the patient lived through the procedure. Blood-letting was a very common practice, as were poultices made from plants and animal innards or feces. But it was the travelling practitioners riding through the night by horse, canoe, and on foot who brought comfort to the early settlers in our area.

In 1864, Oregon Governor A. C. Gibbs and a group of physicians from Portland, Oregon, requested that the Board of Trustees at Willamette University in Salem, Oregon, establish a medical department associated with the university. On February 15, 1865, the Board of Regents at the University authorized such a department, and called it the Willamette Medical Department (WMD). It was the third medical school west of St. Louis. A group of physicians from Portland were appointed as professors.

Oregon didn't get its first medical college, however, until 1867—and it had a bumpy road getting started. In addition, Oregon was slow in getting a process in place that licensed medical practitioners—hence it attracted "doctors" from other states who couldn't meet the requirements to get a medical license elsewhere. Charlatans and quacks flowed into Oregon until legitimate physicians got the state's legislature to create the Oregon Licensing Board in 1889.

In the spring of 1867, lecture classes began with twenty-four students enrolled in the Willamette Medical Department at Salem, in what became known as Waller Hall. (The building is still in use today as the administrative department of the university.) No sooner had classes begun, however, than controversies about the curricula erupted between the medical faculty and the Board of Trustees, nearly closing the medical department. In 1878, with the approval of the university, the medical faculty packed up the entire department and moved the school to Portland—where there was a larger population than in Salem, and a greater opportunity for financial support for the institution. Then in 1887, frustrated with the university, the entire staff of the Willamette Medical Department in Portland resigned.

Oregon Medical College

In an attempt to start a new medical school in Portland, some of the disgruntled professors who resigned from the Willamette University Medical Department joined forces with other physicians in the city to form the Oregon Medical College (OMC) affiliated with the University of Oregon in Eugene, Oregon. Articles of incorporation were drawn up by sixteen local physicians and a charter was obtained from the Board of Regents in Eugene.

The petition, signed by physicians from Portland, Oregon, outlined specifics on the school's organizational: deans of eight specific medical departments were named, and those appointed would constitute the professors for the school. The petition called for a two-year program, with each student applicant to pass an examination prior to matriculation. The petition spelled out that the examination for confirming the degree of Doctor of Medicine

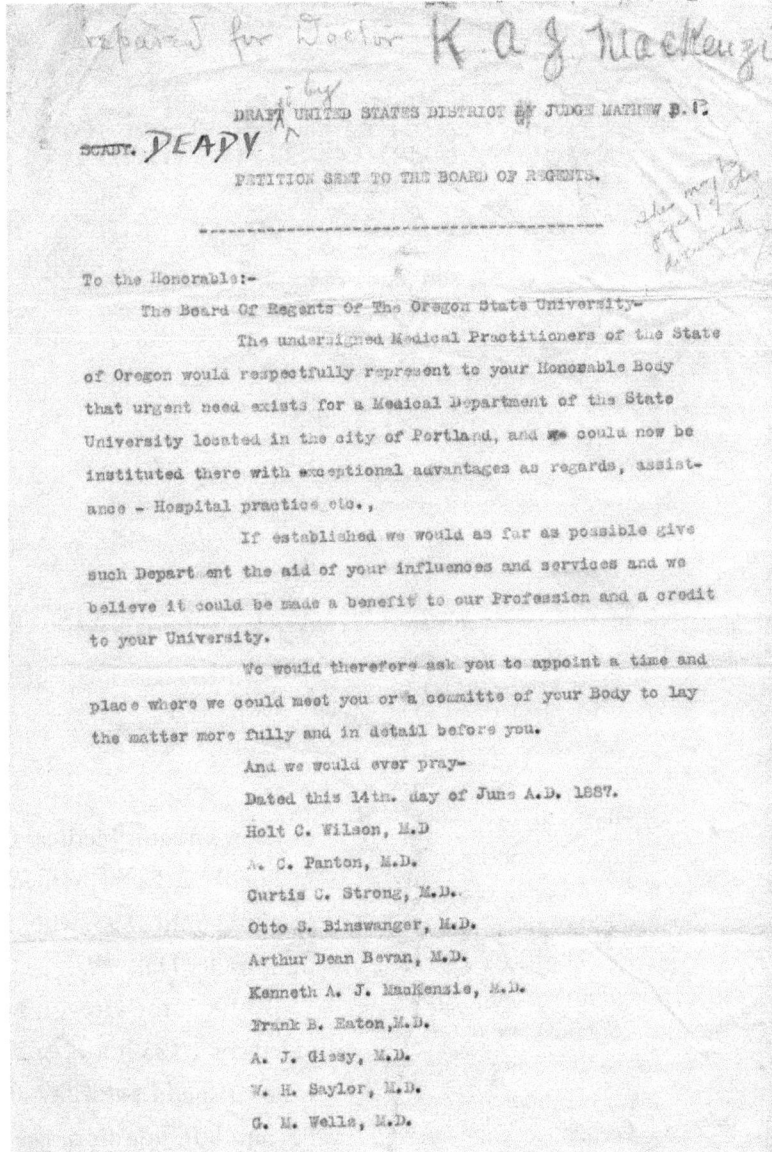

A draft of the petition dated June 14, 1887 to the Board of Regents of the what was then called Oregon State University (aka the University of Oregon—its eventual name), outlining the need for and the establishment of a medical department of the university located in Portland, Oregon. Courtesy of the OHSU (Oregon Health & Science University) archives.

While the above announcement suggests a medical school was associated with Oregon State University in Corvallis, Oregon, I am fairly certain the announcement refers to the University of Oregon Medical School that opened in Portland, Oregon in 1887.

would consist of 100 questions given either in writing, orally, or both. Note the name Kenneth A. J. Mackenzie scribbled in the upper margin. As you will see later, the University named the science building atop Marquam Hill after him.

In October 1887, the new Oregon Medical College, associated with the University of Oregon, opened in a small old two-story grocery building at the edge of a cow pasture on the grounds of Good Samaritan Hospital at the corner of Twenty-third and Marshall Streets in Northwest Portland. The facility consisted of a lecture room on the ground floor, and a dissecting room above. The latter accommodated two or three dissecting tables. Cadavers were hauled up through a trap door in the floor by means of a pulley.

At the time the new medical college opened, the requirements for admission were: "satisfactory evidence of knowledge of the common English branches, including reading, writing, spelling grammar, geography, arithmetic, etc." The requirements for graduation were: "attendance at two full courses of lectures, at least one course of practical anatomy and clinical instruction, and the study of medicine for not less than three years. The candidate [for a degree] must pass examinations."[12]

To avoid conflict with the existing medical school, committees from both institutions agreed that the staff of the new Oregon Medical College would coordinate with the remaining staff of WMD in Portland. Both medical programs stumbled along, providing some semblance of teaching until 1895, when the Willamette Medical Department returned to Salem and into Waller Hall.[13,14]

By 1905, the Oregon Medical College developed a four-year curriculum that provided for 1,185 hours of clinic time for students. The third- and fourth-year students were to spend Saturday afternoons in clinics at the Multnomah County Hospital in Portland. In addition, the third-year class spent some portion of each weekday afternoons and the fourth-year class spent parts of Tuesday, Wednesday and Thursday afternoons in clinics at the Outpatient Department of the medical school.[15]

In the beginning, the Oregon Medical College received $1,000 from its parent university in Eugene for operating funds. The balance of the financial needs came from tuition fees. In 1893, a larger building was constructed to house a growing number of students in this college, but operating funds from Eugene remained dismal. In the 1910 biennium of the Oregon legislature, the University of Oregon Medical College received $10,000 for equipment and $20,000 for maintenance from the general fund, which put the facility on solid financial footing.

As the new medical school continued to grow, it was recognized as a "Class A" medical college at a conference in Chicago in 1910, while the Willamette Medical College was below standard and given a designation of "Class C."[16] The rivalry between the two institutions was reflected in a report written by the president of the Board of Regents of the University of Oregon in Eugene (which was also referred to as the regents of Oregon State University Medical College in Portland). It read, in part:

> *Certainly, if the Willamette University, established by law in Salem, can conduct a school of medicine or anything else at Portland, and grant diplomas to the students therein, the University of Oregon located at Eugene can do the same.*[14]

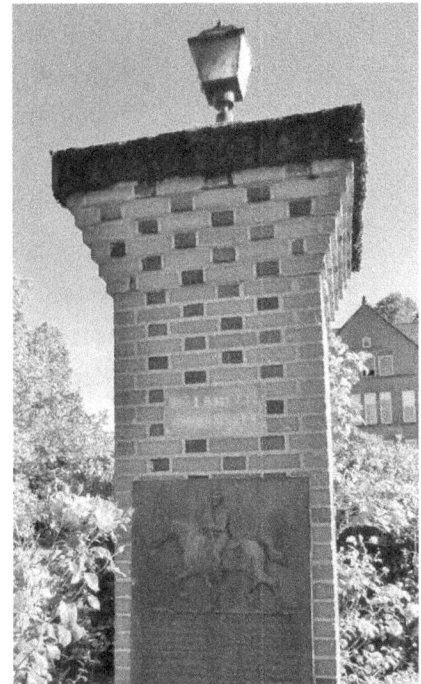

A Merger of the Pioneer Medical Departments

In 1913, the medical departments of the University of Oregon and Willamette University merged to form the University of Oregon Medical School in Portland, dissolving the OMC and WMC. Under the umbrella of the University of Oregon, the newly combined medical schools became the only medical college to offer a full course in medicine north of San Francisco and west of Denver.

Now that Portland had only one medical school, speculation was that the quality of and the financial support of a single medical college would produce higher-quality professionals. The combined medical schools continued to be housed in

The plaque on the Salem campus of Willamette University. The Portland campus of the medical department of Willamette University was permanently closed in the fall of 1895 and a new medical building was erected in 1905 on the Salem campus. In 1967, a plaque was presented to the university by its medical school graduates to commemorate the one hundredth anniversary of the founding of the Willamette University Medical School.

Portland, at the junction of Twenty-third and Lovejoy Streets, until the facility was destroyed by fire on May 29, 1919 as the equipment was being transferred to the new medical facility atop Marquam Hill in Portland.[3,14,15,17-19]

Squabbles with the American Medical Association

As mentioned, during the early period when Oregon had two medical schools, controversy developed between the staff at the universities over the content of the programs, as well as between the American Medical Association (AMA) and the Oregon Board of Medical Examiners.[15] In 1905, Dr. Joseph N. McCormack of the AMA visited Oregon communities where medical practices were evolving and published his findings in the *Journal of the American Medical Association (JAMA)*. It summarized his findings, some of which are captured from his actual journal:

> ... *Their [Oregon] law is weak and is so administered as to give quacks and pretenders no trouble. There was evidence on every hand that the schools of Oregon do not have high standards of requirements, and that their state examinations are such as to make this a dumping ground for low-grade men who fail to pass in neighboring or even distant states. The fees are much lower than in any other state visited on this trip and commercialism ... is more pronounced and widespread. I heard many apparently reputable men say over and over again that they would not think of sending a case to any surgeon who would not divide his fees with them ...*[20]

Obviously, both the faculty at the University of Oregon Medical College, as well as that of Willamette University fired back and threatened to leave the AMA. The article must have touched an already raw

Kenneth A. J. Mackenzie, ca. 1912. Between 1914–1917, Dr. Kenneth J. A. Mackenzie, MD from the medical staff at Willamette University, led an effort to build a new modern medical facility in Portland. He was successful in negotiating a gift of a twenty-acre parcel atop Marquam Hill from the Oregon Railway and Navigation Company. Dr. Mackenzie was also the railroad's staff surgeon. An additional eighty-eight-acre tract of adjacent land was donated by the C. S. Jackson family, the former publisher of the *Daily Oregon Journal*. In 1919, the doors of the University of Oregon Medical School were opened. It was the only medical school north of San Francisco. In 2004, another twenty acres of land along the Willamette Riverfront was donated to OHSU by the Schnitzer Investment Corporation. Photo courtesy of Oregon Health & Science University.

nerve because two years earlier in January 1903, the editor of the Northwest Medicine magazine had written an article along the same themes espoused by Dr. Joseph McCormack. In essence, the article pressed the point about the dismal performance of the licensing tests for graduates of medical schools in Oregon, as well as the fractions within the profession—especially from the physicians within the city of Portland.

In delving into this matter, however, it appears that Dr. McCormack never visited Coos County. As we investigate the history of the pioneer doctors of Coos County, you will see that both the University of Oregon Medical School and the Willamette University Medical School had graduates who ended up in the Coos Bay area.

In 1908, the University of Oregon Medical School changed the requirements for admission to the school as follows:

1. Bachelor's Degree from an approved college or university; or

2. Diploma from an accredited high school, normal school or academy; requiring for admission evidence of completion of an eight-year course in primary and intermediate grades, which listed in its requirements for graduation specified courses in foreign languages, mathematics, English and laboratory sciences; or

3. An examination, plus high school graduation and letters about the applicant's moral character from two reputable physicians.

Above: Marquam Hill in 1920. Photo courtesy of the City of Portland Archives.

Left: University of Oregon Medical School. The Medical Science Building [later known as Mackenzie Hall named after Kenneth A. J. Mackenzie] atop Marquam Hill, ca. 1920s. Photo courtesy of OHSU Digital Commons.

Licensing Physicians in Oregon

Prior to 1888, Oregon had no official medical licensing program for physicians. However, there was a loose-knit organization called the Oregon State Medical Association (OSMA). It was formed in 1874 at the insistence of seventeen physicians, mainly from the Willamette Valley and Portland, who wanted regulations in order to eliminate the numerous hucksters, charlatans, and other non-technically trained people from practicing medicine in Oregon. They wanted to limit the licensing only to those doctors who had graduated from an accredited medical college.

After fifteen years of lobbying by the OSMA, in 1889, the Oregon legislature passed the first official rules establishing a licensing program for physicians and surgeons. The OSMA succeeded in passing a medical regulatory licensing act only after it paid a two-hundred dollar bribe to a legislator (Dr. James V. Pope), who then added an amendment to protect his own medical practice. Among other things, the new law provided licensing to:[21,22]

The official seal of the Oregon Medical Board.

1. Physicians and surgeons who received a diploma from a medical institution in good standing. (It didn't detail whether this meant only in the U.S., or anywhere in the world.) However, the licensing board couldn't discriminate against holders of genuine licenses or diplomas from a licensed medical school or "system" *not* in good standing. At the time, there were what was known as "diploma mills," where diplomas were created for just about any profession as long as the recipient paid the requisite fee. This, then, allowed the licensing of homeopaths or eclectics, etc.); or

2. Anyone, regardless of educational background, by administering a test that evaluated the qualification of the potential practitioner; or

3. Doctors and surgeons already practicing in Oregon at the time the act was passed. They could simply register with the office of the county clerk sixty days after the act's approval and continue their practices; i.e., a "grandfather clause."

In 1895, several amendments were made to the original act; one important addition was the requirement that all applicants had to pass a licensing exam. The revised act also allowed the medical licensing board to revoke a physician's license for unprofessional or dishonorable conduct, including those exempt under the 1889 law. In 1900, the licensing board of three members issued 627 licenses to individuals to practice medicine in the state of Oregon.

The next significant change in licensing doctors came in 1907 when the Oregon legislature extended the licensing board responsibilities to osteopathic medicine, and placed a doctor of osteopathic medicine on the

> Today, the Oregon medical licensing board is composed of nine members, and receives no money from the general state fund. Instead, it's completely self-supporting, with all income generated from licensing, registration, other fees or fines, and data requests. In 2019, the medical licensing board issued 1,753 new licenses in Oregon. That included: medical doctors–1,191; doctors of osteopathic medicine–194; doctors of podiatric medicine–13; physician assistants–260; and acupuncturists–95.[24]

licensing board. (*Author's note: Osteopathic medicine is a distinctive form of medical care founded in America in 1874 by Dr. Andrew Still, MD. It's based on the philosophy that all body systems are interrelated and dependent upon one another for good health. It typically combines conventional treatments with physical manipulation of muscle tissue and bones.*)

In 1908, twenty-three graduates of the two Oregon medical schools took the test for licensing—but only three passed. Something needed to be done. Was it the school's fault, or were the tests for licensing by the state too rigid? Probably a little of each.[15,23]

Early Medical Tools

Pioneer doctors used some of the same kinds of tools that doctors today use—however many of them back then were much simpler, cruder and/or bulkier—and others were downright dangerous.

From Stethoscopes to X-Rays

René Laennec, the inventor of the wooden stethoscope in 1816 wrote:

> *… I rolled a quire of paper [roughly 25 sheets of paper of the same size] into a kind of cylinder and applied one end of it to the region of the heart and the other to my ear, and was not a little surprised to find that I could thereby perceive the action of the heart in a manner much more clear and distinct than I had ever been able to do by the immediate application of my ear …* [25]

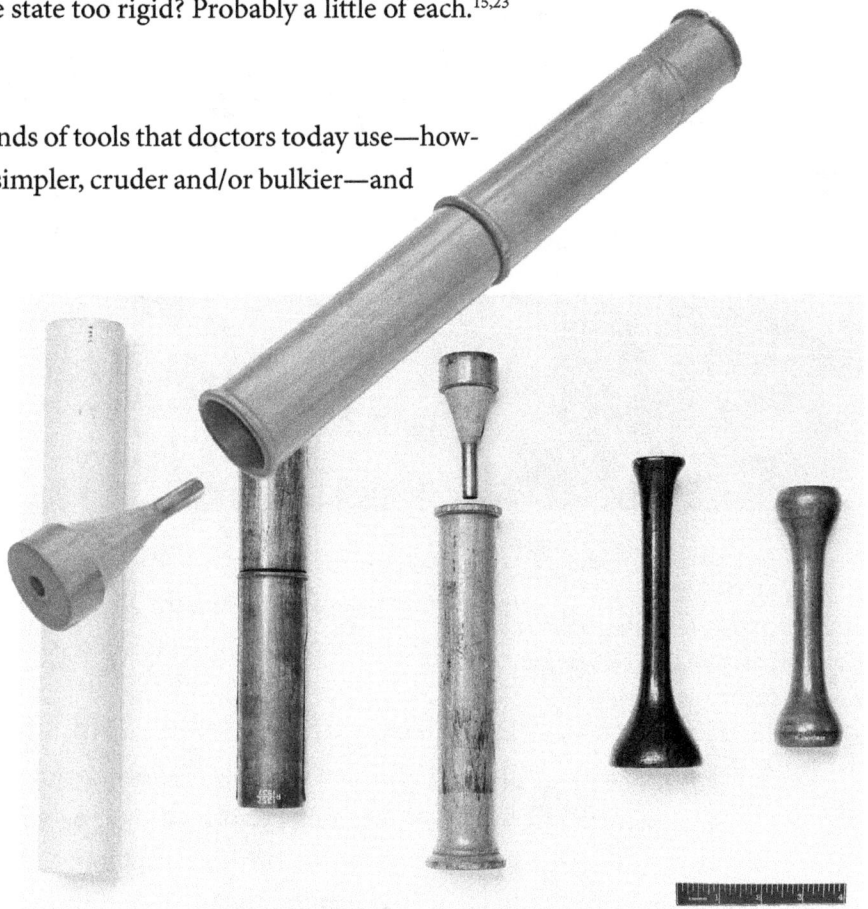

In addition, it was considered taboo for men to place their ear directly over the chest of a female patient. This new instrument eliminated that issue.

Above, right: Early wooden stethoscopes.
Photos courtesy of the Wellcome Collection online museum of health (wellcomecollection.org).
Right: The binaural (used with both ears) stethoscope, ca. 1915. It was designed with a headrest. Photo courtesy of the Science Museum, London.

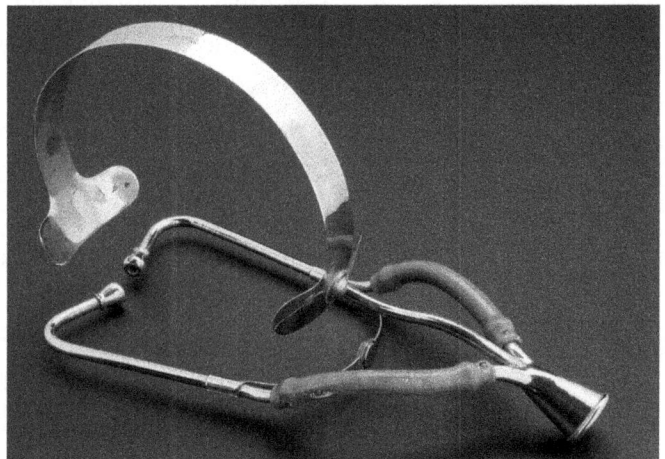

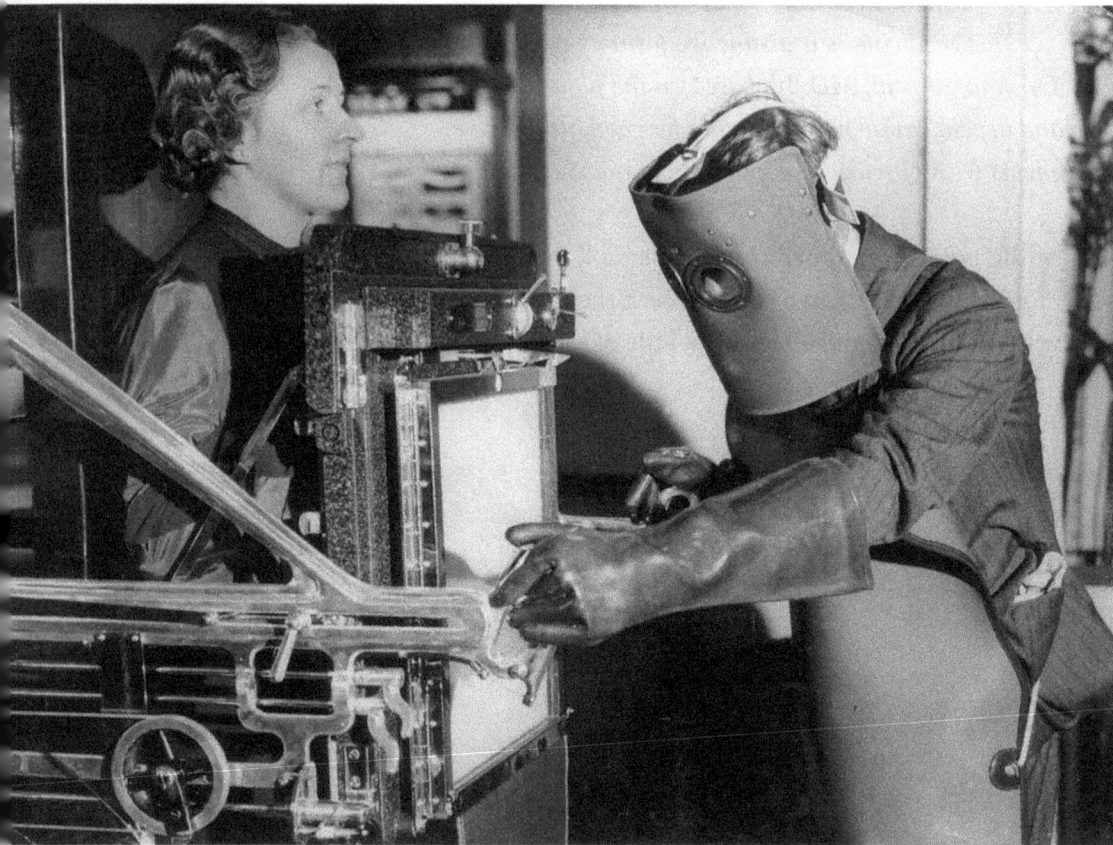

An example of a radiologist taking an X-ray picture of a woman in 1934. Note the bulky gear the radiologist was wearing to protect him from the harmful radiation. Photo courtesy of the Smithsonian.

From a historical perspective, the X-ray machine was discovered accidentally in 1895 by Professor Wilhelm Roentgen of Bavaria, who was experimenting with electrical rays. As he continued to experiment with the rays, he noticed his hand getting red; the rays also seemed to be passing through his hand. Within a few weeks, he found that he could capture images of body parts by placing photographic film between the X-ray's cathode and a fluorescent screen. X-ray machines soon became invaluable for use prior to surgery. At first, the ultimate danger of using the X-rays wasn't understood; and unfortunately doctors and nurses who were exposed to successive doses became quite ill.

The History of the Heart Defibrillator [24-26]

The first recorded example of shocks being used to restart a human's heart was in 1947. The procedure was performed by U.S. surgeon Claude S. Beck. The story goes that a fourteen-year-old boy's heart stopped during surgery. Beck had a theory that the human heart had the ability to start again after it had stopped, and he'd been working on a machine capable of delivering shocks to a heart in order to force such a restart. When the boy's heart stopped, Beck ordered that his research shock unit be brought up from the hospital's basement. The first shock failed to do anything, but when Beck tried a second time, the boy's heart started beating again.

It took a while before anyone tried to improve on Beck's crude model (the original model used two tablespoons with wooden handles to deliver the jolt).[26] Following is a rundown of the main milestones in the tool's evolution, which began at the turn of the twentieth century.

- 1899: Physiologists Jean-Louis Prevost and Frédéric Batelli of the University of Geneva discover defibrillation by conducting tests using dogs. They induced fibrillation (rapid irregular contractions of the muscle fibers of the heart, resulting

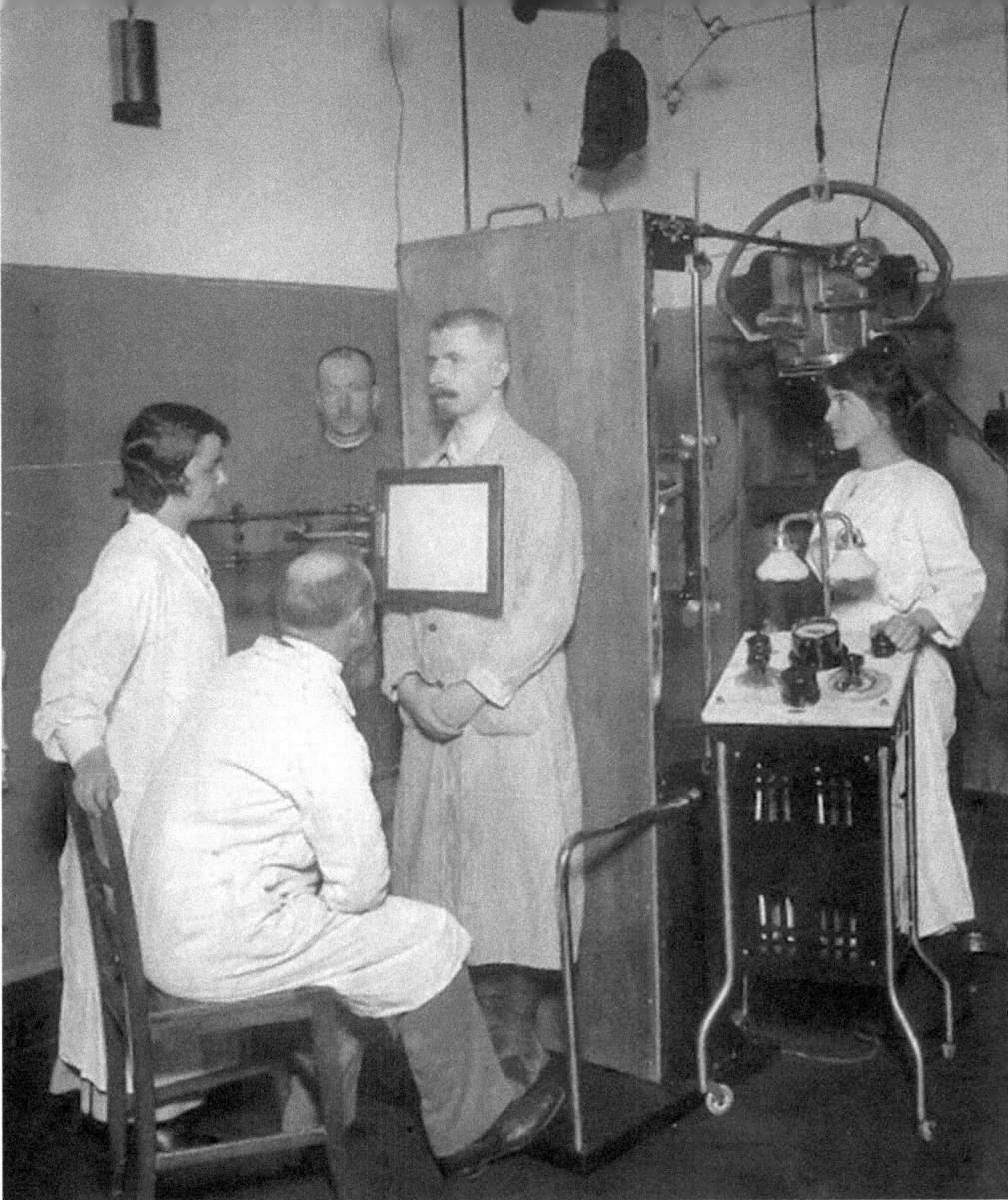

Early radiologists suffered severe injuries from X-rays, resulting for some in the amputation of arms, and even eventual death from cancer. After many medical tragedies, standards of exposure were gradually introduced. Photo courtesy of the Smithsonian.

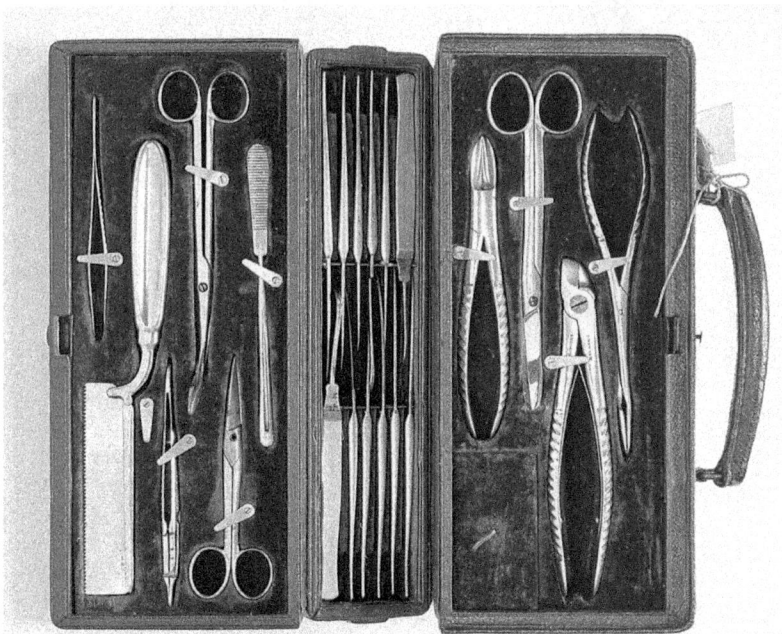

Aseptic (uncontaminated) surgical kit, ca. early twentieth century. Photo courtesy of Wellcomecollection.org.

When the human heart is stopped by any accident, the new self-starter is used as is shown in this picture. Here the needle is being inserted by one of its inventors, C. Henry Hyman. At right is the generator

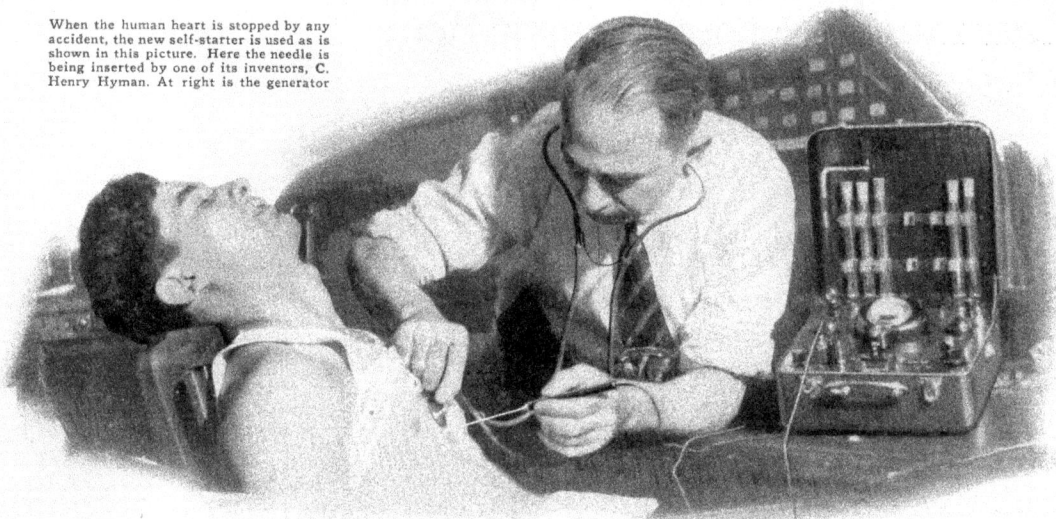

PHYSICIAN INVENTS

SELF-STARTER for Dead Man's Heart

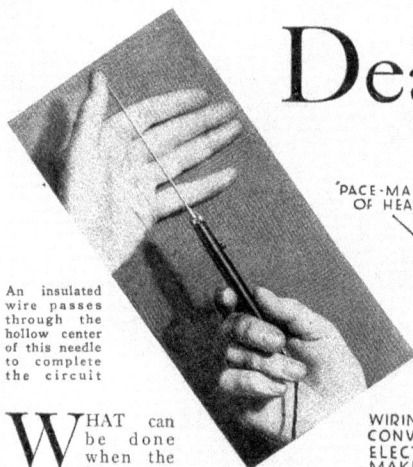

An insulated wire passes through the hollow center of this needle to complete the circuit

"PACE-MAKER" OF HEART

RIGHT AURICLE

LEFT AURICLE

WIRING SYSTEM CONVEYING THE ELECTRIC IMPULSES FROM PACE-MAKER TO THE HEART MUSCLES.

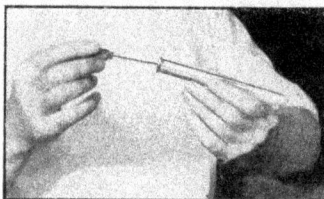

Each needle is kept in a sterilized test tube. Diagram of heart shows position of pacemaker

WHAT can be done when the heart ceases to beat? Under all sorts of different conditions, a doctor often is confronted with this urgent question.

The ambulance physician faces it with the victim of heart stroke, drowning, or accident. The surgeon faces it when the pulse of an etherized patient suddenly stops. The family physician faces it when a baby is still born or when a mother's heart stops during childbirth.

Until recently the only answer was the injection of a powerful stimulant into the heart itself, with the result that, not infrequently, the heart failed to respond.

A new answer has just been furnished by the invention of Dr. Albert S. Hyman, heart specialist of the Beth David Hospital of New York, and by C. Henry Hyman, electrical research engineer.

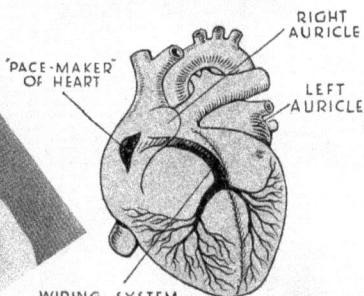

This life-saving device can be compared with the self-starter of a car. When the car's engine stalls, the starter motor turns it over until the cylinders are again firing. In the same way, when the heart stops under any of the conditions named above, the needle of the "Hyman Otor," as it is called, gives the four-cylinder heart engine a rhythmical electrical stimulation. This starts the heart beat and maintains it until the heart's own "electric generator" resumes operation.

This comparison is not far-fetched, for the equivalent of an electrical generator exists in the wall of the right upper chamber (or auricle) of the heart, and a system of "wires" conveys the electrical impulses to the heart muscle. This "ignition system" is called the "pace-maker" of the heart.

The essential feature of the Hyman invention is a hollow steel needle, through which a carefully insulated wire runs to the open point. Both the needle itself and its central wire are connected to the terminals of a light, spring-driven generator, provided with a current-interrupting device. This mechanism can be adjusted to give electrical impulses with the frequency of the heart-beat from infancy to old age.

When the physician faces a case of heart stoppage, he inserts the needle between the first and second ribs into the right auricle of the heart, and starts the generator at the required frequency. The rhythmical current then "cranks" the heart engine by stimulating the "pacemaker" to act in step with the generator, until its normal action is resumed. Usually this occurs quickly.

Medical authorities predict a wide usefulness for the "Hyman Otor."

The first heart defibrillator, the Hyman Otor, described in 1933. The above article appeared in the October 1933 issue of *Popular Mechanics* magazine.

in a lack of synchronism between heartbeat and pulse), then defibrillated by administering high levels of electrical jolts. The results were not favorable, however, because of the high levels of electricity being administered to the dogs.

- 1933: Thirty-four years later, an article appeared in *Popular Mechanics* about Dr. Albert S. Hyman and his "promising new invention," the Hyman Otor. Dr. Hyman's device, which involved inserting a needle with wires into the heart, was compared to "a self-starter for a car." The needle stimulated the heart by way of electrical impulses. The device was tested only on animals, though, and was not accepted by the medical community for use on humans.

- 1947: The first successful defibrillation on a human was reported by American surgeon, Dr. Claude S. Beck. Dr. Beck successfully resuscitated a young patient who had gone into cardiac arrest. Beck used gauze-covered paddles, similar to spoons, to deliver a shock. This, in combination with cardiac massage and drugs, led to the successful resuscitation of the patient.

- 1956: Dr. Paul Zoll, a Harvard cardiologist and widely considered an AED (Automatic External Defibrillator) pioneer, successfully resuscitated two patients by applying electrical charges externally to the chest. (External heart defibrillation was a much less invasive procedure, and clearly less time consuming.[26])

- 1965: Dr. Frank Pantridge, a professor from Ireland, invented the world's first portable defibrillator, which used a car battery to generate electrical current.

- 1978: The first portable external AED was introduced.

Anesthesia

Prior to the development of anesthetics, the most important skill that a good surgeon possessed was speed. Western "frontier" physicians required simple anesthetic techniques using chloroform and/or ether and relegated the task of "putting a patient under" to a nurse or junior medical students. Apparently, (according to *The History of Anesthesia in Oregon* at least) it was the commonly accepted belief of surgeons that "anesthesia could be empirically administered (learned by means of observation or hands-on experience), was technically simple, easily taught, and could be relegated to the least skillful member of the surgical team."

This philosophy held sway throughout the country until the early part of the twentieth century, when full-time professionally-trained anesthesiologists came on the scene. Even with today's commonplace use of anesthesia prior to surgery, a specially trained doctor will assess the patient immediately before the procedure, manage the vital signs during the operation and check in after the patient awakens. Both the surgeon and the anesthesiologist will also caution the patient about the dangers of using drugs to "put the patient to sleep."[27] *The History of Anesthesia in Oregon* gave credit where it was due, noting:

There is little doubt that the more dedicated and skilled self-taught part-time physician anesthetists contributed to their local and regional development of the 'art' of anesthesia. They helped prepare the way for full-time anesthetists.[27]

In the early days of anesthesia use (around 1875), it was common for a surgeon to provide a portion of his fee to the anesthetist, based on each surgeon's inclination. Thus the surgeon had control, as the income of each anesthetist was at the mercy of the surgeon he or she worked with. The ethical issue of this fee-splitting practice raised many issues of conflict of interest, and new surgical interns revolted against taking courses in anesthesia—as they judged such training to be a dead-end with no future. This sparked the creation of the first School of Nurse Anesthesia in the United States. It was founded at St. Vincent Hospital in Portland, Oregon, in 1909. To be certified, nurses spent four months studying various aspects of human physiology. Thirty years later, in 1939, the course of study for nurse anesthesiologists expanded to twelve months.[27]

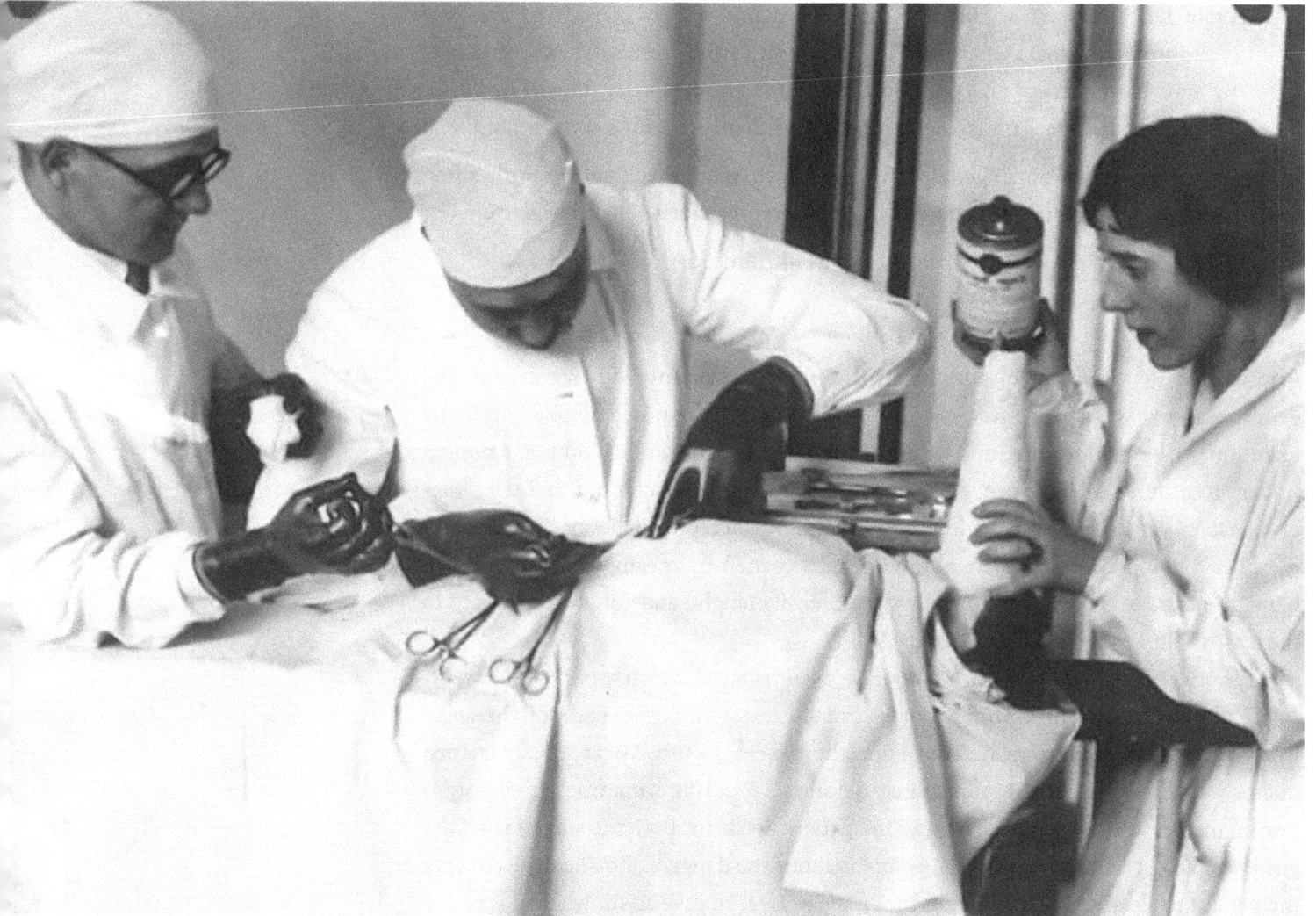

Early operating room, with a nurse anesthesiologist. Photo courtesy of OHSU archives.

PART II

PIONEER DOCTORS OF COOS COUNTY

Once there were medical schools in the region, more doctors naturally set up shop in Coos County. And so we've come to the heart of the book: the individual entries for my group of "pioneer doctors." As noted earlier, for some doctors, I uncovered a plethora of information; for others the record was scarce. But they all combine to create the early medical and community tapestry of Coos County. I've ordered the doctors alphabetically here because it seemed the simplest way to organize them, and have readers find them by name.

But no matter how they're listed, and however long or short their story here, each of these pioneers helped further medical treatment within the early Coos Bay-area community.

Dr. William Cook Angell (1839–1893)

The story of William Cook Angell dates back to the mid-1600s when his sixth great-grandfather, Thomas Angell (1618–1694), immigrated to Rhode Island from England in 1636. He was one of four men who spent that winter at Seekonk in the Plymouth Colony (later Rehoboth, Massachusetts) with Roger Williams (best known for founding the Colony of Rhode Island and advocating for separation of church and state in Colonial America). The group established the settlement of Providence Plantation in the late spring on the upper reaches of Narragansett Bay. Several generations of Thomas Angell's descendants were born and lived in and around Providence, Rhode Island.

William C. Angell was born in Scituate, Providence County, Rhode Island, on October 20, 1839 to Horace B. Angell (1807–1883) and Eunice Lucretia Chase (1844–1889). William was born into a large family of ten children, all born in Rhode Island. Of the ten children who lived to adulthood, three were girls and seven were boys, William being the seventh child. His father was listed as a farmer in the federal census. When William was around twenty-one, he lived with his family in Providence, Rhode Island.

When the Civil War erupted, he enlisted in the army, where he worked and learned medical techniques applied by the military. In 1864, his enlistment apparently finished, he was listed as a junior at Brown University in Providence, where he graduated in 1866. By 1870, he was living in San Francisco practicing medicine and married to Eunice Lucrecia Chace (1844–1889), who hailed from that city. Five children were born to the couple while in San Francisco, with their sixth offspring born in Coquille, Oregon, in 1881.

Dr. William Cook Angell. Photo courtesy of Ancestry.com.

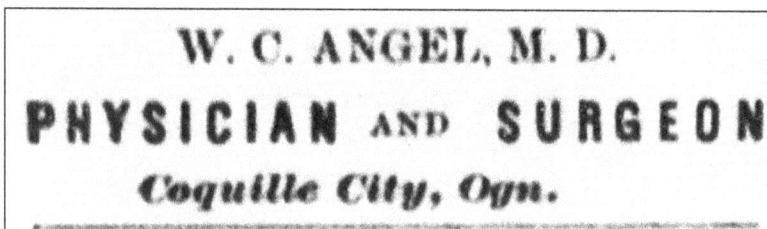

W. C. ANGEL, M. D.
PHYSICIAN AND SURGEON
Coquille City, Ogn.

Advertisement from the January 3, 1880 *Coast Mail*.

From San Francisco, Angell brought his family to Empire City and opened a shop not as a doctor but as a cobbler—though he also dispensed medical knowledge from his shop when customers complained about minor ailments. He soon developed a reputation as a physician, even though he wasn't formally practicing as one. In 1875 Dr. Angel moved to Coquille, Oregon, and there he practiced medicine again for a decade (after which he moved back to San Francisco). His medical office in Coquille was in Leneve's drug store. In 1880, along with Dr. Leneve, Dr. Angell and Doctors Mackay and Cook of Empire City successfully fought a severe diphtheria epidemic in Coos County.[28]

Dr. William C. Angell died in San Francisco on May 20, 1893 at the age of fifty-three.

Ira Bennett Bartle (1871–1943)

Ira B. Bartle was born in Steuben County, New York, on September 16, 1871 to William Bartle (1838–1912) and Hannah M. Baxter (1843–1922). His father was a minister. Ira received his elementary education in the New York public schools, then in 1885, moved with his family to Kansas where he continued his education, graduating from high school in Larned, Kansas, in 1891. He went to college in the Keokuk Medical school in Keokuk, Iowa, graduating in 1894 with a medical degree. Soon thereafter he opened a drug store together with his medical practice in Pawnee Rock, Kansas.

Heading West

In the spring of 1897, Ira joined his brother, Dr. Phillip J. Bartle (1874–1944), a graduate of the Barnes Medical College in 1896, and established a clinic in Great Bend, Kansas. In 1897, the Bartle brothers moved their medical practice to Augusta, Oklahoma. While in Oklahoma, both brothers attended Tulane University in New Orleans, taking advanced courses in medicine. After developing a successful medical practice in Augusta, Ira and Phillip, along with their parents, departed for Eugene, Oregon, in the spring/summer of 1905. There the brothers developed a medical clinic.[30,31]

Dr. Ira Bennett Bartle, ca. 1917. Photo courtesy of the Coos History Museum.

Ira enlisted in the Medical Corps of the U.S. Army as a lieutenant, and by June 1918 had risen to the rank of major before he mustered out. He was stationed at Camp Lewis, Washington. After the war, Dr. Bartle re-entered private practice in San Luis Obispo, California, where he continued to practice medicine until his death in 1943.[32]

In 1907, Dr. Ira Bartle sold his medical practice in Eugene to Dr. D. F. Scalefe and moved to North Bend, Oregon, to open a new practice. When Ira came to North Bend, he was one of only three physicians in town.

… In June 1905, Dr. Ira Bartle wrote an article for medical journals. One subject is new to the profession and is quite a contribution to the Doctor of Science, the subject being: 'Congenital Anemia.' The thin blue blooded babies of which doctors are to a great extent ignorant. The treatment Dr. Ira prescribes is fresh air, light clothing, warm sunshine for the new babies and a sand pile for the child to play in as soon as large enough to crawl …

He was the official doctor of the Simpson Lumber Company at North Bend, served as the United States quarantine officer for a few years, and was elected for two years on the North Bend City Council. He owned a second home up the South Fork Coos River, as well as a cranberry ranch on North Inlet, Coos County. Dr. Phillip Bartle, his brother, on the other hand, stayed in Eugene, where he practiced medicine for another thirty-three years.

Involvement in Water and Transportation Issues

In the early spring of 1911, water samples taken from hydrants in both North Bend and Marshfield were found to be contaminated with colon bacilli (human sewage). While serving on the North Bend City Council (and as the city's health officer), Dr. Bartle was given the assignment to investigate the matter. At the same time, Dr. Everett Mingus was the health officer for the town of Marshfield. Dr. Mingus boiled one of the samples, and after letting it cool, found no resident bacteria present. However, when he took a water sample directly from the faucet in his office and one from his home, he found the office water proved fine—but the one from his home was contaminated.[34]

Once these samples were confirmed to be contaminated, the water board began building a fence around the impoundment reservoir, but both doctors advised those hooked up to city water should boil their water before drinking it, until a better solution could be found. Dr. Mingus also reported that the sample taken from the Lando well on Nob Hill (now Telegraph Hill) was found to be infected and unsafe for domestic use. Over the years as better sanitary rules and regulations were implemented, the incidents of fouled water were reduced or eliminated.[34]

HUMAN OSTRICH AT NORTH BEND[33]

3 Jack knives	3– Small shells	15– Dimes	1– Shingle nail
1– Brass end of knife handle	3– Door keys	17– Horseshoe nails	1– 8-penny nail
1– End of metal fishing rod	1– Small key	1– Fish hook	175– pieces of glass, some
2– Large loaded rifle shells	3– Five-cent pieces	2– Finishing nails	larger than a fingernail

The above represents most of the articles taken from the stomach of a patient, a county charge, at Mercy Hospital in North Bend by Doctors Ira Bartle and Arthur Gale, in the summer of 1908. (The patient was likened to an ostrich because when young, the birds will eat almost anything—especially litter.) The operation, or rather the result, is most remarkable in the history of Coos Bay—and a rare one in the annals of medical science:

… that a man can convert his stomach into a junk yard, savings bank, pocket, and several other things and live to tell the tale is almost beyond the pale of comprehension or belief, but that is the case. Drs. Bartle and Gale and the authorities at Mercy Hospital will vouch for it and in addition, have preserved the articles enumerated as further evidence. The patient had been following the un-human diet for several years but a few days ago he first encountered trouble. He began to suffer from terrible pain in the stomach that became so excruciating he finally went to the hospital. The pieces of glass had penetrated the mucous membrane of the stomach in several places, which probably caused the pain. Some of the articles appear to have been carried in the stomach for a long time. A number of North Bend people saw him swallow various articles, but most of them thought that he was a sleight-of-hand artist and that their eyes had been deceived. The operation proved otherwise …

In 1912, Dr. Bartle, again as a North Bend city councilor, found himself immersed in a challenge as to whether the Southern Pacific Railroad from Eugene to Coos Bay could cross the bay on a bridge or traverse along the eastern shore of the bay, passing through the communities of Glascow and Cooston. Dr. Bartle was president of the North Bend Commercial Club at the time, and as such had much interest in getting the rail line into North Bend. Apparently, the Oregon Central Railway company (aka the Coos Bay and Boise Railroad) had filed an objection with the War Department, purportedly claiming a bridge across the bay would impede water transportation. It seems that the same corporate executives involved in the Oregon Central Railway were also involved in the Glascow Townsite Company with ownership along the east side of the bay. Their objection to the Southern Pacific Railroad bridge was rejected by the War Department, and in 1916, North Bend got its rail access via a large turnstile bridge across the bay.

Partnerships, Logging and War

In 1915, a partnership was formed between Dr. Bartle and Dr. Frank S. Pratt. The latter was a physician with a practice in Gardiner, Oregon, a small community twenty-eight miles north of Coos Bay. Dr. Pratt moved to North Bend sometime in December of that year when Dr. Bartle left the area to undertake postgraduate work in New Orleans, Chicago, and New York.

In October 1916, the Oregon State Health Authority requested that Dr. Bartle examine the Buehner Lumber Company logging camp at Allegany, Oregon, and determine whether it was in an unsanitary condition as had been reported to the state authorities. Upon finishing his inspection, Dr. Bartle noted:

> … The men employed at the camp had no complaint to make on the charges contained in the letter of criticism; the bunkhouses are large and well ventilated, bug proof, of steel, and the kitchen was clean, while the food was wholesome. The location of the toilets is not such as to endanger the health of the employees …[35]

Ad from the *Coos Bay Times,* September 11, 1917.

When America entered the war in Europe in April 1917, there was no official medical corps, but many local doctors wanted to join the war effort to aid soldiers on the battlefields, which were rife with medical challenges old and new. Since WWI was the first war where mustard, chlorine and other noxious gases were employed, doctors had no training in how to treat those injuries. Further, that war was fought in the trenches—where sanitation was horrible. If a soldier got the slightest wound and was not transported to the rear area for cleansing, his chances of survival were exceptionally low.

The federal government asked the Coos County officials to determine how many doctors it needed to keep in the major towns to care for the civilian population. At a meeting of the Marshfield Chamber of Commerce the following was recorded:[36]

> … It was the opinion of the meeting that no married doctor would to go to the war, while any single doctor remained in practice in the [Coos] county … [28]

The Chamber of Commerce further recommended the following doctors be kept home:

North Bend: Two doctors were needed—Dr. Edwards and Dr. Anderson

Coquille: Two doctors were needed—Dr. Hamilton and Dr. Richmond

Myrtle Point: Two doctors were needed—Dr. Pemberton and Dr. Clarke

Bandon: Two doctors were needed—Dr. Houston and Dr. Gale

Marshfield: Four doctors were needed—Dr. Horsfall, Dr. Johnson, Dr. Houseworth, and Dr. White

In June 1917, Dr. Pratt and Dr. Bartle received orders to report to the War Department for enlistment in the U.S. Army. Dr. G. E. Anderson came from Portland and took over the practice of Bartle and Pratt from 1917–1918. Dr. Anderson died in North Bend as the result of blood poisoning from an infected thumb. He died within one week after he was married to a local school teacher. After the war, Dr. Bartle moved to Fort Huachuca, Arizona, and by 1930 was practicing in San Luis Obispo, California.

A Unique Side Interest

Dr. Ira Bartle had an unusual hobby; he propagated latent spores taken from old mission-church walls, which were typically centuries old. Dr. Bartle thought that it might be possible for single-celled organisms to sink into the walls and exist there in a dormant state, in which they would remain potentially alive for extended periods; but even he was skeptical about his theory:

When I first told people about my theory, the whole thing sounded crazy—even to me. But although I didn't have much hope of succeeding, I decided to try.

A few blocks from Dr. Bartle's home in San Luis Obispo, California, was an old Spanish mission built by Franciscan padres in 1772–1774. Some of the basement walls had not been touched since the days of the American Revolution. In 1936, Dr. Bartle decided to test his theory about latent spores' ability to exist in the walls for centuries. Photo courtesy of the *Oakland Tribune,* March 13, 1936.

Dr. Bartle used the following process to test his hypothesis that spores might still be living deep inside the adobe walls:[37]

- The first technique he employed was to flame the surface of the adobe blocks with a blowtorch until it glowed red.

- Next, he sprayed the blocks with a 50 percent solution of phenol as a powerful disinfectant.

- Then a hole was bored three or four inches into the material, and the hole was also flamed and sprayed with disinfectant.

- A small coring auger was inserted into the holes, with care being taken that it did not touch the sides.

- The specimens were then placed in a sterile test tube that contained sterile bacterial media, which supplied food and moisture for any organisms present. All tools used in the operation were sterilized.

- On the fourth day of the experiment, Bartle placed some of the culture from the test tube onto a microscope slide for viewing, where he saw millions of living, moving microorganisms.

From that point on, Dr. Bartle was determined to see from what age or era these microscopic spores could be teased back to life.[37]

Dr. Ira Bartle, ca. 1937. Photo courtesy of the *Los Angeles Times*, February 1, 1937 page 9.

… In the winter of 1937, he traveled to Mexico and the Yucatan, visiting old ruins gathering samples from which he grew cultures, estimated dormant since the time of Christ. He worked jointly with Dr. Charles Lipman, dean of the graduate school of agriculture of the University of California, always dividing his samples with Dr. Lipman, they nearly always getting the same results in practically the same time. Many species of coli bacteria imprisoned in the adobe brick for hundreds of years resumed their normal functions when exposed to moisture and air …

… In 1940, his nephew, Dr. W. B. Neal from Eugene, accompanied Dr. Bartle on a trip into Honduras and Guatemala, visiting old ruins and an extinct civilization, perhaps contemporaneous with that of Egypt. From samples gathered there, Dr. Bartle was able to grow spore life latent for centuries …

So excited was Dr. Bartle from his discoveries that he exclaimed, "These creatures have been dormant for 80 centuries!"

As reported in the February 11, 1937 edition of the *Los Angeles Times*:

... Not Russian traders, as generally believed, but Franciscan padres brought wheat to California, according to an investigation made by Dr. Ira B. Bartle, who is making a study of adobe bricks from the walls of Mission San Luis Obispo, founded in 1772 by Fra. Junipero Serra. Bricks taken from an inner wall of the historic structure and known definitely from mission records to have been built in 1774, were found to contain grains of straw of wheat of a soft, Spanish variety, indicating the grain was growing here as early as 1773 ...[38]

A year later (1938) Dr. Bartle took a sample of soil from an ancient adobe brick from the San Luis Obispo mission walls, placed it in sterile water, and froze it in his laboratory freezer for one year. When the ice melted and the material was examined under a microscope, of the eleven strains of bacteria that were identified before freezing, three had survived and began reproducing as if nothing had ever happened to interrupt that natural event.[39]

Ira Bartle married three times: Laura Belle Gilbert (1880–1967) in 1895; Maude Reta Coke (1889–?) in 1909; and Luz Rafaela Spence (1890–1951) in 1922.

Dr. Ira Bennett Bartle died at San Luis Obispo on November 10, 1943. He was seventy-two years old.

Franklin Chester Birch (1879–1948)

Franklin Chester Birch was born in Orland, Colusa County, California on February 10, 1879 to John Allen Birch (1838–1928) and Elizabeth Ann Ross (1838–1929). He attended public schools in the Sacramento valley. The foundation for his career in medicine was established when he attended the College of Physicians and Surgeons at San Francisco, then later took graduate work in optometry at the Los Angeles School of Optometry. While still living in California's Central Valley, Dr. Birch was associated with his brother, John Wesley Birch (1869–1935), in an optical business in Chico, California.

In 1916, Dr. Birch began operating the only optical shop in southwestern Oregon. His office was located at the corner of Anderson and Broadway in Marshfield. Prior to 1916, Dr. Birch was connected with the Preuss Drug Company in Marshfield. In 1928, the local newspaper carried the following information about Dr. Birch:

... Upon coming to Dr. Birch, every patient is given a most careful examination and tests made which are carefully worked out to discover any possible eye disorder or correction. If Dr. Birch finds that a patient is in need of glasses, his early education and many years of active practice combined with natural

Franklin Chester Birch, ca. 1896.
Photo courtesy of California
State University, Chico.

good professional judgment has unequivocally quali-fied him to make accurate recommendation as to the strength and type of lenses needed.

When selecting rims for glasses, patrons of Dr. Birch have found his suggestions always in good taste. Dr. Birch prides himself in helping people to look bet-ter as well as see better. He has found it unnecessary to conduct eye tests by dilating the pupils. Dr. Birch says that eliminating this factor in optometry is not only a convenience to patients, but thousands of laboratory tests have proven dilation unnecessary and in some rare cases harmful.

From 1916 to 1928, Dr. Birch has prescribed glasses for more than 12,000 residents in Coos and Curry Counties ... [40,41]

Birch's advertisements in the local paper always car-ried the comment: *See Birch and See Better.* His office in Marshfield had the only eyeglass grinding equipment in southwestern Oregon, and by confining his practice to the optical field, Birch had been able to become a recog-nized expert in that field.

In June 1937, Dr. Birch's only son, Frederick C. Birch (1914–1966), completed his pre-medical training at the Willamette University Medical Department in Salem, Oregon, followed by two years of optometry study at the North Pacific College in Portland, Oregon, graduating with honors. A year later he joined his father's practice at Marshfield. Frederick continued to practice optometry in Coos Bay until his death in 1966.[42,43]

Franklin Chester Birch and his sister, Helen Myrtle Birch, ca. 1900. Photo courtesy of California State University, Chico.

Below: An ad from the *Coos Bay Times,* October 4, 1938.

Franklin married twice: his wives were Carlotta A. Berklevelder (1890–?), and Carolyn I. Merryman (1881–1923). Dr. Franklin Birch died in Coos Bay, Oregon, on May 26, 1948, and his son Frederick died in Coos Bay in November 1966.

Dr. Dean Piper Crowell (1894–1983)

Dean P. Crowell was born in LaCrosse, Wisconsin, in 1894 and moved with his parents, George Henry Crowell (1866–1939) and Margaret D. Piper (1868–1956), to Albany, Oregon, in 1908. He attended high school in Albany, and graduated in 1910. He graduated from the University of Oregon with a Bachelor of Arts degree in 1915. While at the University of Oregon in Eugene, he played football under the esteemed coach Hugo Benzdeck (later named into the College Football Hall of Fame). Crowell married Isabella Garland in 1916 in Linn County, Oregon.

After graduation from the university, Crowell attended the Oregon Medical College in Portland for two years, where his academic performance was so good he won a scholarship to attend the Rush University Medical School in Chicago. (Note: Rush Medical College was chartered back in 1837 by it founder Daniel Brainard, MD, and was named for Benjamin Rush, MD; the only physician with medical training to have signed the Declaration of Independence). Crowell graduated from Rush Medical School in 1919, then completed two years of residency at the Memorial and Presbyterian Hospital at LaCrosse, Wisconsin. Following a year's stint teaching classes at the Rush Medical College, in 1922, Crowell went back to LaCrosse and opened a successful medical practice until January 1925, when he and Isabella moved back to Albany, Oregon, to be close to his parents. When he moved to Albany, Crowell brought with him a large inventory of surgical supplies he had assembled while in Wisconsin. He established his practice in leased space on the top floor of the First National Bank in Albany.[44]

In November 1929, Dr. Crowell moved to North Bend to join the staff at the Keizer Brothers Hospital, and became a partner with Dr. Russel C. Keizer following the death of Dr. Phil Keizer (Russel's brother). When Russel Keizer died in 1936, Dr. Crowell was appointed the North Bend city health officer.[45-47]

Activities Beyond Medicine

Just before he moved to North Bend, Dr. Crowell was the president of the Albany, Oregon, Rotary Club. In August 1929, he gave a speech to the Rotarians about the peace propaganda being spread throughout the nation, reflecting upon his serving in the medical corps during World War I:

Dr. Franklin Chester Birch, optometrist, ca. 1937. Photo copied from the *Coos Bay Times*.

... There are various kinds of peace in the world and sometimes 'personal peace' is best kept by carrying a revolver. The same applies to nations. The United States has always been peace minded, that very thing elected Woodrow Wilson for a second time, but it did not prevent this nation from getting into war [WWI]. When all nations become peace minded like the United States, then it is time to scrap armies and navies. There is no man in the world that desires peace any more than I do. Do not become too enthusiastic over peace, but use common sense ... [44]

Dean P. Crowell. Photo courtesy of the Coos History Museum.

Within a few short years, Dr. Crowell became involved in community activities in North Bend. In 1932, he was vice president of the North Bend Chamber of Commerce, and in that capacity was involved in the controversy opposing the re-routing of the Oregon Coast Highway. In February of that year, representatives from the local communities of North Bend, Eastside, Cooston, and Empire met with the Marshfield Chamber of Commerce directors to discuss a petition presented to the state highway commission in Portland. Rumors flew that the purpose of the petition was to have the Coast Highway skirt the east side of the bay, rather than build a large highway bridge across the bay into North Bend (an identical situation that Dr. Ira Bartle faced with the proposal to reroute the Southern Pacific railroad around the east side of the bay—instead of building a railroad bridge across Coos Bay, where it is today).

Petitioners pointed out that the purpose of the petition was to get the state highway commission to build a bridge across the Coos River and not to re-route the Coast Highway. At that time, the only access into Marshfield or North Bend for people living in Glasgow or Cooston was to take one of the two ferries across the bay. Such a bridge across the river would provide those people direct road access into town. The highway commission declined the petition and the vertical-lift bridge across the river (Chandler Bridge) was not built until 1952. In 1936, the McCullough Memorial Bridge across Coos Bay was completed—this provided access into North Bend to people living to the north and east of the bay.[45]

In 1933, Dr. Crowell was elected to the Coos Bay Port Commission and elected as its secretary. During that same year, he took over as president of the North Bend Chamber of Commerce.[46]

In 1935, Dr. Crowell, along with I. N. Hartley of the North Bend National Bank, purchased a used Curtis Wright two-seated monoplane. Both men were interested in promoting aviation in hopes of developing the flying club for airplane enthusiasts in town. The plane was capable of landing at a low speed of twenty-eight miles per hour.

Dick Dickinson of the Coos Bay Aero Club became the club's instructor.[47]

In the fall of 1940, Dr. Crowell, along with Al Langrell, Julius Swanson, Norman E. Johnson, and Rupert Coffman, incorporated a new company by the name of Cape Arago Lumber Company. All five men made up the board of directors. The new concern purchased the old Empire Lumber Company sawmill from the Menasha Woodenware Company. The mill had been shuttered for two years after James Lyons and Howard Irwin left the operation to take over what was known as Mill B. The sawmill equipment in the old Empire Mill was fifty-seven-years-old, built by the Oregon Southern Improvement Company in 1883, but the machines had been well maintained and were in operating order. Eventually the Cape Arago Lumber Company was taken over by Moore Mill and Lumber Company of Bandon, Oregon but the company retained the original name of Cape Arago.[48,49]

Unlike the talk Dr. Crowell gave to the Albany Rotarians back in 1929 on the subject of peace among nations, in 1940 speaking before a gathering of the North Bend Chamber of Commerce, he struck a different chord when speaking about the medical corps:

> *... Dr. Crowell, a major in the medical reserves [serving in the medical corps during WWI], explained the general defensive plan of the U.S. Army, declaring the setup called for a basic unit of regular troops, doubled by the state militia and tripled by the reserves. He added that the regular army, one of the smallest among major nations was the real backbone of national defense ...*
>
> *... Although the medical corps is organized with military efficiency, it must take a back seat in some instances, because war is meant to wound men and not to heal wounds. He explained that artillery and mobile troops are given the preference in locations. Base hospitals in wartime can care for 10,000 troops at a time ...*

Moving His Practice, and Wartime Again

Dr. Crowell had practiced medicine in North Bend for ten years before moving his practice to Marshfield in 1940. (Marshfield did not change its name to Coos Bay until 1944.) In the spring of 1941, Dr. John R. Seeley joined Dr. Crowell's practice. It was located in the Hall Building in downtown Marshfield. When he moved to Marshfield, Dr. Crowell served as chief of staff for McAuley Hospital (we'll discuss this hospital a bit later). Dr. Seeley had been the Coos County health officer for about a year so that the existing county health officer, Dr. Dehne, could take a year off for further study in the East. After Dr. Dehne returned to Coos Bay, Dr. Seeley was able to rejoin Dr. Crowell in private practice. Dr. Seeley was a graduate of Linfield College and the University of Oregon Medical School.

Two years into World War II, Dr. Crowell offered his services to the Army Medical

Corps, but in a letter from the surgeon general it was stated that Dr. Crowell could be of greater assistance to the war effort at home, rather than in an army hospital. Thus for a time he remained in an inactive reserve status. In the spring of 1945, however, he could stay away no longer: he closed his medical practice and enlisted in active duty with the U.S. Navy. His partner, Dr. Seeley, enlisted in the army and served as a captain in the European theatre. Crowell had two sons serving the nation during the war too: Lt. Dean G. Crowell (a West Point graduate) was with the Army Air Corps, and Samuel Crowell was in the navy. A year later, Lt. Commander Dr. Dean Piper Crowell was serving aboard the *USS Sierra* as medical officer.[50-52]

Retirement

In February 1947, Dr. Crowell retired from medical practice and moved with his wife, Isabella, to Portland, Oregon. Still fascinated with flying, he promised local friends that he would keep in touch by airplane. But after moving to Marin County, California, the local paper carried the following:

DOC'S ORDER: LOTS OF AIR, UP IN THE AIR

… Plenty of fresh air and sunshine … that's what the doctor's prescribing for himself. So never a week goes by that people at Marin County Airport in Novato [California] don't see the perky little T-Craft with Dr. Dean Crowell of San Rafael at the controls race down the runway and reach for the clouds … [53]

Dr. Dean P. Crowell died in Marin County, California on April 19, 1983. He was eighty-eight years old.

Dr. Walter Culin (1866–1916)

Walter Culin was born in Philadelphia on June 26, 1866 to John Culin (1829–1879) and Mira Barrett Daniels (1834–1925). Walter attended the public schools in Philadelphia and after graduating, attended the Philadelphia College of Pharmacy, graduating in 1888 with a Ph.G. degree. (In 1821, the Philadelphia College of Pharmacy instituted a program in pharmacy leading to a Ph.G. degree—Graduate of Pharmacy, which required a student to attend the pharmacy college for two years, plus complete a four-year stint as an apprentice with a respectable druggist before the degree was conferred. In 1895, the college replaced the Ph.G. degree with the Doctor of Pharmacy—PD—and the Ph.C.—Pharmaceutical Chemist— degrees requiring three years of college. Dr. Culin's thesis was, "The Solution and Tincture of Chloride of Iron.")

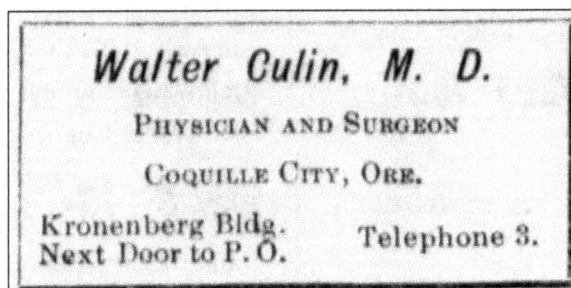

Walter Culin, M. D.

PHYSICIAN AND SURGEON

COQUILLE CITY, ORE.

Kronenberg Bldg.
Next Door to P. O.   Telephone 3.

Ad from the semi-weekly *Herald,* August 5, 1904. On the day this ad was printed, there was only one doctor in Coquille. There was also one dentist, and five lawyers who also ran ads in the newspaper.

During the next two years, Culin attended medical classes, and he graduated from the University of Pennsylvania Medical School on June 1, 1890. Dr. Culin then traveled west and set up a medical practice in the small community of Occidental, in Sonoma County, California, where he stayed from 1892–1894. Dr. Culin came to Coquille, Oregon, to locate his medical practice in March 1894.[31,54-57] Walter Culin married Edith Janvere Taylor (1872–1965) on May 26, 1894 in Marshfield, Oregon.

Dr. Culin also possessed a powerboat he named *Daphne*, which he used to visit patients who lived along the Coquille River. Photo courtesy of *Doctors of the Old West*.

Employing Various Means to Reach Patients

As mentioned earlier, many pioneer doctors reached patients in a variety of ways. When he set up his practice in Oregon, Dr. Culin found that he, as well, had to get creative with the means he used to reach those who needed his help. At the time Dr. Culin moved to Coquille there was over 500 inhabitants (1890 census-494; 1900 census-728). Good roads were few and far between and many used the milk boat and other forms of river transportation.

Dr. Culin often declared that his office looked more like a second-hand store than a doctor's office—as parts of various engines were strewn about along with automobile tires, photographic equipment, and other useful (and perhaps not so useful!) objects. He also had an old Bartlett X-ray machine that had to be turned by a crank to generate electricity while taking an image.[7,58-60]

Leadership Roles and Quarantine Decisions

In early 1907, the Coos and Curry Counties Medical Society was organized with the following temporary officers: president, Dr. C. W. Tower, of Marshfield; vice-president, Dr. Walter Culin, of Coquille; secretary-treasurer, Dr. J. W. Ingram, of Marshfield. In May 1907, the medical society met again to elect new officers as follows: President, Dr. Walter Culin, of Coquille; vice-president, Dr. R. G. Gale, of North Bend; secretary and treasurer, Dr. B. M. Richardson, of Marshfield; councilors, Drs. E. Mingus, J. T. McCormac, and E. E. Straw.[63]

In the spring of 1908, Dr. Culin as the Coos County health officer was called to Sumner, Oregon, a small community south and east of Coos Bay, to quarantine some scarlet fever cases that were reported in a family living five miles from Sumner. A dance

... Dr. Walter Culin can no longer be heard approaching in his [new] Ford car. His friends heretofore could always hear the doctor about 10 blocks away approaching with a series of snorts and groans and rattle of tin [made by his old vehicle]. But Alas! No more will the quiet of our little city be disturbed by the said noise. The doctor has purchased a brand new Ford roadster ... [61]

Another reference to Dr. Culin's proclivity to own an automobile was carried in the April 6, 1912 *Journal of the American Medical Association.* The article describes the frustration Dr. Culin had in dealing with his 1904 vehicle as he attempted to trade it in for a newer model:

After several years of conducting his rounds to rural patients near town by horseback and boat, in 1904, Dr. Culin became the first owner of an automobile in the county—which he used extensively to reach patients close to town. Photo courtesy of the Coos History Museum.

... My first power wagon was bought in 1904; it was the first ever seen in this part of the world. If I were starting in practice again, the first investment that I would make would be in an automobile. I am sure that the time saved pays for the machine, besides the pleasure. I have had several different machines and would buy one that would not run as quickly as one that would [simply] run. The 1904 [cars] are as reliable as the ones made today [1912]. I have not found any difference in machines at the same price.

I use light machines on account of tire expense and trouble; I have run eighteen months without a puncture or tire trouble ... I use distillate for fuel; I never changed brand of cylinder oil and the cylinders never carbonize. Spark plugs last for years and the nine plugs in my engines have never been out of them. [62]

Not only was Dr. Culin a good physician, he must have also been an excellent automobile mechanic. He was once quoted as noting, "I use any spark-plug, but for a one-cylinder engine the plug with a central electrode, shaped like a little gear wheel, gives a great deal more power." [62]

was planned at the Sumner school on the upcoming Saturday night and Dr. Culin proclaimed that there was no danger from the disease and the dance could go forward. He was correct!

Years later, Dr. Culin was called to the Haynes Inlet area northeast of Coos Bay to investigate an outbreak of smallpox. Rumors spread that the local teacher at the Haynes Inlet school was to blame for the outbreak as nearly every family in the area had the disease. Dr. Culin was told that a local physician had diagnosed the teacher with chicken pox. As a result, the teacher was terminated. Several other cases of the pox were reported at Bandon, Catching Inlet, and other locations around the county. Dr. Culin reported that he would wipe out the disease if the county court would back up a quarantine. [64]

In March 1915, Dr. Culin was called to the Empire area to investigate the cause of

> But a pioneer doctor's life wasn't all dealing with ills. Here's a charming little story I found about a treasured tree at Dr. Culin's home.
>
> *... Dr. Culin of Coquille says he had the finest cherry tree in the country at his home. It is a strange variety, being similar to Queen Anne but turns black when ripe. He says it produces about a ton each year; all the children and neighbors feast off it and a myriad of birds enjoy the luscious fruit. He will not permit anyone to drive away the feathered songsters from the cherry tree. He says that high taxes have tempted him to sell the home but when he thinks of the old cherry tree, he pays his taxes and forgets the inclination to sell ... [67]*

recent deaths from typhoid fever. After he investigated the water source used by the affected families, he ordered the spring that fed the homes below Tar Heel to be filled up. A short distance above the spring was a cesspool that drained into the spring. A similar problem was discovered in the Bunker Hill area where several springs provided water to multiple homes in the area.[65]

In October 1915, Dr. Culin was called to investigate the violations of the quarantines for diphtheria in the Bunker Hill area. Apparently, one family moved out of the quarantine area despite the orders from Dr. Horsfall. In a letter from Dr. Culin, he threatened to post guards at Bunker Hill in order to enforce the quarantine. The public was warned that the house vacated by the departing family had not been fumigated and people should stay away. The local district attorney had been requested to take action to enforce the quarantine law.[66]

On August 11, 1916, Dr. Culin was found dead in his bed at his home in Coquille. He had been stricken with apoplexy (or a stroke, as it is known today) and died in his sleep. For many years, he had been the president of the Coos-Curry County Medical Association. He was beloved by all, and his funeral was the largest Coquille had ever witnessed. He was fifty years old.

Dr. George Edwin Dix (1876–1961)

George Edwin Dix was born in 1876 in Woodstock, Ohio, to Peter Dix (1853–1910) and Ella Alberta Chester (1858–1943). Dix's grandfather, Clark Dix, was a pioneer settler in Champaign County, Ohio, having migrated from Mr. Pleasant, Pennsylvania in 1837. George received his primary education from the Dodge Center High School in Dodge Center, Minneapolis where his family had moved in 1897. In 1900, he entered the medical department at the University of Minnesota, graduating in 1904.[68]

Shortly after receiving his medical license from the Minnesota medical board, Dr. Dix became associated with the Northern Pacific Railroad as their assistant chief surgeon at their hospital in Missoula, Montana. Three years later, in 1907, he accepted a contract with the C. A. Smith Lumber and Manufacturing Company operation (aka Coos Bay Lumber Company)

Dr. George Dix. Photo courtesy of the *Encyclopedia of American Biography.*[68]

and the Smith-Powers logging operation at Marshfield, Oregon. He provided hospital, surgical, and medical aid necessary for the employees of the two companies. The arrangement was made such that each employee paid $1 per month as a charge to have the company doctor take care of every employee in the company as well as their families. These were huge companies with over 1,000 men on the payroll. Dr. Dix maintained that relationship with both companies for the next thirty years as the two companies bumped along in and out of financial troubles. Even though he cared for so many people over the years, Dr. Dix kept the relationships at least a bit personal, preferring that his patients call him "Dr. George."

Dr. George Dix. Photo courtesy of the Coos History Museum.

Life outside of Medicine

Aside from his medical practice, Dr. Dix was elected the exalted ruler of the local Elks Lodge in 1910, a position he held for several decades. He took a keen interest in the organization and remained on the board of trustees for years.

In December 1914, the Coos Bay Fish and Game Protective Association was organized for the purpose of assisting in the preservation and propagation of wild game and fish in and around Coos County. In the beginning there were about seventy-five members in the association. Dr. George Dix was elected president; Dr. Ephraim E. Straw, vice president; and William J. Conrad, secretary-treasurer. The purpose of the organization was to study the conditions of the local streams and upland areas to ascertain what species of wild birds, game, and fish were best adapted to the environs and then through cooperation with the Oregon State Game and Fish Commission replenish those stocks. Not only was the organization tasked to propagate different species, they were responsible for their protection until each species could fend for themselves.[69]

That winter, Dr. Straw received two dozen young Chinese pheasants from the state game commission. One crate of chicks went to the Frank Rogers' place on the South Coos River, where they were cared for until the next spring and then released. The other crate of chicks went to Dr. Dix's ranch on the Coquille River near Bridge, Coos County, Oregon.

George Dix married Sara L. Lakeman (1880–1965) in 1918 in Seattle, Washington. No children were born to that marriage.

In 1919 Dr. Dix purchased a ranch (the old Mark Davis farm at the forks of the Coos River) not far from Marshfield, and with the assistance of G. H. O'Connor, began raising Holstein dairy cattle under the brand name of Brookmead. In 1939 and again in 1941 he acquired additional acreage to add to the farm. Ill health

Ad from the Coos Bay Times, October 27, 1908, page 3.

DR. GEORGE E. DIX

Caricature of Dr. Dix as seen in the December 13, 1913 edition of the *Coos Bay Times*, page 5. The image was part of a special edition that highlighted several people in Coos Bay.

ultimately forced him to sell the operation in 1952 to the Brunell brothers.[70]

Dr. Dix also served in the Spanish-American War in 1898–1899. He was the first chairman of the Coos County American Red Cross, which was organized in 1917, and was a charter member of the local Rotary Club. He belonged to the Coos Bay, Curry County, and Oregon Medical Societies as well as the American Medical Association, the Academy of Medicine in Portland, Oregon, and the American College of Surgeons. He was a thirty-second degree Mason.[68,72]

Clearly, Dr. Dix was heavily involved in the community. And besides his medical and dairy work, he was involved in other business matters. In 1925, in conjunction with other prominent businessmen in the bay area, ground was broken for the construction of the Marshfield Hotel (aka Tioga Hotel), with stock being issued to capitalize the construction with $250,000. Dr. Dix was chairman of the board of directors at the time along with board members Ben. F. Fisher, John Goss, W. J. Conrad, A. E. Adelsperger, Benjamin Ostlind, Joseph Williams, Ben R. Chandler, and E. P. Lewis. The ground upon which the hotel was built required scores of pilings to be driven down to bedrock to support the nine-storied structure. As the story goes:

… The idea [of building a new hotel in Marshfield] is said to have been conceived by a group of prominent Marshfield men accustomed to eating together in the old Chandler Hotel dining room. These men usually stayed at the Benson Hotel in Portland when in the northern city on business and they wanted to see Marshfield with a hotel as fine or finer than the Benson.

The Depression wreaked havoc on the project and the work was abandoned in 1928 when more money was needed after the superstructure was finished. Standing gaunt and dismal for nearly twenty years, the gray concrete building bore the brunt of many jokesters whose attempt at humor gouged deeply the feelings of those who not only had lost money but were disappointed in the failure of the well-meaning project.

In 1947, the building was sold to W. A. Rushlight, a Portland businessman, for $500 with Coos County having waived the unpaid taxes to ease selling the building and returning it to the tax rolls.[73]

In 1922 Dr. G. B. Dowland arrived in Marshfield and joined the practice with Dr. Dix, as Dr. Manzer, former partner with Dix, had left the area for Seattle. In 1939, Dr. Dix retired from practice, but because of the shortage of doctors during WWII, he returned to medicine and partnered with Dr. Robert Dixon, retiring again in 1947.[49,74,75,76-79]

Dr. Dix died in Eugene, Oregon on March 27, 1961. He was eighty-four years old.

A DAIRYMAN, TOO

On December 27, 1938, the Coos Bay Times carried the following article about Dr. Dix's Brookmead Dairy operation on the south side of the Coos River:

... To keep the milk pitcher on the table morning, noon, and night well-filled with safe milk is the best insurance that one can have for every member of the family. Dieticians and physicians everywhere recognize body-building qualities of milk—but not just any milk. Milk can be dangerous as well as beneficial. Realization of this fact has been made by Dr. George E. Dix, a practicing physician and owner of Brookmead Dairy, who feels that the safety factor in milk is the most important phase in the successful operation of his picturesque dairy.

After four short years of development, including the introduction of the most modern scientific methods of processing milk, the 1938 business has been the largest in the history of the dairy. It is indeed unfortunate that every man, woman, and child in the Coos Bay area cannot have the experience of casually walking over the beautiful expanse of succulent pasture to see the improvements that have been made at the 160-acre Brookmead Ranch with its modern buildings—all basically important to the operation of this dairy. While every business is founded on a basis of financial success, there is outstanding evidence that in the development of Brookmead, Dr. Dix made this a secondary consideration. His business has been built to an enviable position as the leader in safe and nutritious milk for Coos Bay area residents.

Riding along the dike road, Dr. Dix points out the lush ninety acres of bottom ground where the grass is worth $200 per acre per grazing season. Dr. Dix has owned this ranch since 1918. When we visited the milking shed not one misstep was found in the entire process. Sixty cows were observed in their stanchions quietly chewing their cud, another thirty were observed in the nearby pasture awaiting their turn. There is frequent testing for various bovine diseases. The milk from this dairy is safe to drink whether pasteurized or raw.

The milk is transported in sterilized cans with the volume used for raw milk immediately placed in refrigeration and the balance put into one of the most scientifically modern pasteurizing plants known to the dairy industry. Once pasteurized, the milk is automatically bottled and then goes directly into refrigeration until delivered to the customer.

In summary, it can be said that $75,000 has been expended in preparatory work and arrangement for safe milk for Coos Bay residents. Housing quarters for the employees are modern. Ten pasture lots are fenced off with four- to sixteen-inch drain pipe underlaying the soil every 100 feet for proper drainage ...[71]

Dr. Robert James Dixon (1895–1963)

Robert James Dixon was born in San Francisco on August 8, 1895 to Mathew A. Dixon (1862–1943) and Alice F. Stevens (1866–1959). He received his elementary and secondary education in Santa Clara County and completed his medical training at Stanford University. He married Lucy Mary Powers (1895–1986) in 1922; she was the daughter of Albert Henry Powers (1862–1930) and Johanna Elizabeth Hogan (1866–1948). (Albert Powers was a partner with C. A. Smith in the Smith-Powers Logging Company at Marshfield, Oregon.) Two daughters were born to Robert and Lucy.

Shortly after completing his medical training, Dr. Dixon came to Coos Bay in 1923 and established a successful practice in the First National Bank building in Marshfield. Six years prior to coming to Coos Bay, he had enlisted in World War I.

In 1924, when funds were being sought for building the Methodist Hospital (aka Wesley Hospital, later known as the McAuley Hospital) in Marshfield, Dr. Dixon—along with other prominent citizens of the area and Drs. L. G. Johnson, A. B. Peacock, H. M Peery, William Horsfall, Everitt Mingus, George Dix, and J. I. Mershon—worked to raise the sufficient funds (about $65,0000) so that an additional $70,000 loan could be obtained to finish the hospital building. The original estimate needed to build the facility

This portrait of Dr. Robert Dixon was taken from the *Coos Bay Times* July 31, 1928, page 72.[80]

DOCTORS TO ENTER SPITTING MEET

… Southwestern Oregon physicians were challenged today by Dr. Donald M. Long, past president of the [Coos] County Medical Association and Marshfield health officer, to come on out and do your darnedest against him in the international intercollegiate and unaffiliated spitting derby at noon Saturday behind the Marshfield post office. This included all pharmacists. Dr. Long marked a spot on his office wall where he expects to hang the professional men's divisional champion certificate that will allow him to demonstrate his prowess at all medical conventions, clinics, army and navy infirmaries, medical campuses, and nursing schools. He named Dr. Robert J. Dixon as his second, terming him one of the finest artists I know at downstream wading on Coos River, indicating that his second also can flick a fly off a piece of fish bait at fifteen paces.

Asked how he gained prominence in expectorating, Dr. Long said, 'I'm a one-track spitter, I cling to the spewing technique and find it's a pip. Because of my pro-allied sympathies, I generally employ a little English from the looser lip. As a babe, my name was actually Groositifitis, but when they saw my potentialities in expectorating, they changed it to Long … [83]

Three judges were handpicked for the challenge: Professor W. R. Hyslop of the botany department at Oregon State College, Bob Ward of the *Seattle Post-Intelligencer*, and Clarence Osika, principal of the Coquille High School. According to the local interviewer, Bob Ward said:

… his Uncle McWarter, known as the St. Patrick of East Feliciana parish, could hit a snake between the eyes at twenty paces on a calm day. A cousin named Snortwurfle was a carpenter and never owned a hammer. He spat the nails into place, first taking a healthful chaw to work up steam … [83]

was $135,000. A later estimate put the actual construction cost of the new hospital of around $175,000.[82]

In 1958, Dr. Dixon received a lifetime membership in the Southwestern Oregon Medical Society for being an active member of the society for thirty-five years. A certificate was presented to him by the society's president, Dr. Raymond McKeown.

Dr. Dixon died in Coos Bay in March 1963, after serving the area some forty years as a physician and surgeon. He was sixty-seven years old.

Dr. Jacob "Dr. Jake" Pinkerton Easter (1842–1932)

Jacob P. Easter was born on September 12, 1842 in Highland County, Ohio, to John Burnett Easter (1805–1868) and Mary Ann Miller (1808–1896). Nine children were born to the couple, of which Jacob was the seventh. All the children were born in Highland County, Ohio, where their father was a farmer and a carpenter. Jacob spent his early years working on his family farm, and when the Civil War was in full swing, he enlisted in the Union Army on June 13, 1863. He served for two years as a private in the Light Artillery Brigade of the 24th Independent Battery, Ohio Volunteers, until he mustered out on June 26, 1865.

After the war, Jacob returned to his father's farm and found himself behind the plow as if the war years never existed. During this time, he enrolled in a private school in order to prepare for college. He then studied six months at Franklin College in Wilmington, Ohio, studying medical subjects. According to a local doctor, it seemed that Jacob had a natural ability to care for the sick, so he

This portrait of Dr. Dixon, ca. 1960s, was taken from the obituary column in the *Coos Bay Times*, March 2, 1963, page 1.[81]

In an interview given by Jacob P. Easter in 1927 and in his own words:

I was born on September 12, 1842 in a little log house with just one room and a loft with no kitchen or stove; the fireplace occupied most of one end of the house where Mother did the cooking. That room was kitchen, dining room, parlor, and bedroom. A trundle bed was kept under Father's and Mother's bed except when occupied by the three youngest children. At that time, there were eight children; another was born the next year.[84]

A 1932 interview with Dr. Easter continued his recollection of growing up:

… I spent my boyhood on the farm with axe, grubbing hoe, and plow helping to clear 300 acres. I attended school three months in the winter. In 1860, we had a literary society in an empty log house on Father's farm. We met every week; it was a community affair. It was there that I put on the program for an oration (I was a born Abolitionist). I tried to make a speech for Lincoln but was scared stiff. Two weeks later, I was again on for an oration and my subject was Lincoln. I had been gibed and twitted by my school mates of the Democrats and my fighting blood was up and when the night came I delivered the goods to a full house. That gave me the name 'The Lincolnite.' Well, I have been proud of that name always. My first vote I cast for president of the United States was for Abraham Lincoln … [84]

enrolled at the Physio-Medical College of Medicine in Cincinnati, Ohio. He graduated in February 1869 and started a practice in Wilmington, Kansas. He was known as "Dr. Jake."[84]

In 1880, he moved to Burlingame, Kansas, but because of some health issues, on June 20, 1883, he moved to Portland, Oregon, and then to Coos County. He settled in Coquille City. Records show that he was appointed the postmaster at Angora, Coos County, in 1888. Like so many early pioneer doctors, Dr. Easter visited his patients by all means of transport—by foot, by horse, by boat—often staying overnight with the sick, or even for a few days until the infirmed got better.

He also was known to interact with wilder creatures. As reported in the March 31, 1885 edition of the *Coquille City Herald*, page 3:

> ... *Dr. Easter killed an old bear and captured two nice cubs last week. He is raising the cubs.*
>
> *Anyone wishing a couple of nice young bears for pets can have the same at very reasonable prices ...*

In 1900, the federal census shows Dr. Easter in Dunn, Jackson County, Oregon, but he'd moved back to Coquille by 1910. In 1923, he moved to Portland to work with the Portland Electronic Clinic.[84,85]

In an interview about Prohibition that was carried in the *Coos Bay Times* in 1927, Dr. Easter was quoted as saying:

When the question of Prohibition was first up in Oregon, I organized the Temperance League and went all over the county delivering lectures in school houses and logging camps. Coos County has been dry ever since, but for the foreigners and bootleggers. I have preached in Oregon and six months in Washington. I have received in all just $750. I owe no man anything.[84]

Dr. Easter married at least three times—and possibly four. He wed his first wife, Nancy Jane Frump (1843–1873), on July 25, 1867 in Ohio. A year after Nancy died, he married again ... this time to Martha A. Musgrove (1837–1915). Two children were born to the first marriage, and four children were born to the second. One of the children from the second marriage, Chester Franklin Easter, became a doctor with a practice in Portland, Oregon, along with his wife, Mabel, also a doctor. When Jacob Easter's third wife (Viola P. Strang) died in 1929, he moved to Portland to live with his son Chester. In 1930, he married yet again and moved with his bride to Clatskanie, Oregon.[86]

Aside from his clinical practice in Coquille, he was the superintendent of the Coos County farm for indigent teens from 1886 to 1994. The job paid $1,400 per year. Before leaving Burlingame, Kansas, for Oregon, Dr. Easter was involved in the local Osage County poor farm. It was a natural extension of his experience in Ohio that he became involved in the Coos County indigent farm. During the time Dr. Easter was in charge of the farm, it stopped being a burden to the county and became profitable. As a side note, Dr. Easter was an ordained minister in the Church of Christ and around 1885, he began preaching in Coquille in a little church in town.

Dr. Jacob P. Easter died on July 13, 1932 in Portland, Oregon. He was eighty-nine years old.

Dr. George Dillard Elgin (1831–1916)

George Elgin was born in Clark County, Kentucky on May 23, 1831 to William Harrison Elgin (1802–1862) and Clementina Duvall (1810–1844). His father moved with the family to Missouri in 1839 and settled on a farm in Howard County, near the Moniteau River, six miles north of Rochefort. After graduating from Howard County High School George studied medicine under the supervision of John Wilcox, MD. George also attended lectures in the medical department at the University of Virginia in 1849–1850 and received his medical diploma from the University of Missouri in 1851.[87]

> … For many years, Dr. Elgin lived on his mining claims on Sixes River, where the traveler always found the latch string hanging on the outside of his cabin. He was a man of education and refinement, and it is said that a disappointment in his younger days caused him to live the secluded life he did, and prevented him from taking the position among his fellow men that his attainments fitted him for … [91]

In 1860, Dr. Elgin moved to California where he practiced medicine in Yolo and Lake Counties. By 1872, after trying his hand at gold mining on the Sixes River in southwestern Oregon, he moved to Myrtle Point, Oregon and set up a practice there. He was a contemporary of Doctors Tower and Leneve. One of Dr. Elgin's most prescribed medicine to his neighbors was cascara bark and Oregon grapes for laxatives. By 1890, he again became interested in gold mining operations on property located on the Sixes River and the 1910 census had him living in Eckley, Oregon, near the headwaters of the Sixes River. The census showed his profession as physician but other sources suggested he had retired from medicine when he moved to the mountain home above the river.[88-90]

Feeling ill, in February 1915, Dr. Elgin caught the beach stage out of Port Orford for Bandon, where he caught the boat to Portland and the train to the east. Dr. Elgin died at his sister's home in Rocheport, Boone County, Missouri, on May 15, 1916. He was eighty-four years old.

Dr. Alfred Jesse French (1910–2001)

Alfred J. French was born on January 4, 1910 at Falls City, Polk County, Oregon, to Clyde F. French (1878–1960) and Sarah Alice Judson (1887–1981). Alfred was the second son born to that marriage, and he had eight siblings. He was named after his grandfather, Alfred Jesse French (1838–1912). The family moved from Kansas in the early 1900s, finally settling in Salem, Oregon, in 1905. Alfred's father, Clyde, taught school for nineteen years. He was president of the Salem Teachers' Association and president of the teachers' union; he also served two terms as a Salem city alderman.

Alfred attended public schools in Polk County, Oregon, as well as in Yakima County,

Janet Stowall-French and Dr. Alfred J. French. Photo courtesy of Ancestry.com.

Janet Stowall-French and Dr. Alfred J. French, later in life. Photo courtesy of Ancestry.com.

Washington, as his family moved around. As shown in the 1930 federal census, the family had settled back in Salem, Oregon, where Alfred graduated from Willamette University in 1932, followed by the University of Oregon School of Medicine in 1936—where he was elected to Alpha Omega Alpha Medical Honorary Society. He completed his internship at the Multnomah County Hospital in Portland. Alfred married Janet Stowell in Salem, Oregon, in 1939.[92,93]

In 1937, Dr. French was a junior partner in the medical practice of Drs. A. B. Peacock, John M. Simpkin, and Donald M. Long located in Irving building in Marshfield. Aside from the years spent in the military during WWII, Dr. French practiced medicine in the Coos Bay area from 1937 to 1985. When the Sisters of Mercy took over the Wesley Hospital in Marshfield in 1939, Dr. Horsfall was the chief of staff, Dr. Leslie Johnson was vice-chief of staff, and Dr. Alfred French was secretary.

In September 1942, Dr. French, along with Drs. John Keizer and Fred Anderson, took the oath as members of the United States Army. Prior to their enlistment, the doctors had performed physical examinations on men called up for active duty. They were all commissioned as first lieutenants, along with Dr. John Seeley. During the war, Dr. French served as a flight surgeon. By 1944, Dr. French had risen to the rank of captain in the air medical corps and was stationed at Montgomery, Alabama. After being released from military service in 1946, he spent one year at Sweet Home, Oregon, as a local physician, then in 1947 returned to Coos Bay and rented space in Dr. Donald Long's office.

In 1957, Dr. French was elected chief of staff at the McAuley Hospital, along with Dr. Roger Flanagan as assistant chief of staff and Dr. Donald McCowan as secretary. French remained as chief of staff until the hospital was closed. Dr. French was an active

In September 1950, two men were swept overboard from the destroyer escort, USS *Gilligan*, when it was hit by a rogue wave as it attempted to cross the Coos Bay bar in a storm. The coast guard lifeboat was dispatched with Dr. Alfred French aboard, seen here as he attempts to transfer to the *Gilligan* to treat other injured men. Two sailors who were swept overboard lost their lives. Photo courtesy of the *Coos Bay Times*, September 25, 1950, page 1.[94]

PIONEER DOCTORS OF COOS COUNTY OREGON

member of the Southwestern Oregon Medical Society and the American Association of Family Practitioners. He was elected as a fellow in that organization in 1977.

At the time Dr. French took over as chief of staff at McAuley Hospital in 1957, there were twenty-two physicians active on the hospital staff:

> *Drs. Bernard Barkwill, William Corrigan, Chares Cottel, Robert Dixon, John Flanagan, Roger Flanagan, Alfred French, John Garner, Norman Harris, Douglass Johnson, William Kean, Ennis Keizer, Charles Lindsay, Amelia Lipton, Donald Long, Donald McCowan, Raymond McKeown, Richard McLean, Jack Pennington, Edwin Quinn, Eugene Sorum, and Anson Stage.*[92]

In 1957, twelve doctors were appointed to the courtesy staff at McAuley:

> *Drs. Carl Albertson, Edgar Berg, Norville Butler, Donald Courtney, Marshall Kennedy, Alan Loeffler, Ellsworth Lucas, Elmo Peterson, Ralph Meincke, Victor Westover, David White, and Pewter Wolfe.*[92]

Dr. Alfred J. French. Photo courtesy of the Coos History Museum.

In 1960, Drs. French, Corrigan, John Flanagan, and Roger Flanagan joined together to build a new medical clinic at 6th and Commercial Streets in Coos Bay. But while they coordinated in the construction of the new clinic, they did not form an official association.

In August 1985, Dr. French retired from the practice of medicine, after a career of forty-eight years. At his retirement party, he noted that he'd been responsible for many births in Coos County, and could count many where he attended to four generations of the same family. A tribute to Dr. French was written by Anita and Robert Hale and printed in the July 9, 1985 *Coos Bay World*:

> *… Dr. French abundantly fulfilled the definition of the ideal family doctor. Superior practice of medical science accompanied by loving care and empathy for his patients were outstanding attributes of Dr. French …*[95]

Dr. Alfred J. French died on February 16, 2001 in Portland, Oregon, where he and his wife Janet had moved in 2000. He was ninety-one years old.

Dr. Arthur Gale (1877–1936)

Arthur Gale was born on December 21, 1871 in Detroit, Michigan. His father was Benjamin Gale (1832–1906), of London, England; his mother, Carolyn Thornton (1832–1906) was born in Canada. Arthur came west as a young man and in 1902 married D. Gans (1876–1951).

After marriage, Arthur entered medical school, and graduated from the University of Oregon at Portland in 1910. His first practice was at Madras, Oregon, where he joined Dr. H. B. Haile. From there he went to Bandon in 1912 and opened his own clinic over the Orange Pharmacy. He practiced in Bandon until his death just after the catastrophic Bandon fire in 1936. While there was another Dr. Gale (R. G.) in North Bend in 1907–1908, there was no family relationship.[96]

Dr. Arthur Gale died at the Mast Hospital in Myrtle Point on December 28, 1936. He was sixty-five years old.

Dr. Arthur Gale with daughter Elizabeth, ca. 1918.

DR. ARTHUR GALE
Physician & Surgeon
Office over Orange Pharmacy. Office phone, 352. Residence phone, 353.

BANDON, OREGON

An ad in the semi-weekly *Bandon Recorder,* October 21, 1913.

Dr. Gale was among Bandon citizens who fought the fire that destroyed the town on September 26, 1936, giving aid to the ill and injured while his home and office were consumed by the flames. Some believe it was the inhalation of smoke and foul air during the fire that weakened his lungs and contributed to his demise. He had been on duty long hours during and after the fire, having reestablished his office in the temporary medical center. He was sixty-five years old at the time of his death. In January 1937, Dr. Edward Thorstenberg from Powers, Oregon, moved to Bandon and purchased the office equipment and medical practice of the late Dr. Gale.[98,99] Photo courtesy of the Oregon Historical Society.

An example of the medical prescriptions given to patients by licensed physicians during Prohibition. In this particular case, the script was issued by Dr. Gale for gin to be taken by the patient three times per day. While the production, transport, and sale of liquor was illegal during Prohibition, the National Prohibition Act allowed alcohol to be consumed for medicinal and religious use. It required a prescription that cost $3 from a doctor plus another $3 to $4 to get it filled by a pharmacist. The doctor could prescribe up to a pint of a certain kind of liquor. This was one of the few legal exceptions to the thirteen-year ban on alcohol initiated in 1920 by the 18th Amendment. Courtesy of the Bandon History Museum.

… Dr. Arthur Gale, a physician who for thirty years had responded to the needs of Bandon's ill at all hours, in any weather, and without thought of the patient's ability to pay, answered his last call at 8:10 last night at the Mast-Wilson Hospital. His death came as an aftermath of the Bandon fire, it is said … [97]

Dr. Verne Leonard Hamilton (1883–1940)

Verne Leonard Hamilton was born on April 5, 1883 in Nelson, Nuckolls County, Nebraska, to Charles Leonard Hamilton (1855–1919) and Fannie Luella Ryden (1861–1960). His father was a minister who lived in Nelson around the turn of the twentieth century, but moved west to Portland, Oregon, around 1910. Charles soon moved to Marshfield, where he became the pastor of the Methodist Church; he died in 1919 in that town.

Verne Hamilton had six siblings; two of his brothers were also medical doctors (Royden Ryden Hamilton and Charles William Hamilton) and one was a dentist (John Wesley Hamilton). In addition, his brother-in-law (Clarence Ulm Snider) was also a physician. Several of the brothers' spouses and sisters worked alongside their husbands as nurses. The other siblings settled around the Columbia River near Portland. For instance, Royden first went to Medford, Oregon, after graduating from medical school, but spent most of his career in Portland. Charles William spent most his medical career in Hood River, Oregon, save for a short stint as the local physician in Myrtle Point, Oregon; he died in Coos Bay in 1946. John Wesley, the only dentist in the Hamilton family, set up his dental practice in Portland, but died in Tillamook County in 1961. Dr. Clarence Snider, husband of Nellie May Hamilton, enlisted in the army, received his medical training in the service with additional studies at Willamette University, and died in San Francisco, California in 1952.[101]

The year after graduating with a medical degree from Willamette University in 1913, Dr. Verne Hamilton moved to Tillamook County, Oregon, where he took a position in the local hospital. He was in the last graduating class from the medical college at Willamette University before it merged with the University of Oregon Medical school in 1914. There were thirteen members in his graduation class.

Moves and Leadership Roles in Oregon

Like most rural towns along the Oregon coast at the time, timber dominated the economic scene and many towns suffered the boom-bust cycles of resource-based industries. As such, one of the large logging camps in that area closed and put the hospital where Verne was employed out of business. But Dr. Hamilton found the Pacific Coast too attractive to get very far away from it, so he moved to Coquille around 1914 and set up his medical practice upstairs over the Farmers and Mercantile Bank. On one occasion in 1914, while Dr. Russel C. Keizer was away, Dr. Hamilton took over the Smith-Powers emergency hospital associated with their logging camps in Coos County.[102,103]

In 1919 Dr. Hamilton became the mayor of Coquille. But in 1921, he formed a partnership with Dr. Abram L. Houseworth in Marshfield and moved to that town. In December 1922, the local paper announced that Hamilton was moving to The Dalles, Oregon. As he was making arrangements to dispose of his fourteen-room hospital building in Coquille, he was quoted as saying that he disliked leaving Coos County, but the opening at The Dalles was such that he could not overlook it. Shortly after moving to The Dalles, Dr. Hamilton, along with his brother Dr. Charles W. Hamilton, were instrumental in building a new hospital in that town.[104]

In 1929 Dr. Hamilton left The Dalles and moved to Klamath Falls to open a practice in that town, where his brother, Royden, had practiced for several years before he moved north to Portland. Dr. Verne Hamilton stayed in Klamath Falls for only a few years, however, before returning to Coquille in 1934.

Twenty years had passed since he'd started his original medical practice in Coquille, and much had changed. No longer was he using a horse as the mode of transport to visit patients. He purchased a two-wheeled Moto-Scooter that was powered by a small gasoline engine. He claimed it got one hundred and twenty miles to the gallon. Both Dr. and Mrs. Hamilton were often seen scooting around town in his newfangled gadget.[105]

In 1936 Dr. Hamilton was involved in building a second hospital in Coquille.

TWO COQUILLE PHYSICIANS TO BUILD $50,000 HOSPITAL[107,108]

… Work was started today on the new Belle Knife Hospital to be located on the intersection of Front and Taylor Streets in downtown Coquille, in the Farmers and Merchants Bank building and Richmond building.

The hospital is the property of Dr. V. L. Hamilton, who today announced that he has leased the home of the defunct Coquille bank from George A. Ulett, with option to purchase, and will remodel it and the adjoining building belonging to Dr. James Richmond to make a hospital that will be open by October 15th. It will replace the present Knife Hospital located at 327 South Beach street.

Dr. Richmond and Dr. Hamilton are forming a partnership in which Dr. Richmond will specialize in surgery and Dr. Hamilton will take care of general practice. The doctors will occupy the first floor. The second story of both buildings is to be remodeled to contain eighteen beds and the surgery room. A third story will be added in 1938. When all is completed, including an elevator, the hospital will handle thirty-five patients …

In 1934, Dr. Verne Hamilton applied for a patent for his creation of an antacid formula medication. It was developed by him while in Coquille:[106]

Serial No. 357.197 Vern Leonard Hamilton, doing business as

Alka-Algae Company

Coquille, Oregon

Filed October 17, 1934

The term Algae is disclaimed apart from the other features of the mark shown.

For Medicinal Preparation Used as an Anti-acid and Recommended for Treating Gastric Ulcers, Hyperacidity Colitis and Chronic Constipation Claims used since April 1933.

Soon after the new Coquille hospital was up and running, Dr. Hamilton moved back to Portland to pursue the development of his new stomach medicine—Alka Algae. His interest in the hospital was taken over by Belle Knife, whose name the hospital bore.

On September 13, 1940, Dr. Verne Leonard Hamilton died of injuries suffered when he was struck by an automobile while walking across a highway at the north end of McMinnville, Oregon. He was fifty-seven years old.

Dr. Walton Haydon (1856–1932)

Dr. Walton Haydon was born in Devon, England in 1854 to George Henry Haydon (1822–1891) and Clarissa Risdon (1830–1917). His father was a barrister (lawyer), and head of the Bethlem Hospital in London. According to one source, the Haydon name has been traced back to the year 1066. The family still bears the coat of arms granted by the king of England in 1412. Walton was tutored by governesses until he was ten years of age; then he attended a public school in London. He received his medical training at the University of London, and after completing his medical schooling, he traveled throughout Europe.

An Adventurous Life as a Young Surgeon

Dr. Haydon even served as a surgeon aboard a voyage to the Arctic in 1875. The trip took over a year, and during that time he collected multiple plant specimens. That was the first year of his employ with the Hudson Bay Company as they explored Canada. For several years, he was surgeon and superintendent at Moose Factory at the southern end of James Bay, Ontario, for the Hudson Bay Company. At the time Dr. Haydon worked at Moose Factory, one or two ships arrived from England each summer bringing supplies for the entire year. He stayed at Moose Factory for several years.[109-112]

In 1878, Walton married Nina Jane Vetch. Six children were born to the couple; each in different parts of Canada except for one: Walton Haydon Jr., who was born November 24, 1894 in Oregon—and hence was a U.S. citizen by birth. In 1883, Dr. Haydon left the employ of the Hudson Bay Company after covering a large expanse of the James River and Hudson Bay territory. While traveling throughout parts of Canada, he collected butterflies and plants for Charles Darwin, who wanted to study the variations in animal and plant life. At that time, Haydon developed an interest in photography and prepared his own wet plates and his own chemicals.

Dr. Walton Haydon. Photo courtesy of the Coos History Museum.

Settling in Oregon

In 1893, he left Canada and immigrated to the United States along with his wife and six children. The family first settled in Portland, but a year later Dr. Haydon came to Bay City (now called Eastside, Oregon, located on the eastern shore of Isthmus Slough). Within two years the family moved to Bandon, Oregon. Dr. Haydon came back to the Bay Area in 1903 and practiced his trade until his death in 1932.

Dr. Haydon was an ardent botanist and naturalist and explored the rich fauna and flora of the Coos County region.[109]

Ad for Dr. Walton Haydon as copied from the weekly *Coast Mail*, September 26, 1903.

Dr. Haydon was also reported to be quite a good cook, and several close friends would often gather at his home for a good meal and stimulating conversations. One might imagine the stories he could tell about his escapades throughout the wilds of Canada! Some of these close friends included George Flanagan, Jim Flanagan, Dr. William Horsfall, Charles Nicholson, and many others.

Dr. Walton Haydon (left of post) and Dr. George Dix (above beer bottles). Photo courtesy of the Coos History Museum.

Sadly, when a fire swept through the Marshfield Front Street district in 1922, Dr. Haydon's collection of plants was destroyed. However, he had made copies of all the material descriptions and sent them to an old professor of his in England, so all was not lost. The fire was described by the local *Coos Bay Times* newspaper:

… Fire which started at 4 o'clock Sunday morning [July 23, 1922] swept a large portion of the Marshfield waterfront, destroying 25 business buildings and four residences and causing a loss of probably $200,000. The city hall and many of the city records and maps were lost.

For a time, it appeared that the entire business section of Marshfield would be wiped out. The port tug Fearless kept three lines of hose working and the bar dredge Michie was called from the lower bay. Hundreds of people gathered to help save the contents of some of the buildings, but in many cases, the occupants were away for weekend visits and lost everything.

Probably the greatest personal and community loss was the destruction of the offices and apartments of Dr. Walton Haydon, physician and distinguished scientist who was away over Sunday. He had the only complete records and specimen collections of mineral, sea products, and plants of this part of the state. His library was one of the rarest and a collection of curios gathered from all over the world was famous throughout the coast. His collection of photographs was priceless and never to be replicated as were the finest microscopes and other scientific apparatus; all gone …

A FUNNY LITTLE PAIN

Scientist sent from afar to study the Oregon Coast were referred to Dr. Haydon. At various times he made notable collections, some of which he presented to the University of Oregon. He was above all, however, a humanist. He watched the world roll madly by with an observant but tolerant understanding. Friends liked to gather in his Front street office in Marshfield and rearrange the universe. A few were privileged to go with him on his long exploratory rambles. He was a good companion because he enjoyed every minute of living.

Regrets would be out of order in speaking of a man who looked on both life and death as an extremely interesting adventure. Yet the tall, rugged gray-bearded old gentleman in the rough clothes was almost one of the landmarks of growing Oregon. Wealth and fame he did not seem to desire. He seemed to say that the important thing is to be interested; if you are interested, you will be interesting ... [111]

Dr. Walton Haydon came to Bandon, Oregon, in 1897, and then to Marshfield in 1903—where he practiced up to the time of his death in 1932. Photo courtesy of the Coos History Museum

Dr. Walton Haydon, pioneer physician, writer, and naturalist died at his home in Empire, Oregon, on December 14, 1932. He was seventy-eight years old.[109]

He was remembered as "... *The English gentleman with a large pipe and pockets full of butterfly nets and collection boxes ...*"[7]

Dr. Henry (aka Heinrich) Mazzeny Hermann (1812 [or 1816]–1869)

Dr. Henry M. Hermann was a member of the old Baltimore colony group that settled in Broadbent, Oregon before there was a town of Myrtle Point. The community was along the South Fork Coquille River. Henry Hermann was reported as being born in 1812 in Hesse Cassel, Germany. (Some, however, e.g. his son Theobalt Manell Hermann in 1922, recalled that his father's birth was in 1816—perhaps records were sparse back then in Germany.) Henry graduated from the University of Marburg with a medical degree in 1831, and afterwards occupied the chair of professor of Anatomy and Demonstrator of Surgery at the same university.

Fleeing Germany for Baltimore

Hermann was a participant in the failed German revolution of 1834–35 and eventually fled his native land bound for Baltimore, Maryland.[56]

The following story was told to Fred Lockley by Henry's son, Theobald Manell Hermann (1845–1928), and reported in the *Portland Journal* in 1922:[113,114]

… My father [Dr. Henry Hermann] was born in Hesse-Cassel, Germany. All of his people were army people and he was to follow in his father's footsteps and become an army officer. When he was not over nine- or ten-years- old, his uncle broke a leg. Father visited him. The leg was so painful that he asked my father to take the bandage off so he could secure relief from the pressure. My father did so. After an hour or so, he asked Father to replace the bandage. Presently the doctor came. When he looked at his patient's leg, he asked, 'Who took the bandage off?' My father, very much subdued by the doctor's look and tone, said, ' I did.' 'Who put the bandaging back again?' inquired the doctor. 'I did' answered my father. When my uncle confirmed my father's statement, the doctor said, 'You shall study medicine. You have a deft touch. You will make a famous surgeon.'

My father shook his head and said, 'No, I am to be an army officer.' The doctor said, 'Let me tell you something. I want you to think seriously over what I tell you. A physician and surgeon spends his life helping others. His life is devoted to service. He heals the sick and succors the suffering, whether they can pay him or not …

… My father pondered the doctor's words … and against the wishes of his relatives, decided to study medicine. While in college he found that the right of free speech and free press was forbidden. One could not write or speak of his own beliefs but could say or write only what the authorities said should be believed …

As the interview went on it was apparent that Henry, along with other students, rebelled against the rules and were arrested. Fortunately for Henry, the judge who heard his case was a friend of the Hermann family and determined that the case against young Henry lacked sufficient evidence for a conviction. The interview continued:

… One night the judge came to my father's room and said, 'I am taking my life and liberty in my hands to come here to warn you … In an hour the soldiers will be here to seize you. A ship is leaving for America. Go quickly. I cannot save you if you are again arrested and tried … My father, along with a fellow student, went to the ship and met the captain, who agreed to transport them to America. They were hidden is a wooden cask called a hogshead until they were well out to sea. That was in 1834 when my father was about eighteen years old …

Henry Hermann and his sailing companion arrived in America and for several years lived in Baltimore, where he continued his medical studies. He owned a drug store in town that was very profitable. To add more to his growing wealth, Dr. Hermann took a job as a physician at a local coal mine near Cumberland, Maryland. While working at the mine, he met his future wife, Elizabeth Hopkins (1821–1900). They were married on November 20, 1840. And from this union, nine children were born—six in Maryland and three in Coos County, Oregon. Being a well-educated man himself, in 1856, Dr. Hermann moved his family back to Baltimore so that the children could be provided a better education.

Heading to West, to Oregon

In an effort to escape the depression that gripped the east coast of the United States in 1857, Dr. Hermann and John Ousterhous set out the next year for the West Coast to evaluate a site for a future settlement. They had three basic requirements for a new German colony in mind: *1. A mild climate; 2. Pure water; and 3. An area free from cyclones.*

His first inclination was to settle in the Willamette Valley, where other settlers were moving, but in 1858, after missing a boat that would transport them from San Francisco to Portland, they rented horses and started overland for the Willamette Valley. As fate would have it, their route took them to Roseburg, Oregon where they met miners who described the conditions in the Coquille valley. They departed with a small group from Roseburg and found what became the future colony site on the South Fork of the Coquille River, near the current community of Broadbent. In March 1859 Dr. Hermann sailed back home to Baltimore from the mouth of the Umpqua River for the long journey by sea.[60]

Once back home in Baltimore, on April 11, 1859, a small group of families set sail back to Oregon via the Bahamas, Jamaica, and the Isthmus of Panama. They then loaded aboard another sailing vessel on the Pacific side of Panama; they stopped in Mexico, then San Francisco, and finally they disembarked at Port Orford, Oregon. From there, they traveled by wagon, horse, and foot to Hermann's promised land, arriving in May–June 1859. It was originally called Hermannsville, until 1908 when Charles Broadbent built his cheese factory there, and the name was changed to Broadbent.[115]

Settling in the Coquille Valley

As transcribed from a handwritten document by (David) Binger Hermann (1843–1926), Dr. Hermann's eldest son, in his autobiography the following was taken:

> … *In April 1859, seven families and several single men left Baltimore, Maryland, hoping to build a new life in Oregon's Coquille valley. Known as the Baltimore Colony, this group of families was led by Henry Hermann, a German-born*

physician who wanted to escape the stresses of city life and find a more healthful life in the far west ...[116]

When Dr. Hermann arrived in the Coquille valley, he purchased the old homestead of Harry Baldwin and lived in Baldwin's cabin until his house was completed. They were not the first to settle along the South Fork of the Coquille River, but they made the first permanent settlement. Those who preceded them were miners who were chasing the discovery of gold in 1853, as well as trappers and herdsmen who were living in log cabins built on the grassy prairies adjacent to the river. Most of the Baltimore Colony men were of the background that they knew very little about the woods or how to make lumber, etc., but they learned.[117,118]

Theobald Manell Hermann continued with his story about his father, Dr. Henry Hermann:

> *... Father had shipped his library, his surgical instruments, and a supply of drugs from Baltimore on a clipper ship that was bound for San Francisco by way of the Horn. It took six months to make the trip. Father secured a scow to transport his library, his surgical instruments, and his drugs. In the swift current of the river [Coquille], it foundered within a mile of the landing. The medicines, especially powders and such things as Epson salts, melted away and were lost. Many of the books were ruined. Some of the instruments he did not recover until the following summer.*
>
> *Father was the only doctor in this part of the country and went on horseback or by canoe all over the coast, his district including the country as far inland as Roseburg and as far south as Port Orford ...*

One of the lineal descendants of Dr. Hermann who lived in the Coquille valley was Virgil Hermann. I knew Virgil myself, as he and I had served on the Coos County Planning Commission in the early 1970s. He was reported as saying:

> *... The old vacant house, which was built of split red cedar by Dr. Hermann in 1861 is both a delight and something of a dilemma. It is an official pioneer dwelling—the oldest structure in Coos County. But it has grown dilapidated over the years and is now almost more trouble than it's worth to fix up. Dr. Hermann lived and practiced medicine in the house until his death in 1869 ... "[119]*

Once Henry settled into his homestead on the South Fork, he became interested in agriculture and experimented with many crops—tobacco, sugar beets, flax, almonds, cherries, berries of many kinds, and artichokes. He had 150 hives of bees at one time and sent samples to San Francisco. Transportation down the Coquille River and onto waiting sailing vessels presented an insurmountable problem for the Baltimore Colony farmers, including Dr. Hermann. The only product that could be shipped to the California markets without spoiling was livestock, as they could be driven to the safe harbor at Marshfield, loaded aboard a sailing vessel headed for San Francisco. As Dr. Hermann devoted more and more time to his agricultural ventures, his homestead grew to 320 acres.[54]

In the fall of 1923, the descendants of Dr. Hermann gathered for a big family reunion at Camas Valley, a few miles west of the town of Roseburg, Oregon. Dr. Hermann's son, Binger Hermann, then eighty-years-old, gave a talk to the family concentrating on two main topics: his father and celebrating the completion of a road between Coos County and the Umpqua Valley:

> … It was then that old Doctor Hermann, remembering expedients he had seen in the Alleghany mountains, seriously proposed, in printed form, that Coos County and the Umpqua Valley should be connected by a hardwood tram railway, with homemade cars propelled by horse power. Three days' time in winter and two long days in summer was the horseback schedule of time between Coquille River, with one day additional from Coos Bay to Roseburg over the trails in such a journey. And now like a dream in the "Arabian Nights," but three or four hours complete, these same widened points, by easy, safe and pleasant transit over splendid road-ways …[118]

AN ODDITY

… When Binger Hermann died in 1926 and his will had been accepted by the courts, all the property was equally divided among his [three living] children, except for a few articles of personal property that was divided between the sons and one brother in Myrtle Point. Among those effects are some legal pleadings in Abraham Lincoln's handwriting, a piece of napkin stained with the blood of that president and a lizard preserved in alcohol, the lizard having been taken alive from a man's stomach by Dr. Henry Hermann, Binger Hermann's father …[121]

To add some detail to the early roads throughout Coos County, in 1916 Louis J. Simpson, from Shore Acres in Coos County and known for his habit of driving his automobiles fast, the following was recorded by the local newspaper:

> … L. J. Simpson and Jesse Barton drove to Roseburg and on to Portland in record-breaking time. Mr. Simpson was at the wheel most all the way. Reuben Mast joined him at Coquille and drove the car from Bridge. Mr. Simpson drove to Bandon in 1:15 from Marshfield, from Bandon to Coquille in 1:01, Coquille to Roseburg in 4:15, and from Roseburg to Portland in nine hours, including a stop for dinner. Simpson was driving his Buick automobile, one of his favorites …[120]

The cost of the sixty-one-mile roadway was $1,750,000 and connected Roseburg to the paved Pacific Highway.

Dr. Henry M. Hermann died at Broadbent, Oregon December 16, 1869. He was fifty-seven years old.

"Dr." Jonathan Frazier Hodson (1811–1903)

Jonathan Frazier Hodson was born in Indiana on April 26, 1821 to Enos C. Hodson (1790–1853) and Lavina Frazier (1793–1862). In 1844, Jonathan married Emily Ann Parris (1831–1855) in Jefferson County, Iowa and two children were born of that marriage. In 1850 he crossed the plains with an oxen team to California, where he stayed a year or two, before going back East by way of the Isthmus of Panama. There was no record about what happened to his first wife and children, but in 1857, he married Eliza J. Ross (1832–1916) in Marion County, Iowa, and in 1858 he again crossed the plains with his new wife and a young son, coming this time to Oregon.

Settling in Oregon

After living in Deer Creek in Douglas County, Oregon, for a year, Hodson came to Empire City in 1861 or 1862, where he owned and managed a hotel. About this same time, he acquired land east of Coos Bay near the South Fork Coos River. At the time the Coos River country was still a wilderness, and travel was mainly by Indian dugout canoes. Eliza and Dr. Hodson had seven children, one born before they left Iowa and the rest born in Oregon.[122,123]

Jonathan Hodson. Photo courtesy of Find a Grave (www.findagrave.com)

Jonathan Hodson had studied medicine in books and under the supervision of other doctors, but had no official education on the subject. For many years, however, he dispensed his medical knowledge and homemade remedies among the area settlers— being sometimes called as far away as Scottsburg, Oregon (today about a 45-mile drive northeast of Coos Bay) to help fellow homesteaders. Over time, Hodson acquired the title of "doctor" for which he became known locally, even though, as noted, he never did train formally.

Life Beyond Medicine

Hodson was a member of the Masons and the Odd Fellows, and helped organize the first lodges of those orders at Coos Bay. He left both organizations in the late 1870s, though, and joined the United Brethren Church, which opposed secret societies.

He also built the first grist mill in Coos County on his property adjacent to the Coos River. It ran by water power and was a great convenience in the early days.

"Dr." Jonathan Hodson died at his home on the Coos River on August 14, 1903, at age eighty-two. He had been in failing health for four or five years, and had been bedridden for several months prior to his death.[123]

Jonathan F. Hodson; ca. 1890. Photo courtesy of Ancestry.com.

He was buried at the Coos River Cemetery, and those who attended the burial were carried upriver on the *Alert*. Besides his widow, four sons and four daughters survived him—save for one son, John M. Hodson, who had died several years before at Myrtle Point.

"Dr." Jonathan F. Hodson (left) and his brother James F. Hodson. Jonathan Hodson's brother was a blacksmith. Photo courtesy of Ancestry.com.

Dr. William Horsfall (1867–1958)

Reverend William Horsfall. Photo courtesy of the Coos History Museum.

William Horsfall Jr. was born in Lancashire, England in 1867 to William Horsfall (1839–1921) and Sarah Howard (1847–1935), and at the age of four moved with his parents to America in 1871. His father entered the Theological Seminary at Kansas City in 1880, and became a missionary at Baxter Springs, Cherokee County, Kansas. Within two years, the family moved to Miles City, Montana.

A Move to Oregon, and William Jr. Becomes a Teacher, Then a Doctor

Soon the family moved again, this time to Newport, Oregon for Reverend Horsfall's health; and then to Marshfield in 1886, where the elder Horsfall conducted services in the old Lockhart building on Front Street. William Jr. was twenty years old when the family came to Coos Bay.[124,125]

William Jr. taught school at Kentuck, Oregon, after he graduated from the Bishop Scott Academy in Portland, Oregon. The Kentuck school was a small, rural one-room schoolhouse adjacent to a slough to the east of the Coos Bay. He continued to teach school at Kentuck until he entered medical school, graduating in December 1892 from Cooper's Medical College in San Francisco. (In 1908, the school was merged into Stanford University, and became known as the Stanford University Department of Medicine.)

After graduation, the newly minted Dr. Horsfall returned to Marshfield to establish a medical practice. Dr. Horsfall also worked at the Mayo Clinic in Minnesota for a while, but returned to Coos Bay in 1893, set up his office on Front Street in Marshfield, and served that community as a physician and surgeon for the next sixty-four years.[126-128]

Dr. William Horsfall Jr. married Lydia Elizabeth Yoakam (1875–1963) on April 7, 1896 at Marshfield in a ceremony officiated by his father. The new Mrs. Horsfall became well known in the area as an accomplished musician. Her grandfather, John Yoakam, had also been well known locally: he crossed the prairies in the covered-wagon days, and settled with his family on a homestead near Empire City. (John Yoakam died on January 14, 1876 at Marshfield. He was so well respected that at his burial site on the Coos River, over four hundred mourners gathered to pay their last respects.)[129]

William and Lydia Horsfall had three children:

- William Horsfall III (1898–1942), was a book-keeper for a time during the 1920s for a gold mine operation in Calaveras County, California before moving to Los Angeles. He later married a woman named Genevieve Madonna, but his mother had the marriage annulled. Embittered, William did not talk to his parents for five years. He then married Frances Bonnie Smith (1895-1969).

- Colonel George Horsfall, MD (1900–1968) first married Alice Mortensen (1906–1994) but they divorced and he married Helen Linstruth. Dr. George Horsfall served in several medical capacities in the military throughout Europe and the far east, and by the late 1950s he was the commanding officer of the U.S. Army Medical Center at Fort Lee, Virginia.

Reverend William Horsfall and Sarah Howard. Photo courtesy of the Coos History Museum.

William Horsfall Jr. Photo courtesy of the Coos History Museum

Dr. William and Lydia Elizabeth (Yoakam) Horsfall later in life. Photo courtesy of the Coos History Museum.

- Marion Horsfall (1902–1993) never married. After college, she taught school in Glendale, California, for many years, but in the early 1950s she returned to Coos Bay to care for her aging parents.

When WWI broke out, Dr. William Horsfall was appointed the representative of the Volunteer Medical Service Corps for Coos and Curry Counties. (Dr. Bartle, who we have learned about earlier, served as the representative for Lane County), and according to a local newspaper article, Dr. Horsfall served in the U.S. Naval Reserve Medical Corps as medical officer in charge of the Coos Bay Naval Radio Station from 1917–1919.

A Resourceful Doctor

Even as a young practitioner, Dr. William Horsfall was unusually courageous and resourceful. For instance, back in 1894, he performed an appendectomy on the kitchen table in a lonely cabin in the Coquille valley. It was probably the first successful operation of its kind performed in Coos County. Another example of Dr. Horsfall's creativity was reported by Emil Peterson back in 1948:

Dr. William Horsfall.
Photo courtesy of the Coos History Museum.

… It was during the early years of his practice that he received an urgent call from South Slough. A woman had been gored by a cow. The report didn't indicate how badly she had been hurt. The doctor had to go prepared for any emergency.

The trip to South Slough meant a long horse and buggy ride. Dr. Horsfall had become engaged to marry Miss Lydia Yoakam, a teacher in the Marshfield school. He invited her to accompany him. She accepted the invitation and they made the long drive over the old wagon road through Empire and on to South Slough.

At the farm home, the doctor found the woman in bed. The wound was a bad one. It meant a major operation. There was no hospital within several hundred miles. What was to be done had to be done in that little farm home; water heated; an operating table had to be improvised—it was the kitchen table. An anesthetic must be administered. The doctor needed an assistant.

Ad in the *Bandon Recorder* for Dr. William Horsfall's Hospital in Marshfield, 1905. The hospital opened in 1904 with nine beds.[130] There was no further information about this hospital.

Miss Yoakam had remained in the buggy, waiting. The doctor pressed her into service, saying that he must have help. She replied that she was a teacher of music, not a nurse. This being an emergency, however, she did her part under the doctor's instructions, while he completed the operation successfully ... [124]

Reflecting on his memory of meeting Dr. Horsfall, Emil R. Peterson wrote:

... In his professional work, he [Dr. Horsfall] would go at any and all times—night or day—whenever and wherever duty called. Sometimes afoot with a lantern,

HOUSE CALLS VIA A SWIM

... And there are those who even recall when Dr. Horsfall, without aid of rowboat or makeshift oars, made many trips across the bay by swimming the long stretch. In fact, in years gone by, Dr. William Horsfall was such an outstanding swimmer that he taught every moppet in town how to hold its breath under water and now to swim across the mudflats on the east side ... [131]

... It was years ago that Dr. William Horsfall would make one of the toughest night calls of all. He'd be summoned to Eastside to deliver a baby and started the trip over by row boat. It is recalled that at one time he lost an oar and unable to make the trip by row boat, he leaped overboard, held the little black bag over his head and swam to Eastside to deliver the new baby ... [132,133]

To prove that genetics do indeed carry through to future generations, the story of Dr. Horsfall's son Dr. George Horsfall and Oregon's Crater Lake proves the point:

... Dr. George Horsfall [1900–1968], while on his way to California, established two records at Crater Lake when he was the first Oregon man to ever swim the lake from the landing to Wizard Island, a distance of one and three-quarter miles, and set a record by swimming the distance in fifty minutes. Four other men have made this swim, it was reported. Dr. Horsfall stated the water was ice cold ... [134]

Apparently, young George Horsfall was not only a superb swimmer, but he could hold his own in a boxing or wrestling match.

Sketch of Dr. William Horsfall traveling to a patient in the dark with his medical bag and lantern.124. Courtesy of the Coos History Museum

sometimes on a bicycle, perhaps in a row boat across the bay or a stream and then by horseback on trails through woods and over hills. When roads permitted, he went with horse and buggy. Later there came the gas boat and the auto, but for many years there will were places where boat or auto could not reach and the doctor had to continue by the old means of travel ... [124]

In 1901, Dr. Horsfall purchased property at the corner of Third and Central in Marshfield and built their home where the family lived for two decades. Then in 1923, Charles Hall organized the Coos Bay Building Corporation as a vehicle to construct a building to accommodate the Coos and Curry Telephone Company. On July 23, 1923, the company purchased the property on which the Horsfall home stood and the residence was moved to South Second and Johnson. As the local newspaper reported, the Horsfalls lived in the house during its two-week journey down Second Street. Once the lot was cleared at Third and Central, the Hall Building was constructed in 1924.[135]

Loved by the Community

In 1939, Dr. Horsfall was the recipient of the Coos Bay Lions Club Number 1 Citizen of the Year award. At the time of the award, Horsfall had been in continual practice for fifty years. At the ceremony, there were elaborate citations extolling his numerous activities and service to the community over the decades. People were also reminded that Dr. Horsfall practiced on the bay when many calls were made on horseback, riding over the hills to Empire, Charleston, Libby, and similar points. To attend to those that were waterbound, he used a rowboat for calls along the Coos River, as well as the Catching, Willanch, Kentuck, Haynes, and Larson Inlets.

The local paper also reported on commitment and his generosity, as follows.

If testimonials could be solicited from people, I vision them coming in by the hundreds to tell of charitable works done to families where there was no hope of repayment, of long hours spent at the bedsides of the ill no matter how poor, and of unfailing friendliness which carries the doctor on long trips about the countryside.[136]

Another such tribute was carried in the local newspaper a couple of days after Dr. Horsfall had died:

... She said she felt he [Dr. Horsfall] saved her life, along with the lives of her brothers and sisters, when they were typhoid fever victims living in their ranch home on Willanch Slough. She recalled the doctor visited them every day for two months. He made the trip across the bay to Cooston in his rowboat and rode from there on a horse ... [137]

Yet another tribute posted in the Open Forum in the local newspaper back in 1939 was a poem about Dr. Horsfall (author unknown):

Coos Bay doffs its hat today to one we delight to esteem
Sometimes there comes a man who may, passing along life's turbulent stream,
Stand out from others in bold relief to share our sorrows, assuage our grief.

Fifty years! How swiftly they go for one who labors here below,
And knows that gold is never the end but serves all men and calls them friend.

No humble cottage has been too bare, that he did not hasten to enter there.
No storm has ever been too wild to keep him away from a suffering child.
No trail has been too rugged or steep, his rendezvous with pain to keep.

He has taken from life, as he went along, his share of joy from an inner song.
His garden is always gay with flowers; birds sweetly sing in its leafy bowers.
He knows the thrill of the morning trail; a gentle-eyed deer, a covey of quail.

He knows the flash of a silver trout; he knows the joy of a hunter's shout.
He has stood on a cliff in a quiet place and thrilled to the ocean breeze on his face.
He has watched the sun in glory go down, into the sea of midnight blue,
Away from the struggles and trials of town, his strength and courage to renew.

Most anyone can make a rhyme, few, like him, have lives sublime.
Oh, for the gift of a golden pen, to write him all the thanks of men.
Lacking this, I can only say: Coos Bay doffs its hat today.[138]

By: I.O.

In October 1952, the local *News-Review* paper reported on yet another honor.

MEDICAL SOCIETY OF OREGON HONORS
DR. GEORGE E. HOUCK
AND DR. WILLIAM HORSFALL

… The unsung heroes of medicine are the family physicians of the nation who have given years of devoted and competent service to their communities. Each has served his community for about sixty years. Both have practiced in two eras of medicine, the age of empiricism, still lingering in the 90s, and the later scientific period of the present century. In this fruitful transition from empiricism to science, both continued to employ their unusual talents in the art of medicine, while eagerly embracing the new scientific methods. Thus, both continued to bring to their patients the warmth of the heart while utilizing the cold efficiency of the new service … [140]

Dr. Horsfall was an active member of the Eagles Lodge, Aerie 538, in Coos Bay. He was appointed the lodge's physician in 1904 and thereafter elected for fifty-three consecutive years. At an elaborate ceremony in 1958, Dr. Horsfall was given a diamond studded Eagles pin along with a plaque bearing a silhouette of a horse-drawn carriage amid fir trees and an "Ode to Our Doctor" that also called him "Our Beloved Brother Dr. Horsfall"—declaring to each and all he is a friend. The introduction speech given at the celebration captured the basic essence of Horsfall when the commentator simply said: "The doctor has never overlooked an opportunity to do good." Afterward, the Eagles Lodge retired Dr. Horsfall's regalia. Courtesy of the Coos History Museum.

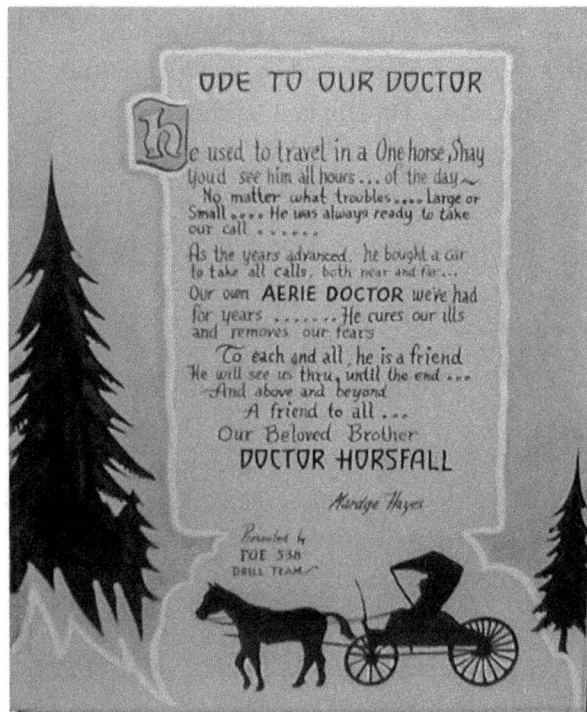

ODE TO OUR DOCTOR

He used to travel in a One horse Shay
You'd see him all hours ... of the day—
No matter what troubles.... Large or Small.... He was always ready to take our call......

As the years advanced, he bought a car to take all calls, both near and far...
Our own AERIE DOCTOR we've had for years........ He cures our ills and removes our fears

To each and all, he is a friend
He will see us thru, until the end...
...And above and beyond
A friend to all ...
Our Beloved Brother
DOCTOR HORSFALL

Marilyn Hayes

Presented by
FOE 538
DRILL TEAM

A Summer Place

Dr. Horsfall and his brother. Photo courtesy of the Coos History Museum.

Dr. William Horsfall (in photo below on left) was quite an outdoorsman. He had a summer home on a lake in the sand hills north of North Bend, Oregon, where he found enjoyment in nature during spare hours from his medical practice in Marshfield.

In 1906, this land had been withdrawn from homestead for use as coal lands, as well as for the Umpqua National Forest lands. In the application for a homestead in 1909, Dr. Horsfall noted that he had resided on the land from 1903–1906. The application went on to state that his family had moved onto the property full-time beginning in 1907 and that he travelled back and forth to the property every Friday and Monday from 1907–1909. In 1910, the property was given over by the federal government to Dr. Horsfall from the public domain. An inspection report by the General Land Office in January of 1910 noted that the land contained a good house, barn, chicken house, well (with windmill), and forty acres that were fenced. Apparently Horsfall and two of his neighbors had successfully raised cranberries in the marshland too.

Dr. William Horsfall Jr. died on March 21, 1921 at Bandon, Oregon, at the age of eighty-two. He was often referred to as the "Dean of Doctors" in Coos County.[141]

The Horsfall family (L to R standing): Helen Linstruth, second wife of Colonel George Horsfall; George Horsfall Jr. (youngest son of Colonel George Horsfall); Colonel George Horsfall; Dr. William Horsfall (oldest son of Colonel George Horsfall); and Marion Horsfall. (L to R seated): Lydia Yoakum Horsfall and Dr. William Horsfall Jr. Photo courtesy of Coos History Museum.

4—1023-R.

The United States of America,

To all to whom these presents shall come, Greeting:

WHEREAS, a Certificate of the Register of the Land Office at ROSEBURG, OREGON, has been deposited in the General Land Office, whereby it appears that full payment has been made by the claimant

WILLIAM HORSFALL

according to the provisions of the Act of Congress of April 24, 1820, entitled "An Act making further provision for the sale of the Public Lands" and the acts supplemental thereto, for the **SOUTH HALF OF THE SOUTHWEST QUARTER OF SECTION TWENTY-EIGHT AND THE EAST HALF OF THE SOUTHEAST QUARTER OF SECTION TWENTY-NINE IN TOWNSHIP TWENTY-FOUR SOUTH OF RANGE THIRTEEN WEST OF THE WILLAMETTE MERIDIAN, OREGON, CONTAINING ONE HUNDRED SIXTY ACRES,**

according to the Official Plat of the Survey of the said Land, returned to the GENERAL LAND OFFICE by the Surveyor-General:

NOW KNOW YE, That the UNITED STATES OF AMERICA, in consideration of the premises, and in conformity with the several Acts of Congress in such case made and provided, HAS GIVEN AND GRANTED, and by these presents DOES GIVE AND GRANT, unto the said claimant and to the heirs of the said claimant the Tract above described; TO HAVE AND TO HOLD the same, together with all the rights, privileges, immunities, and appurtenances, of whatsoever nature, thereunto belonging, unto the said claimant and to the heirs and assigns of the said claimant forever; subject to any vested and accrued water rights for mining, agricultural, manufacturing, or other purposes, and rights to ditches and reservoirs used in connection with such water rights, as may be recognized and acknowledged by the local customs, laws, and decisions of courts; and there is reserved from the lands hereby granted, a right of way thereon for ditches or canals constructed by the authority of the United States.

IN TESTIMONY WHEREOF, I, **WILLIAM H. TAFT,**

President of the United States of America, have caused these letters to be made Patent, and the Seal of the General Land Office to be hereunto affixed.

GIVEN under my hand, at the City of Washington, the **SIXTH**

(SEAL)

day of **FEBRUARY** in the year of our Lord one thousand

nine hundred and **ELEVEN** and of the Independence of the

United States the one hundred and **THIRTY-FIFTH.**

By the President: *Wm H. Taft*

By *M. P. LeRoy* Secretary,

John O'Connell

Acting Recorder of the General Land Office.

RECORD OF PATENTS: Patent Number **175850**

6—2171

Land patent from the federal government public lands to William Horsfall, signed on behalf of President William M. Taft on February 6, 1911. Courtesy of the General Land Office files.

Left: U.S. Forest Service marker. The public campground, the lake, road to the beach and the beach itself all carry the name "Horsfall." It's one of the most visited sites along the Oregon coast.

Below: The approximate location of William Horsfall's homestead land near what is now called Horsfall Beach within the Oregon Dunes National Recreation Area. The property was located in the S ½ SW ¼ of Section 28 and the E ½ SE ¼ of Section 29 all in Township 24 South, Range 13 West of Willamette Meridian, Coos County, Oregon. Photo courtesy of Google Earth, 2019.

Aproximate Location William Horsfall Homestead Land 1911

Horsfall Lake

Dr. William Horsfall's medical bag.

Dr. Abram Leman Houseworth (1871–1951)

Abram L. Houseworth was born in Missouri on January 29, 1871, the son of James William Houseworth (1841–1916) and Elizabeth Mitchell (1840–1927). He was a twin brother to John L. Houseworth (1871–1932); he had three sisters and an older brother as well. Their father, James, enlisted in Company B, Eighty-first Indiana Infantry at the beginning of the Civil War; he participated in several battles throughout his enlistment. James survived the war, but was killed in 1916 by falling from a wagon and breaking his neck while traveling home from his mining operation in Colorado.

The James William Houseworth family. From left to right, first row: Estella Rachel, James W., Elizabeth (Mitchell), Theodore Edwin, Second row: Frances Olga, John L., Abram L., Lucy Gertrude. Photo courtesy of Ancestry.com.

From the Midwest to Oregon

Abram Houseworth graduated from Harper University in Harper, Kansas. In 1895, he received his medical degree from the University of Louisville, Kentucky, and on December 24, 1896, he married Huldah Gunn and moved to Cashion, Oklahoma, where he had a medical practice for some twelve years. In 1907 Dr. Houseworth moved his family to Marshfield, Oregon, where he practiced medicine for another twenty years and was active in community affairs. Abram's

Dr. Abram Leman Houseworth on left, with twin brother, Dr. John Leon Houseworth on right, ca. 1905. In the fall of 1910, John visited Abram at Marshfield. They looked very much like one another, save for the fact that John was a bit heavier than Abram. Several of the townspeople thought they were talking with Abram when they were actually talking to John. Hopefully, they got the same medical advice from either![142,143]
Photo courtesy of Ancestry.com.

twin brother, John Leon Houseworth, also became a doctor and settled in the Los Angeles, California, area.[142]

Soon after arriving in Marshfield, Dr. Houseworth performed an operation to remove the prostate gland from one of his patients. It was probably the first operation of its kind ever performed in Coos County. Dr. Edwin Straw, another pioneer physician in the area, assisted in the operation. It was a complete success.[144]

Dr. Houseworth was president of the Coos and Curry Medical Society in 1921, along with being appointed as medical officer in the Oregon National Guard with the rank of captain. In 1922, he was elected as president of the State Medical Society of Oregon.[146,147]

Dr. Abram L. Houseworth died on May 18, 1951 in Wichita, Kansas at the age of eighty.

Ad from the October 27, 1911 *Coos Bay Times*, page 3.

Doctors Abram and John Houseworth and wives, ca. 1920. Photo courtesy of Ancestry.com.

DR. HOUSEWORTH INSTALLS NEW SURGICAL APPARATUS

… Dr. A. L. Houseworth has just completed the installation of the new Carbon Dioxide Snow [an early cryotherapy tool], a treatment for the removal of birthmarks, skin discoloration, etc. The new device is very effective and eliminates the danger hitherto attached to these operations. It is attracting much attention. It is also used in the removal of small tumors… [143]

Dr. Abram Houseworth's home in Marshfield, ca. 1910. Photo courtesy of the Coos History Museum.

Huldah and Dr. Abram Houseworth, ca. 1912, Marshfield, Oregon. Photo courtesy of Ancestry.com.

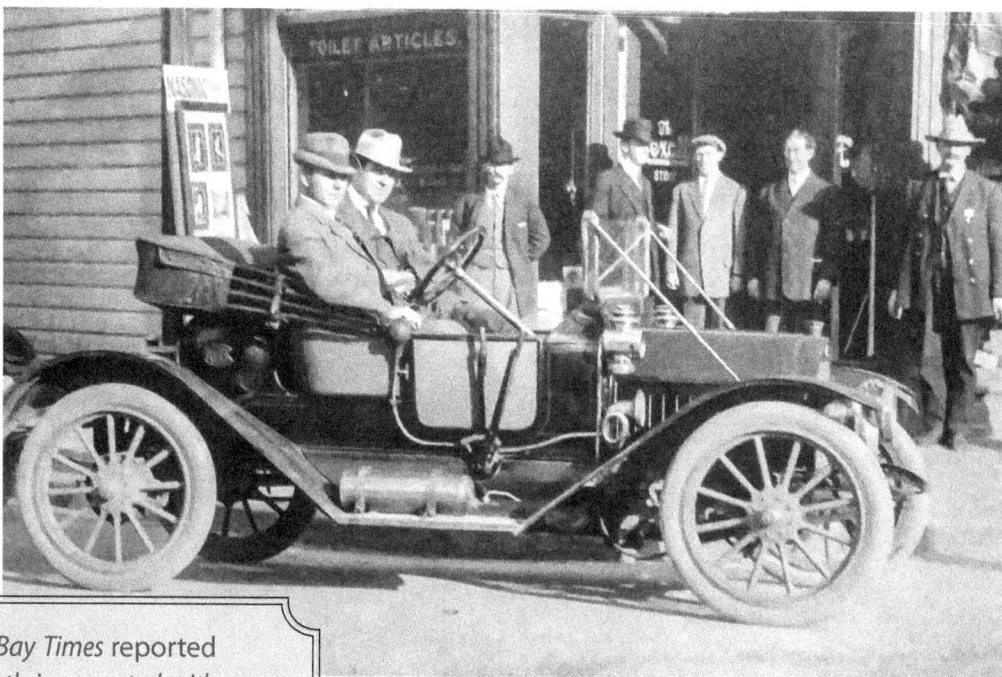

... [In 1914 the *Coos Bay Times* reported that] *Dr. A. L. Houseworth is presented with a novel piece of jewelry. It is a large gold ring made out of Coos County gold. It was presented to him by George W. Shelly, who secured the gold dust from a mine he is interested in near Myrtle Point. The ring is a large one and in place of a setting bears the word 'Oregon' in raised gold letters, the letters of a different hue ...* [145]

Dr. Abram Houseworth showing off his new Buick, ca. 1913. Photo courtesy of Ancestry.com.

Dr. Leslie Gloyd Johnson (1887–1950)

Leslie G. Johnson was born on April 10, 1887 in Stockton, California to William Wynn Johnson (1860–1922) and Martha Jane Gann (1868–1920). Sometime before 1900, the family moved to Portland, Oregon, where his father was the business manager of the *Oregon Daily Journal*. Leslie graduated from Portland High School in 1903 and received his medical training and degree from the University of Oregon medical department in Portland in 1909. In the graduation announcement, he was listed as the head of his class. In October 1909, Leslie married Leta L. Drain (1887–?) at Astoria, Oregon. (The town of Drain, Oregon was named after her grandfather.)[96,148]

Immediately after graduating from the university, Dr. Leslie Johnson went to Myrtle Point, Oregon, to set up a medical practice in that community. He was a member of several fraternal organizations including the Masons, the Woodmen of the World, Modern Woodmen of America, the Royal Neighbors, as well as the local grange.

Around Christmastime, 1915, Dr. Johnson moved from Myrtle Point to Marshfield. He located his office between that of Doctors Toye and Houseworth, in the Irving block of town. Dr. Pemberton from Curry County acquired Dr. Johnson's Myrtle Point practice. When the McAuley Hospital opened, Dr. Johnson was the first chief of staff.[150]

Dr. Leslie Johnson, 1916. Photo courtesy of the *Coos Bay Times*.

Dr. Johnson was very active in getting an airport built at Eastside, Oregon. He started the campaign to build one in the field to the north of Eastside, first to accommodate low-flying forest patrol planes that regularly flew the coast in search of forest fires. Later the army got involved in support of the effort and in 1931, Dr. Johnson headed a committee to raise the funds to make one of the runways suitable for winter use. The plan called for spreading coal slag on the dirt runway to help seal it from winter rains. The year before, Dr. Johnson received his certification to give physical examinations to pilots.

Dr. Leslie Gloyd Johnson died on July 31, 1950 in Springfield, Lane County, Oregon. He was sixty-three years old.

Dr. Leslie G. Johnson. Photo courtesy of the Coos History Museum.

The following demonstrates the risks doctors faced when prescribing liquor as "medicine."

DR. L. G. JOHNSON ENTERS PLEA OF GUILTY AND EXPLAINS CIRCUMSTANCES

… Dr. L. G. Johnson of Myrtle Point, one of those indicted in connection with the Myrtle Point liquor prescription trouble, yesterday appeared before Judge Coke, pleaded guilty and was given the minimum fine of $50, which the court later remitted. Dr. Johnson was indicted on a technical charge, that of having written a prescription for brandy on a regular prescription blank instead of on a certified blank prepared by the state … [149]

The Keizer Family Doctors and Nurses 1857–2020

| Doctors/Dentists | Nurses | Niether Dr. nor Nurse |

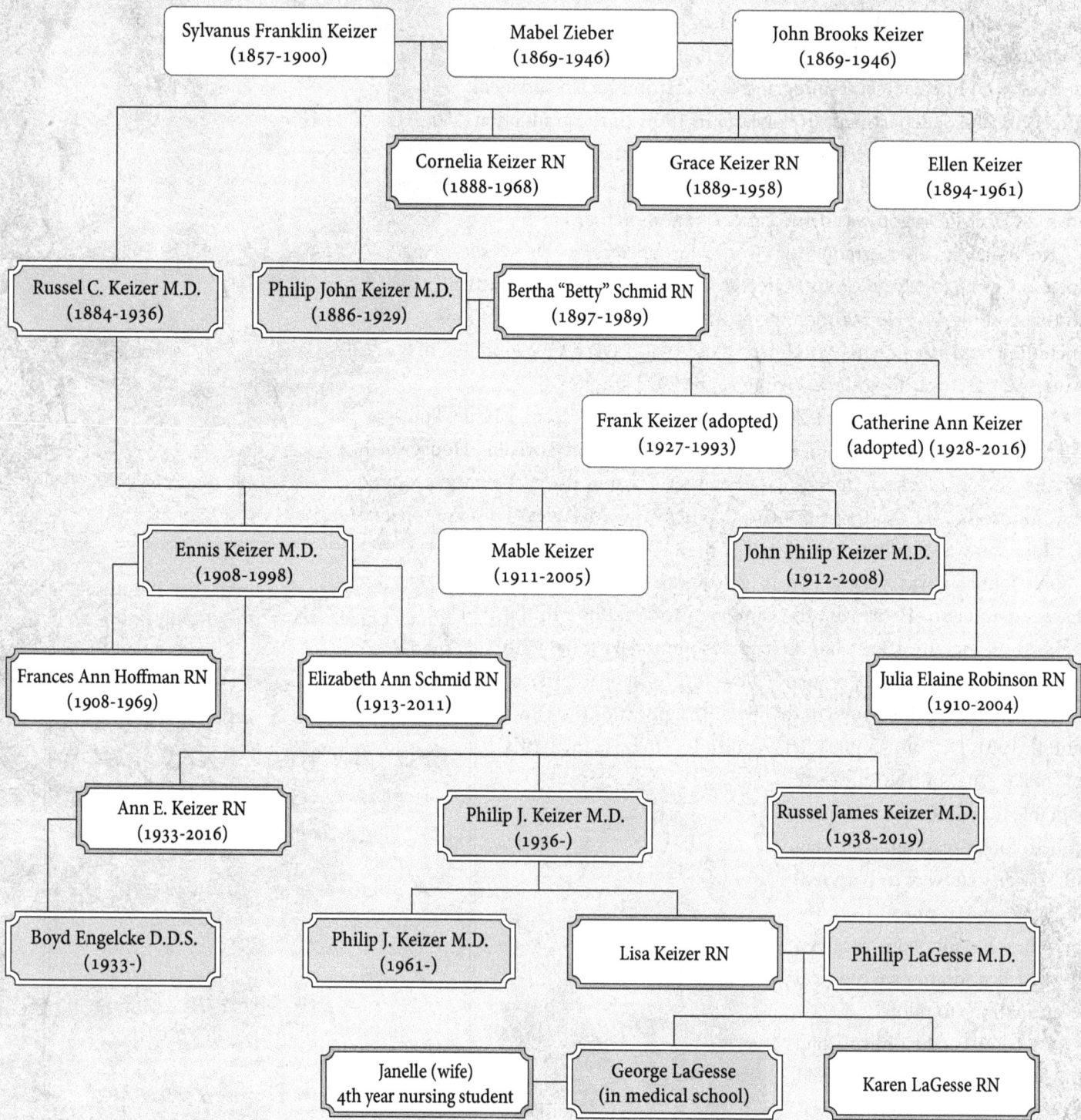

Sylvanus Franklin Keizer (1857-1900) — **Mabel Zieber (1869-1946)** — **John Brooks Keizer (1869-1946)**

- Cornelia Keizer RN (1888-1968)
- Grace Keizer RN (1889-1958)
- Ellen Keizer (1894-1961)

Russel C. Keizer M.D. (1884-1936)

Philip John Keizer M.D. (1886-1929) — **Bertha "Betty" Schmid RN (1897-1989)**

- Frank Keizer (adopted) (1927-1993)
- Catherine Ann Keizer (adopted) (1928-2016)

Ennis Keizer M.D. (1908-1998)

Mable Keizer (1911-2005)

John Philip Keizer M.D. (1912-2008)

- Frances Ann Hoffman RN (1908-1969)
- Elizabeth Ann Schmid RN (1913-2011)
- Julia Elaine Robinson RN (1910-2004)

Ann E. Keizer RN (1933-2016)

Philip J. Keizer M.D. (1936-)

Russel James Keizer M.D. (1938-2019)

- Boyd Engelcke D.D.S. (1933-)
- Philip J. Keizer M.D. (1961-)
- Lisa Keizer RN
- Phillip LaGesse M.D.

- Janelle (wife) 4th year nursing student
- George LaGesse (in medical school)
- Karen LaGesse RN

There were nine direct and indirect "docs" within the Keizer family, who hailed from the Coos Bay area. There were/are also eleven registered nurses within the family. Some of the doctors and nurses are still practicing as of 2020.

The Keizer Family Doctors and Nurses

The story of the Keizer family starts back with Thomas Dove Keizer (1793–1871) and Mary Gurley (1793-1853) in North Carolina. They were married in 1813 and the couple had ten children. John Brooks Keizer was the oldest son and fourth in line after three sisters; he was born in North Carolina in 1924. John's siblings were born in North Carolina, Tennessee and Arkansas.

Thomas Dove Keizer and Mary Gurley. Photos courtesy of Ancestry.com.

The Keizer Family Moves West

Around 1830, Thomas and Mary began migrating west, first stopping in Giles County, Tennessee. In 1833 they moved on to Van Buren County, Arkansas, on their way to connect with the Dr. White wagon train leaving Independence, Missouri, in 1842 bound for Oregon. The Keizers arrived too late to leave with White's party, and had to wait a year in order to connect with the Oregon Emigration Company (aka the Jesse Applegate wagon train) in 1843, also bound for Oregon. The Oregon Emigration Company was the first wagon train to complete the overland trek to the Willamette Valley. They were credited with blazing the western portion of the Oregon Trail for wagons.[151]

At the time they left Independence, the extended Keizer family consisted of 22 members: five sons, five daughters, along with eight grandchildren, two sons-in-law (Sam Penter and John Ford) and John Ford's brother, Nimrod Ford; and the family's prized Morgan horses. The entire wagon train consisted of about 900 people with 120 wagons. After six months on the trail, the Keizer family arrived in what is now the city of Keizer, Oregon—named for the family patriarch, Thomas Dove Keizer. The settlement sits a few miles north of Salem, Oregon.[152]

Statue of Thomas Dove Keizer located in Keizer, Oregon. Photo courtesy of the city of Keizer.

The John Brooks Keizer Sr. and Sylvanus Franklin ("Frank") Keizer Families

John Brooks Keizer Sr. (1824–1870) provides the direct lineage to the current Keizer physicians in Coos County, Oregon. He was the oldest son of the family patriarch, Thomas Dove Keizer, and his wife Mary Gurley. John Brooks Keizer Sr. married Mary Jane Herren in 1851.

Sylvanus Franklin Keizer (aka Frank, 1857–1900) was born near Salem, Oregon to John Brooks Keizer (1824–1870) and Mary Jane Herren (1832–1909).

Frank married Mabel Zieber in 1883, and the couple had six children (Bertha, Russel C., Philip John, Cornelia, Grace Zeiber and Ellen May). The Keizers were a growing and prominent family in the Willamette Valley around Salem.

However, in 1898, gold was discovered near Nome, Alaska and it drew Frank Keizer from Oregon in search of the precious metal. Two of Frank's brothers also went to Nome. The following story about Frank Keizer's trip to Nome was relayed by Frank's grandson, Dr. Philip John Keizer, in an interview conducted by the Author of this book in June 2020:

… Frank Keizer was my great grandfather. He was in Seattle headed for Nome and they had an epidemic of meningitis and when he got on the boat to Alaska, he came down with the disease and died on the boat. The captain wanted to get rid of the body so they buried him at sea. He never made it to Nome. So, as the custom was, his brother John [John Brooks Keizer Jr. (1870–1927)] married Frank's wife, Mabel Zieber Keizer … [153]

No children were born to the marriage of John Brooks Keizer Jr. and Mabel Zieber-Keizer.[154]

The First Keizer Doctors

The first of the Keizer physicians to arrive in North Bend, Oregon, was Philip John Keizer in 1914, followed by his brother, Russel C. Keizer in 1919. They were the two sons of Frank Keizer and Mabel Zieber, and the brothers began a long line

John Brooks Keizer Sr. (1824–1870) Photo courtesy of Ancestry.com.

Mabel (Zieber) Keizer, wife of Frank Keizer and John Brooks Keizer Jr.[154] Photo courtesy of Ancestry.com.

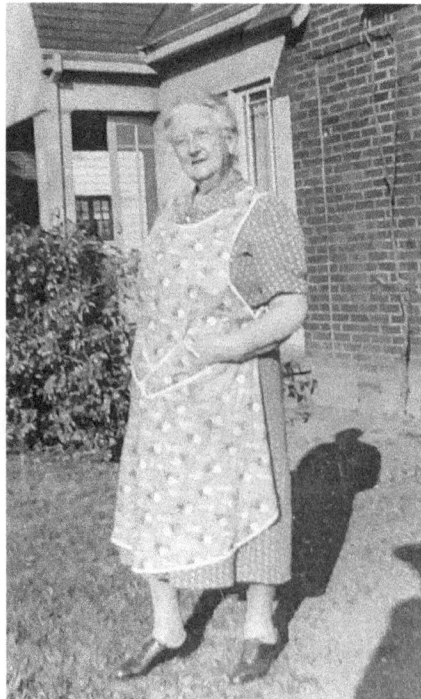

Right: Mabel (Zieber) Keizer. Photo courtesy of Dr. Phil Keizer.

of Keizer doctors in the community. Three of Frank and Mabel's daughters went into nursing, and over the years, several other Keizer women also became nurses. House calls became part of the tradition of this family of medical practitioners. And a deep and abiding sense of community and compassion for others provided a rich heritage in the Keizer family.

In 1984, Ennis Keizer (Russel's son, and Frank's grandson) captured the abiding theme within this medical dynasty at his retirement at age seventy-five when he said: *"... There's a great deal of satisfaction in being a doctor. It's kind of nice to go home and have someone say, 'If it hadn't been for you ...'"*

Dr. Philip John Keizer Sr. (1886–1929)

Philip J. Keizer was born on April 7, 1886 on a farm near Salem to Sylvanus Franklin (Frank) Keizer (1857–1900) and Mabel Zieber (1863–1946). As mentioned, the marriage of Frank and Mabel Keizer produced six children, among them were two doctors and two nurses. Philip John attended a local grammar school near Salem and graduated from the Portland YMCA high school, after which he enrolled at the Willamette University College of Medicine. After spending three years at the medical college, he finished his final year of medical training in Portland, when the Willamette University medical department merged with the University of Oregon Medical School—where he received his medical degree shortly before coming to North Bend in 1914.

Dr. Russel Keizer, his older brother, was already a licensed physician practicing in Portland, Oregon. Russell moved to North Bend around 1920 to join his brother, and assisted in building the Keizer Brothers Hospital. Aside from the twenty-two months serving in the U.S. Army during WWI the brothers maintained a successful medical practice in the area for many years. (See the chapter on Hospitals for more detailed description of the Keizer Brothers Hospital.)

Philip J. Keizer, ca. 1918.

A Full Life in North Bend

When Dr. Philip John Keizer returned from the war in 1919, he helped start the Sunset Post of the American Legion, and at one time was the post commander. He served as mayor of North Bend from 1923–1926, was elected commissioner several times to the Port of Coos Bay, and served a term as president of the Coos Bay Chamber of Commerce. He also served as Coos County coroner. He was an accomplished musician, too, while in Salem he played in the Cole McElroy jazz band.

On January 8, 1923, the *Coos Bay Times* reported the following:

WALK 34 MILES THROUGH STORM

... Dr. Phil Keizer, mayor of North Bend, and Ira Padrick arrived in North Bend last night on the fishermen's special train which they caught at Gardner, foot-sore and weary from a thirty-four mile hike from Mapleton, Oregon, where the incoming train is stalled.

Dr. Keizer said this morning that the train would not have left Eugene, but it was hoped to effect a transfer of passengers. However, this was found impossible and return to Eugene was cut off as well, as the track washed out behind the train an hour after it had crossed over, so rapidly were the waters rising everywhere.

Mapleton was flooded so that a boat plied between the station and the hotel. Many rooms of the hotel were occupied by the town-people, who were flooded out of their own homes. Dr. Keizer said that Padrick and he thought the hotel looked risky, as the flood waters were all around it and great logs were being carried past it by the rapid current.

PHILIP JOHN RETURNS FROM THE FRONT, AND FROM THE DEAD

... On July 17, 1917, Phil Keizer left for France where he was a captain in the gas and flame division of the U.S. Army until the war ended. July played a prominent part in his war record as it was in that month in 1918 that relatives in North Bend received word that he had been missing in action, which, though somewhat dispelled by the fact that letters written after his supposed disappearance were received, was not found to be untrue until the Armistice had been signed. Dr. Keizer returned from France in July 1919, the possessor of a wonderful war record for service and ability ... [155,156]

CAPTAIN KEIZER KILLED

... The telegram notifying Captain Keizer's relatives of his death read as follows: 'I deeply regret to inform you that Captain Phil J. Keizer, 30th Engineers, is officially reported as killed in action July 13 [1918]...'Dr. PJ Keizer of North Bend is reported from France as killed in action. No details of the casualty have been received. But according to a post card mailed after the notice of Dr. Keizer's death to his wife, this could not have been true. Signed: Harris, Acting Adjutant-General ... [157]

Dr. Philip J. Keizer courtesy of Dr. Phil Keizer
Photo courtesy of the Coos History Museum.

About 10:00 p.m. the waters seemed to be going down, and it was reported there were still rooms at the hotel, so the two men left the train and went by boat to the hotel. The next day, they planned to go by boat on the Siuslaw River and started out but found the river too dangerous. They were put ashore and walked the railroad track ...

To provide against hunger, the hikers carried a loaf of bread, some cheese, and some chocolate and they stopped once at a farm house along the way for a cup of coffee. About a mile this side of Kroll, they left the track because of the darkness. They walked over the mountain at the big tunnel and also at Canary. The latter tunnel was blocked by a slide at each end and was filled with water to a depth of eight feet.

They passed a work train up the line from Gardiner and the men aboard told them that the fishermen's special train was to make the trip to Marshfield that night. Keizer and Padrick resolved to make renewed effort to reach Gardiner in time to catch the train which left Gardiner about 7:45 p.m. They made it with 10 minutes to spare ...[158]

Bertha (Betty) Schmid, Nurse and Wife of Dr. Philip John Keizer

In 1919, Betty Schmid graduated from the Multnomah Hospital Nurses Training School in Portland, Oregon, and came to North Bend to work as a nurse at Mercy Hospital. After three months she left the hospital and went to work for Drs. Phil and Russel Keizer, whose offices were in the old Mittleton building at the corner of Virginia and Sherman in North Bend.[159]

When the Keizer brothers completed the construction of their hospital in 1923, Betty moved to the hospital to be in charge of the nurses. But Betty wanted more involvement in the hospital—she also wanted to specialize in anesthesiology—so she enrolled in graduate work at the Lakeside Hospital in Cleveland, Ohio. The day she graduated in 1925, she married Dr. Phil John Keizer. Two children were adopted by Phil and Betty: Frank, born 1927, and Catherine, born 1928.

Sadly, just four years after they were married, Dr. Keizer died from complications of surgery at the Good Samaritan hospital in Portland, Oregon, on October 13, 1929. He was only forty-three-years-old. Betty continued to work in the hospital, and was probably one of the oldest nurse anesthesiologists in the state, if not the nation. She was instrumental in the successful operation of the Keizer Brothers Hospital and was involved in hundreds, if not thousands, of surgical operations.

Coincidently, Dr. Keizer's death occurred a few hours after Dr. Edwin Straw, who served as mayor of Marshfield and was on the staff of the Keizer Brothers Hospital. (We will read more about Dr. Straw in a bit.)[160]

Dr. Russel C. Keizer (1884–1936)

Russel Keizer was also born to Franklin Keizer and Mabel Zieber, on August 2, 1884 in Marion County, Oregon. He was the older brother of Philip John Keizer. Russel was reared in Marion County, where he attended public schools. He enrolled at the University of Oregon Medical School in Portland and graduated with the class of 1918. He stayed in Portland for one year, practicing medicine with Dr. Sabin before coming to North Bend to join his brother's (Dr. Phil Keizer) practice. When Dr. Philip J. Keizer died in 1929, Dr. Dean Crowell, a former classmate of Russel's, became a partner in the Keizer hospital.

As my interview with Dr. Philip John Keizer continued in June 2020, he relayed another story about his grandfather, Russel C. Keizer:

… My Grandfather, Dr. Russel [Russel C. Keizer] besides being a physician and surgeon was an inventor. He was a smart guy. He invented the first three-dimensional movies and you didn't have to wear glasses or anything. What he did was attach two movie cameras on a wooden board; he would wind them up, focus one on the distance and the other one was focused up front. On one of the cameras he put on a red lens and I think the other camera was only black and white. He would then take

Dr. Russel C. Keizer. Photos courtesy of Dr. Phil Keizer.

DR. RUSSEL KEIZER AND THE RED CLOUD MERCURY MINE

The earliest discovery of quicksilver (aka mercury) in Oregon as far as is known was at the Nonpareil and Bonanza mines of Douglas County in 1865. The Nonpareil was developed in 1877 and the Bonanza in 1879. Furnaces were built on both properties for the production of quicksilver, but the records are sparse. Apparently, an early settler in the Rogue River Valley found cinnabar (the red rock material from which quicksilver was extracted) in the "meadows" of the Gold Hill district of Jackson County in 1878. Some production was made there with retorts (a container or furnace for carrying out a chemical process on a large or industrial scale) and sold locally to placer gold miners in the region.

The quickest, cheapest, and easiest method for extracting gold from gold-bearing ore is to mix the crushed ore with mercury. The chemical adheres to the gold, forming an amalgam, which is then burned over a blowtorch or open fire to vaporize the mercury and isolate the gold. The process can be very dangerous as the vapors can cause serious health hazards.

Red Cloud Mine (hg), Douglas County, Tiller-Drew Area

"… Former Name: Mother Lode Mine

Location: Near the center of the NW1/4 Section 21, T. 32 S., R. 2 W., W. M.

Production: 6 flasks recorded; probably 63 produced

History: Cinnabar was discovered in the area in 1907 by R. W. Thomason, Lewis Thomason, and William Sasse. Some development work was done between 1908 and 1911 by the Scotia Development Co. No production was made and the prospects lay idle until 1932. The Research Mining Co. operated the mine from 1932 through

movies simultaneously with the two cameras perfectly lined up …
Next, he had two projectors, again attached to a board, lined them
up and zeroed them in and it came out three-dimensioned …

In 1929, Dr. Russel Keizer served on the North Bend school board, and also served as the Coos County coroner.

In the spring of 1936, Dr. Russel Keizer was asked to deliver a talk to the senior class at North Bend High School. He offered the following observations about getting into and sustaining a career in medicine:

… It takes application and ability to survive in the field of medicine … only 60 out of 300 who apply to the University of Oregon Medical School are accepted, [and] after you graduate, you need an honest heart to stay with the profession or you might as well give up …

Russel died from complications of a stroke on November 4, 1936. He was fifty-two years old. He was very popular, and the church where they held his funeral was overflowing with people.

Dr. Russel C. Keizer.
Photos courtesy of Dr. Phil Keizer.

1934, producing 39 flasks with a small 3-pipe retort. In 1935, the property was purchased by Dr. Russel C. Keizer. During 1936–1938 at least 14 flasks were produced from his operations and from those subsequent leases. In 1940, the property was acquired by the Red Cloud Mining Co. …"[161]

During the years that Dr. Russel C. Keizer owned the Red Cloud mine (he'd bought it simply as an investment), he made several trips to the area to inspect the mine. One story relayed by his son Dr. Ennis Keizer to his son Dr. Phil Keizer added color to the mercury mining operation at the Red Cloud mine. Dr. Phil Keizer shared the details with me as such:

… The story about the mercury mine was told to me by my dad [Dr. Ennis Keizer]. My dad said that my grandfather [Dr. Russel C. Keizer] had hired the Coos Bay Iron Works in Coos Bay to fabricate a unique piece of machinery to extract the pure mercury from the cinnabar ore. Mercury was valuable back then, but it was a difficult process to get the mercury out of the ore. Anyway, one day, my dad and my uncle John [Philip John Keizer] went along with my grandfather to the mine. They were digging on the claim and putting the ore in the machine but it wasn't working right. There was smoke or steam coming out machine into the air. The boys were walking around and noticed that on the thimbleberry and salmonberry leaves there were little round balls of pure mercury. The kids didn't know what it was so they went back to the car and got a jar and began tipping the slippery silver metal into the jar. They didn't say anything to their dad and after a while they had filled the whole jar full of pure mercury …

I'm sure that some facts have been tweaked over the years, but the story seemed worth repeating.

Dr. Ennis Keizer (1908–1998)

Ennis Keizer was born on November 26, 1908 in Portland, Oregon, to Dr. Russel Keizer and Laura Rees. When Dr. Russel Keizer moved his family to North Bend in 1920, Ennis was enrolled in the public schools there, and he graduated from North Bend High School in 1926. Ennis graduated from the University of Oregon in 1930, and from the University of Oregon Medical School in Portland in 1933.

In 1932, he married Frances Ann Hoffman (1908–1969), and from that union produced two more Keizer doctors and one Keizer nurse. (After Frances died in 1969, Ennis married Elizabeth Ann Schmid (1913–2011) in 1970.)

When Ennis returned from his internship at Ancker Hospital in St. Paul, Minnesota in 1934, he joined his father's medical practice. Ennis also worked in the Keizer Brothers Hospital, managing it after his father and his uncle (Dr. Philip John Keizer) passed away; in fact, there was a Keizer doctor working in that hospital during its entire existence.[162]

Dr. Ennis Keizer. Photo courtesy of the Coos History Museum.

Extensive Medical and Community Involvement

Ennis always liked to keep busy. He was the medical director of the Life Care Center in Coos Bay; the South Coast Hospice; the Visiting Nurses Association; the Bay Area Home Health; the South Coast Health Council; as well as the Coos County Council on Alcoholism. He also served on the Coos County Welfare Commission for many years, and was its chairman for eleven years. If that was not enough, Ennis served one term on the North Bend City Council in the 1940s, and was the Coos County coroner from 1936 to 1942. He served an eight-year term on the Oregon Welfare Commission beginning in 1960. He was president of the Oregon Academy of General Practice, and director of the American Academy of General Practice as well; and for those commitments and many more, Ennis Keizer was named the citizen of the year in in 1982 by the Coos Bay-North Bend Rotary Club, and again in 1988 by the North Bend City Council.[163]

North Bend Medical Center

In 1945, Ennis, along with his brother John Philip and six other doctors who worked at the Keizer Brothers Hospital, formed the North Bend Medical Center, Inc. It occupied the building that currently houses the North Bend School District administration facility. In 1978, it was announced that the North Bend Medical Center would relocate to property in Coos Bay near the new Bay Area Hospital, and build a new clinic costing $2.3 million. They retained the connection to their home city by naming the new facility the North Bend Clinic, even though it was located within the city boundary of Coos Bay. The new clinic was designed to house twenty-three doctors. Just recently, the clinic underwent a major expansion with satellite clinics added throughout Coos and Curry Counties.

The Keizer Brothers Hospital in North Bend was sold in 1953 to a nonprofit corporation that operated under a community board of directors until the Bay Area Hospital opened in 1974.

In 1978, Dr. Ennis Keizer was still practicing medicine at the age of seventy at the North Bend Medical Center. It was reported that he was the oldest practicing physician in the area.

Dr. Ennis Keizer died on December 20, 1998 in North Bend, Oregon at the age of ninety.

Dr. John Philip Keizer (1912–2008)

John Philip ("John P.") Keizer was born on October 9, 1912 in Brooks, Marion County, Oregon, to Dr. Russel C. Keizer and Laura May Rees. John grew up in North Bend, Oregon, and attended public schools in the area. Upon graduation from the local high school, he enrolled at the University of Oregon in Eugene for two years, then transferred to and graduated from Oregon State University. He then enrolled at the University of Oregon Medical School in Portland, and received his medical degree in 1937. He also took post-graduate work at the State of Wisconsin General Hospital.

In 1938 John Philip married Julia Robinson (1910–2004), who received her registered nursing training at the same hospital in Wisconsin. Shortly after their wedding, the couple returned to North Bend, whereupon Dr. John P. Keizer joined the staff at the Keizer Brothers Hospital along with his older brother, Dr. Ennis Keizer.[164]

In August 1941, Articles of Incorporation were filed with the Commissioner of Corporations at Salem, Oregon, for the "Flying Six," a group of aviation enthusiasts in North Bend. Incorporators of the nonprofit organization were Dr. John P. Keizer, Dr. Ennis R. Keizer, Dr. E. E. Boring, Dr. L C. Garner, John Hawkins, and Harold Hoar. After the war the Flying Six group expanded and acquired their first airplane.

Dr. John Philip Keizer. Photo courtesy of Dr. Phil Keizer.

Dr. John P. Keizer, along with Doctors Fred Anderson, (brother) Ennis Keizer, and Alfred French all took their oath of office for the U.S. Army Medical Corps at the Chandler Hotel in Marshfield, and were commissioned as first lieutenants in October 1942. Dr. John Seeley, also from the area, was commissioned in the army a month earlier. Within a year John P. Keizer was promoted to captain (in December 1943), and

was at that time attached to the air base at Stockton, California.

In 1951 Dr. John P. Keizer and family moved to Portland, where he served as chief in charge of the Children's Eye Clinic from 1953 to 1954. In 1954, he began a private practice in Portland. He later added a satellite office in King City, south of Portland. He was certified by the Board of Ophthalmology in 1956. While in residency at the OHSU in Portland, he headed a research program on the effect of oxygen on the vision of premature babies, in an effort to curb an increasing rate of blindness in infants.[165]

Dr. John Philip Keizer died in Longview, Washington, on June 8, 2008. He was ninety-five years old.

Dr. John Philip Keizer. Photo courtesy of Dr. Phil Keizer.

Dr. Russel J. Keizer (1938–2019)

Russel J. Keizer was born on April 18, 1938 in North Bend, Oregon, the son of Dr. Ennis Keizer and Frances Hoffman. He attended the local public schools and graduated from the North Bend High School in 1956. From there he went to the University of

Portland for his undergraduate studies, graduating in 1960. Like his other family members, Russel attended the University of Oregon Medical School in Portland, where received his medical degree in 1965. He performed the requisite residency in orthopedic surgery at the Washington University in St Louis, and served as a major in the U.S. Army in Savannah, Georgia.[166]

Dr. Russel Keizer started as an orthopedic surgeon in Portland in 1972, but returned to his home in North Bend and became associated with the North Bend Medical Clinic in 1993. He then moved to Astoria, Oregon, to establish a practice until he retired in 2007. At the time, he served as the chief of staff at Columbia Memorial Hospital in Astoria.

He was a member of Rotary for forty-five years, with perfect attendance. He was also a member of the Astoria Knights of Columbus and served on the board of directors of Columbia River Maritime Museum.

Dr. Russel J. Keizer died at the age of eighty-one in Portland, Oregon, on June 11, 2019.

Dr. Russel J. Keizer; photo courtesy of Dr. Phil Keizer..

Dr. Philip John Keizer (1936–)

Philip J. Keizer was born in North Bend, Oregon, in 1936 to Dr. Ennis Keizer and Frances Hoffman. He attended public schools in the area. Phil Keizer married Ann Clarice Petterson on June 22, 1958. Soon after their marriage, the young couple moved to Portland so Phil could attend the University of Oregon Medical School. While Phil was studying at the university, Ann taught biology at Wilson High School in Portland.

In 1962, Phil received his medical degree from the University of Oregon. The couple then moved to St. Paul, Minnesota, so that Dr. Keizer could complete his internship. In 1967, the couple moved back to North Bend, where Dr. Phil Keizer joined his father, Ennis, in his practice at the North Bend Medical Center.[167]

Dr. Phil Keizer served in many different capacities before his retirement in 1999. In 1978, he was associated with the North Bend Medical Center, and served as chairman of the building committee for the new North Bend Medical Center clinic just one-quarter mile from the new Bay Area Hospital. He was chairman of the surgical department at the hospital as well. He was a member of both the Coos Bay-North Bend Rotary and the Holy Redeemer Catholic Church.

Dr. Philip John Keizer. Photo courtesy of Dr. Phil Keizer.

In 2009, Dr. Philip Keizer gave a speech to a group of North Bend High School students, sharing some of his memories of being a physician. One story went as follows:

A patient [came in to see me] with an attitude and a bullet in his belly. He was a member of the Hells Angels motorcycle club and he didn't want surgery, but realized he'd die without medical attention. He said OK, I'll let you operate on me. But if you screw up, I'll kill you! I pointed my finger at the man and said he better be nice because I was about to save his life. Good thing the operation went well as the patient had six holes in his gut.

Another story relayed by Dr. Phil Keizer to me (June 8, 2020):

… There was this young woman who lived in Charleston and after she was married they had a little baby girl. The family moved to Paris, France where she had a tubal ligation, because she didn't want to have any more children. It wasn't long thereafter that the cute little daughter died of something like Leukemia and they wanted to have another baby. But all the gynecologists in Paris wouldn't touch her and said it could not be done, no way! That was back in those early days.

So, she called my dad [Dr. Ennis Keizer], long distance and told him about it and he said: 'come on home and I'll see if I can make it work'. She came back to North Bend to see my dad. He operated on her and took these "Looped Glasses," kind of like magnifying glasses and then he used this real fine eye suture and ever so slowly and carefully put the fallopian tubes back together.

He said he couldn't guarantee anything but a short period of time later, she became pregnant and delivered a daughter.

When my dad died [1998] and they had a big reception after the funeral, this young good looking woman from Paris or wherever comes up to me, and told me the story. That was really great ...[153]

One more story from Dr. Phil Keizer June 8, 2020):

... Do you remember when the ship hit the Highway 101 bridge that goes across Coos Bay [McCullough Bridge-December 4, 1986] and they had to close down the bridge for six weeks and reroute traffic around the east side of the bay? Those people that lived in North Bend and worked north of the bay had a long way to go to get home. No one was allowed to cross the bridge.

On Saturday night I was working in the emergency room at the Bay Area Hospital when a fight broke out at the Lakeshore Lodge bar in Lakeside at one in the morning [12 miles north of the McCullough Bridge]. A couple of young guys went outside and one of them stabbed the other in the chest [heart] with a knife.

They called the Reedsport ambulance and found this guy with a knife in his chest with blood squirting out with each pulse, so they put a bandage over it to stop the bleeding. That wasn't going to work and the kid was starting to fail. There was no way the Reedsport hospital could handle it and no way to get him to Eugene in time, so they thought they would go to Coos Bay.

When they got to the McCullough Bridge, the policeman that was there were instructed that no one could go across the bridge. So they refused to let the ambulance go over the bridge. They radioed me and I told them they had to get the man to the hospital quick. So, I called the Coast Guard to send the helicopter but the only place where they could land safely was at the Menasha Paperboard mill. That all worked and they brought him directly to the hospital. The kid was almost dead.

So I threw my coat off, rolled my sleeves up and with bare hands and the help of my physician assistant cut open this kid's chest. Blood was squirting all over the place and we were giving him O-negative blood just to keep him alive. That heart was really beating fast. We could find the hole [in the heart] and thank God it missed the coronary arteries.

Anyway, I was able to get my assistant to get his hands around the heart; it scared everybody in the emergency room. Blood was going everywhere, all over me. I told my assistant to put his hands around the heart and squeeze it for a second and I had a stitch ready in my hand. I would say: 'NOW' and I would put the stitch in to start closing the hole in this guy's heart. He would let go and blood would again start squirting all over the place. I said: 'AGAIN' and I put another stitch in.

I sewed the patient back together and saved his life. His blood pressure started coming back up and he survived ...[153]

Dr. Philip John "PJ" Keizer Jr. (1961–)

Philip John "PJ" Keizer was born in Portland, Oregon, to Philip John Keizer and Ann Clarice Petterson. He attended local schools in Coos Bay, graduating from Marshfield High School in 1979. In 1983 he received his Bachelor of Science degree from the University of Notre Dame in South Bend, Indiana.

In 1986, PJ received a master of science degree in radiation health from Oregon State University and went to work at the Hanford nuclear plant located on the Columbia River in Benton County, Washington. That facility was decommissioned in 1987, and PJ moved to the Trojan Nuclear Power Plant in Columbia County, Oregon, as a health physicist. While there, he invented a program that could scan barrels of radioactive isotopes that would tell what isotopes were in the barrels, and identify their half-lives.

After Trojan closed in 1992, PJ was hired as a consultant for the closure of the Stockton, California, nuclear power plant. Once that project was completed, he enrolled in the Saint Louis University Medical School and received his medical degree in 1994. He completed his residency in radiology at St. Luke's University of Missouri in Kansas City. Eventually PJ returned to Coos County, and he practices his specialty in Coquille, Oregon.

As you can see, the Keizer family had quite an impact on our area. Not only did they provide exceptional medical care for a century, they were deeply involved in the communities.

Dr. Philip John "PJ" Keizer. Photo courtesy of Dr. Phil Keizer

A BROTHER WITH A DIFFERENT KIND OF EXPERTISE

PJ's younger brother, Ted Keizer, did not pursue the medical profession. His claim to fame came from speed hiking and mountain climbing in ultra-marathons. At one time he held at least eight world records for covering long distances in the shortest time. His nickname was "Cave Dog"—but that's another story. One such marathon was called the Mighty Mountain Megathon in Colorado. While living in Colorado in 1998, Ted began training for the event, which required speed climbing all the local peaks over 14,000 feet in altitude—known as the "14ers." The Mighty Mountain Megamarathon required climbers to summit each peak under his or her own power, and also ensured a certain amount of vertical elevation was gained for each summit.

In early September 2000, Keizer, with the help of his team (known as the "Dog Team"), set out to break the Mighty Mountain Megamarathon record. During his record-breaking attempt, Keizer unintentionally fell asleep on the trail three times. Despite these minor setbacks, Keizer completed the Megamarathon of climbing 55 "14ers"—and broke the record with a time of 10 days, 20 hours, and 26 minutes! That record held until 2015, when it was broken by a full day.

Another event, the Barkley trail race in Tennessee, covered a distance of 100 miles. Ted Keizer set the record for the event in 2003—he was two hours faster than the previous record holder. He also became only the fourth finisher ever of the grueling Barkley Marathons in 2003 in what was a then record of 56 hours, 57 minutes, and 52 seconds.

PJ and their father, Dr. Phil Keizer, went along for support.

Front row (L-R) Ellis Leep (1844–1938), Curtis Leep (1854–1936); Back row (L-R) Selby Leep (1845–1920) and Dr. Kersey Leep (1855–1924). Photo courtesy of Julie Leep.

Dr. Kersey Armston Leep (1855–1924)

The Leep Familiy's Early Days in America

The story of the Leep family of Myrtle Point, Oregon, starts back with the birth of John Wesley Leep (1733–1845) in Manheim, Germany. At the age of twenty-four, he left his parents and fifteen brothers and sisters in Germany and boarded a cargo ship as a stowaway for America, arriving in 1757. He married twice, and between the two marriages had ten children—one of whom continues the line to our Leep doctors in Coos County today.

When the Revolutionary War started, John Wesley enlisted in the Continental Army, and when the war of 1812 rolled around, it was all the family could do to stop him from enlisting to help the American cause. He was seventy-five years old![56]

Ten years after the close of the war of 1812, John Wesley Leep Jr. was born, the third oldest of eleven siblings. He seemed to have inherited many of his father's pioneering traits. A Virginian by birth, John Wesley Jr.'s early days were passed at Carrollton, Carroll County, Kentucky, where he combined general farming with horticulture. About 1856 he moved back to West Virginia and took up farming near Newark, Wood County, but in 1868 he left for Missouri, settling on a farm near Windsor. Two years later he died there, at forty-eight years of age. He was survived by his widow, Sarah June (nee Wise) Leep (1821–1890), a native Virginian, who died at Halfway, Baker County, Oregon.

Kersey Armston Leep

In the family of John Wesley Leep Jr., there were seven sons and three daughters—among whom Kersey Armston Leep was seventh in order of birth, born on December 23, 1855. Kersey graduated from high school at Carrollton, Kentucky in 1876. In 1878 he began attending the Louisville Medical College, where he hoped to take the complete course of study, but ill health forced him to abandon his plans.[54]

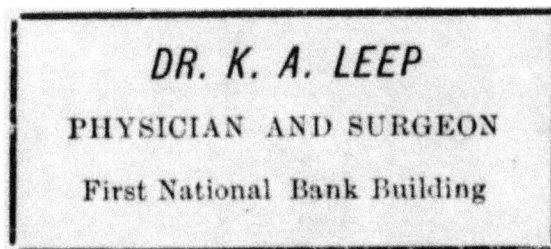

DR. K. A. LEEP

PHYSICIAN AND SURGEON

First National Bank Building

Ad for Dr. Kersey A. Leep from the *Coquille Herald*, February 16, 1911.

Believing he would benefit by a change of climate, as well as find opportunities in the new and growing West Coast settlements, in 1879 Kersey came to Oregon, where he filed for a homestead on one hundred and sixty acres in Union County, and then started to raise cattle. Although focused on ranching, Kersey never lost interest in science. In addition to his partially completed medical course he had been a constant student, endeavoring to increase his knowledge of professional topics by self-study. In 1886, Kersey Leep married Emma Gaylord (1864–1883) in Union County, Oregon. No children were born to that marriage.

After Emma died, Kersey married Catherine "Katie" Reed (1867–1887) in 1886. She was a native of Boulder, Colorado. Catherine and Kersey had one child, Roland Vivian Leep (1887–1929), but she died shortly after giving birth to Roland. During 1889 Kersey took a lecture course at the Willamette University, and the following year he settled at Myrtle Point, Coos County, where he established a medical practice—but without a medical degree. (Yes, you could do that back then.) Kersey married a third time in 1892 to Sarah Ellanora Endicott (1868–1930). She was the daughter of a local farmer in the area.[7]

Into the family of Kersey and Sarah, five children were born: Homer, born in 1893; Hallie, 1895; Freda, 1898; Kersey A. Jr., 1900; and Stuart Lyle, 1909. Wishing to further increase his medical knowledge, in 1892 Kersey Sr. went to St. Louis to take lecture courses at the Marion Sims Medical College. The college granted him an MD, and in 1893 he, along with his wife and family, settled in Eugene, Oregon, where Kersey Sr. began practicing medicine again—this time as a full-fledged doctor. The family stayed in Eugene until 1911, when he returned to Myrtle Point, and built a small hospital (likely connected to his clinic, as that was common back then).

Noteworthy among the associations of Dr. Kersey Leep's life have been his fraternal relations, which included membership in the Woodmen of the World, the Independent Order of Odd Fellows, and the Masons, in which he is identified with Myrtle Lodge No. 78. Kersey was an active member of the Democratic Party and was nominated for state senator in 1900. The office of mayor had been offered to him more than once, but he always declined the honor, feeling that his professional interests required his constant attention. However, he consented to serve on the Myrtle Point City Council for seven years.[54]

Dr. Kersey Leep died in Myrtle Point, Oregon, at the age of sixty-eight on November 3, 1924.

Dr. Roland Vivian Leep (1887–1929)

As noted earlier, Roland V. Leep was born in Pine Valley, Union County, Oregon, on September 5, 1887 to Dr. Kersey A. Leep and Catherine Reed. After Roland's mother died, he was taken in by an aunt until he joined his father and stepmother Ellanora Endicott at Myrtle Point. Roland received his education in the public schools in Myrtle Point and graduated from the Agricultural College at Corvallis, Oregon.

While at college, he was a leading athlete. He was a letterman in football and basketball—and as a sprinter, was one of the fastest in college circles. He stayed at Corvallis for a few years studying pharmacy, and then went to Portland to enroll in the University of Oregon medical college (OMC). He graduated with a medical degree on May 1, 1911 and did one year of residency at the St. Vincent Hospital in Portland.[96]

In January 1912, Dr. Roland Leep opened a medical practice in Bandon, Oregon, with Dr. Smith J. Mann, and soon built a small hospital in the central district of the town.

In June 1916 Roland married Agnes Catherine Hughes (1896–1974). Throughout his short career (cut short by his untimely death in 1929; see sidebar), Roland kept current with developing medical procedures. Shortly before his death, he attended clinics at the Mayo brothers' hospital in Rochester, Minnesota.

Dr. Roland Leep was also a good businessman. He owned a large cranberry bog south of Bandon, and was a stockholder and director of the

Dr. Roland V. Leep. Photo courtesy of the Bandon History Museum.

DR. R. V. LEEP
Physician & Surgeon
Office in Rasmussen Building.
Phone 72.

BANDON, OREGON

Ad in the semi-weekly *Bandon Recorder* December 16, 1913.

In 1924, Leep escaped death by bear:

BEAR ATTACKS DR. LEEP BANDON MAN KILLS BRUIN JUST IN TIME[168]

… While hunting deer on the Hughes brothers ranch near the mouth of Sixes river, Dr. R. V. Leep was attacked by a large black bear. The animal appeared suddenly from behind a large snag and less than fifty feet from the hunter. It took three shots to stop the bear. He was only a few feet away from the doctor when he was stopped.

The bear had been on the ranch for more than two years but was too clever to be caught. He had been living on hogs and sheep and it was estimated he had cost the Hughes brothers several hundred dollars …

Leep's clinic was above the Rexall drug store on the main street of Bandon, Oregon. Photo courtesy of the Bandon History Museum.

Bank of Bandon. According to local newspapers, he was an avid outdoorsman. He loved to hunt and fish and was a member of several duck-hunting clubs in Coos and Curry Counties.

Dr. Roland V. Leep died on June 29, 1929 at Bandon, Oregon, at forty-one years of age. In 1937, a new hospital was built in Bandon. It was named the R. V. Leep Memorial hospital. (To learn more about it, see the section on hospitals).

In 1929 Roland Leep wasn't so lucky; he was accidentally shot and killed while out hunting sea lions:

BANDON MAN IS VICTIM OF GUN SHOT ON REEFS[169]

... Facts relating to the accident Saturday which resulted in the death of Dr. Roland V. Leep were stated by Ed Capps, one of the party when they arrived back at the wharf at four o'clock in the afternoon. Mr. Capps stated that the party of five consisting of Dr. Leep, Dr. Shoot, Sr. Sabin, Arthur Rosa, and himself arrived at the dock about five o'clock Saturday morning and engaged Louis Peterson and Harry Jensen to take them to the seal rocks in their motor boat. While on their way to the rocks they shot several shags with their shot guns and stacked the supposedly empty guns in the stern of the boat.

When they reached the rocks, the five men landed on the one known as Camp rock and were standing in a group while light-lining the guns from the boat to the rock. The rifle was first successfully landed, then Dr. Leep's Winchester shot gun and one of the others were tied together and started up the line, when the doctor's gun exploded. The whole charge of shot struck Dr. Leep in the breast, killing him instantly. Mr. Capps stated that they were about 50 feet from the gun where it discharged ...

"Dr." Samuel L. Leneve. Photo courtesy of Ancestry.com.

"Dr." Samuel Lemon Leneve (1829–1901)

The lineage of Samuel Lemon Leneve in America dates back to the late 18th century, when his grandfather Samuel Leneve (1774–1831)—let's call him Samuel the elder—came over from France with his brother John and family. They came to this country about the time Lafayette and his troops came to assist the Americans during the Revolutionary War. Samuel the elder was only about three years old when they landed in America.

Samuel Leneve the elder married Katherine Arrington (1775–?) and together they migrated to Tennessee, but after one year moved west to Kentucky. From there, Samuel moved to Shakers Prairie, Indiana. His last move was to Lawrence County, Illinois, where Samuel the elder resided until his death in the spring of 1831.

Samuel Lemon Leneve, (or, Samuel Leneve the younger, the main subject of this entry) was born in Vermillion County, Illinois. His father was Obadiah Leneve (1800–1884)—the oldest son of Samuel Leneve the elder and Katherine Arrington. The younger Samuel's mother was Mary Polly Lemon (1803–1925).

Heading to Oregon

Samuel L. Leneve married Elizabeth Willey (1830–1920) in 1846 in his home town, and in 1851 the young couple, by then with two young children, headed west across the plains in a covered wagon pulled by a team of oxen, to Portland, Oregon. The trip took nine months to complete.

In the spring of 1853, the Leneve family arrived in Myrtle Creek, Oregon, where they stayed until moving to the Coquille area in 1861. In total Samuel and Elizabeth had twelve children; most of them lived and raised their families in Coos County.

"Dr." Samuel L. Leneve purchased 160 acres where the town of Coquille now stands. In 1865, the family moved to Parkersburg, Oregon, on the north side of the Coquille River upstream from Bandon, but moved back to Coquille City around 1872. At first, Leneve sold medicines from his farm, until about 1870, when he opened a drug store on the south side of Front Street in Coquille. He also practiced general medicine, delivered babies, and performed minor surgery.

Although he performed these medical services and was called "doctor" by most in the community, Samuel L. Leneve in

Samuel Lemon Leneve and his wife Elizabeth Wiley. Both photos courtesy of the Coos History Museum.

actuality had no formal training—although he'd learned some about medicine while living in Illinois, and had read several books on various medical topics before coming west. But basically, he was just a druggist that dispensed medical advice and treatment!

Leneve also served as Coquille postmaster for several years.[54,57,170,171]

Leneve's Drug Store

As noted earlier, around 1870 Samuel Leneve opened a drug store in Coquille. The store was a bustling presence for quite a while, but it was later destroyed by a fire that swept through the business district of Coquille. As relayed by Samuel L. Leneve's grandson in *Pioneer Coquille Merchants*:

> … R. S. Knowlton, as well as my grandad, owned and operated a drug store—the only difference being the fact that Grandad practiced medicine along with the

"Dr." Samuel L. Leneve. Photo courtesy of the Coos History Museum

The Leneve Drug Store in Coquille, Oregon. In 1886, Dr. M. M. Murphy's office was upstairs above the drug store. Dr. Murphy was a graduate of one of the earliest medical colleges in Europe. Photo courtesy of the Coos History Museum.

As follows are several advertising testimonials for certain medicines carried by Samuel Leneve's drug store:
Coquille City Herald, January 28, 1896:

In the late war I was a soldier in the First Maryland Volunteers, Company G. During my term of service, I contracted chronic diarrhea. Since then I have used a great amount of medicine, but when I found any that would give me relief it would injure my stomach until Chamberlain's Colic, Cholera, and Diarrhea Remedy was brought to my notice. I used it and will say it is the only remedy that gave me permanent relief and no bad results follow. I take pleasure in recommending this preparation to all of my old comrades, who while giving their services to their country, contracted this dreadful disease as I did, from eating unwholesome and uncooked food. Yours truly, A. E. Bending, Halsey, Oregon. For sale by S. L. Leneve, druggist.[172]

Coquille City Herald, July 14, 1896:

Oregon Kidney Tea is nature's own remedy for kidney troubles. For sale by N. G. W. Perkins, of Myrtle Point and Dr. S. L. Leneve of Coquille City.[173]

Coquille City Herald, November 26, 1895:

Sore Throat. Any ordinary case may be cured in one night by applying Chamberlain's Pain Balm as directed with each bottle. This medicine is also famous for its cures of rheumatism, lame back and deep-seated and muscular pains. For sale by Dr. S. L. Leneve, druggist.[174]

Dr. Leneve in his Masonic regalia.

drug business. Prior to the fire, my Dad [John W. Leneve] was associated with his father as a pharmacist, filling the prescriptions that Dr. S. L. prescribed for his patients ... [57]

Samuel Leneve died on March 17, 1901 in Coos County, Oregon. He was seventy-five years old.

Dr. George William Leslie (1870–1936)

George W. Leslie was born in 1870 in Lewis County, Kentucky, to Albert Leslie (1841–1928) and Rebecca Ellen Ritchie (1846–1942). He graduated from the American School of Osteopathy at Kirksville, Missouri, in 1902 and moved to Marshfield the next year, where he became a charter member of the local Chamber of Commerce.

The Osteopathy College in Kirksville was the first school in the country that followed the teachings of Dr. Andrew Taylor Still (1828–1917), who had started the school in 1892. Dr. Still believed that osteopathy was a necessary discovery because the current medical practices of his day often caused significant harm, and conventional medicine had failed to shed light on the causes and effective treatment of disease. His theories were rooted in diagnosing and treating the musculoskeletal system. He believed that physicians could treat a variety of diseases in this manner, and spare patients the negative side-effects of drugs.

Dr. Leslie came to Marshfield in 1903 and opened his first office in the Garfield block of town. He also maintained offices in Coquille and Myrtle Point. In the fall of 1924, Dr. Leslie moved his office to the First National Bank building in Marshfield, on the second floor.

He was an active member of the Masonic and Elks Lodges. For relaxation, Dr. Leslie had a ranch near Florence, Oregon.[175] He was also one of the largest individual prop-

Dr. George W. Leslie. Photo from the *Coos Bay Times*, 1936.

erty holders in Marshfield, having over thirty residences and apartments that he leased to local residents.[176]

Bringing Legitimacy to Osteopathy

When Dr. Leslie first came to Oregon, there were only one or two osteopaths in the state. Because of his and other doctors' efforts, a state law was enacted placing osteopathy on the same footing as the medical doctor degree and giving osteopathy one member on the state board of medical examiners.

Anatomy lab at the St. Louis College of Pharmacy. Photo courtesy of the Osteopathy College in Kirksville, Missouri; photo by Drake; ca. 1893

Dr. George W. Leslie caricature as seen in the 1916 *Coos Bay Times*.

An ad from the *Coos Bay Times*, March 29, 1909.

Today osteopathic physicians practice alongside their MD colleagues. However, this was not always the case. Osteopathic medicine faced the same skepticism as most new medical philosophies and ideas. The State of Michigan became the first to recognize the legitimacy of the practice, but it took years of tenacious work to accomplish the feat of having DOs (Doctors of Osteopathic Medicine, as they are now called) licensed in every state in America. Today, there are over fifty osteopathic medical schools throughout the country.

DEFINITION OF OSTEOPATHY (1906)[177]

As system of drugless healing by which a practitioner through an accurate knowledge of anatomy and physiology and by appropriate manipulation aims to adjust structure so that nature can restore normal conditions of functions to the body.

Right: Ad from the *Coquille Valley Sentinel*, December 2, 1921 page 8.

Left to right: Ray Kaufman, Dr. George William Leslie, Dr. James Thomas McCormac, I. S. Kaufman, and Alva Doll. Photo courtesy of the Coos County Museum

Dr. Donald Malcolm Long (1906–1994)

Donald M. Long was born on June 19, 1906 in Webster, South Dakota, to Charles Henry Long (1880–1950) and Lottie Ibach (1880–1956). He was a graduate of the School of Pharmacy at Oregon State University and received his medical training from the University of Oregon school of medicine in Portland, Oregon. He married Dorothy Simpson (1911–2004) in 1933, and they moved to Marshfield, Oregon, to establish a medical practice in 1936. Three children were born to the marriage. When he first arrived in Marshfield, Long joined the offices of Drs. Peacock and Simpkin.[178,179]

In 1951, Dr. Long had a new office constructed for his medical practice. It was located at Third and Market in Marshfield. In 1956, he was elected to the executive committee of the Board of Trustees of the Oregon Physicians' Service. He had served on the board for several years along with Dr. Raymond M. McKeown of Coos Bay. And in 1976, he was appointed medical director of the St. Catherine's residence facility. In that capacity, he was responsible for coordinating the medical care of the residence as well as tending to the employees.

In 1949, Dr. Long gave a speech on socialized medicine to a gathering of the Coos Bay Rotary Club:

... Dr. Long noted that the subject of socialized medicine in America was not new. In 1946, a bill was introduced in the U.S. Senate, re-introduced in 1947 and again in March 1948, sponsored by Oregon Senator Wayne Morse. The proposal is now being recommended by President Truman. 'What is Socialized Medicine'; Dr. Long described it as a plan for government control of all doctors, clinics, hospitals, drug stores, and other now independently operated medical facilities.

As to when and where socialized medicine originated, Dr. Long declared it to be nearly as old as socialistic doctrines propounded by Karl Marx 100 years ago. Great Britain introduced governmental control of medicine in 1911; New Zealand has been experimenting with 'free medical service–something for nothing' for ten years. Behind the current legislative activity are government bureaus and administration personnel, so-called progressive legislators, certain international labor organizations and governmental malcontents, Dr. Long declared.

Summarizing his arguments, Dr. Long asserted the proposed document to be of more political significance than medical value. He reiterated that there would not be sufficient personnel and medical facilities to meet increased public demands. The system would produce 'assembly line medicine' with consequent lowering of medical standards ...

How apropos are Dr. Long's comments to the current debates about health care in America?

The "Flying Physician"

Donald M. Long (seated), the "flying physician" and a member of the Coos Bay Pirates organization. Photo courtesy of the Coos History Museum.

Among other interests, Dr. Long was an avid airplane enthusiast. In 1946, he made his first solo flight out of the Lakeside, Oregon airport—a grass landing strip, no less! He was the second member of the Lakeside Flying Club to complete that part of the licensing process, the other being pilot Dr. Gordon Nash from Coos Bay. Dr. Long had ordered a Piper cub for delivery sometime during 1947. In 1948, he purchased a different plane, this one a four-seater Stinson painted canary yellow. He soon completed his requisite hours to obtain a private flying license and on a flight taken in March 1949, to Crescent City, California, he had to make an emergency landing on the beach because of fog. He and his passengers had to walk two miles up the beach to Port Orford, where they spent the night in the Castaway Inn. He was the chapter president of the National Aeronautical Association for Coos Bay. Later on, he became the local doctor who gave physical exams to certify that men and women were fit to fly private and commercial airplanes, as well as control tower operators.[179]

Long was a fifty-year member of the Coos Bay–North Bend Rotary Club as well as the American Medical Association. He also took an active role in the Little Theatre on the Bay. He continued to practice medicine until his retirement in 1989.

Dr. Long died in North Bend on May 14, 1994 at the age of eighty-seven.

Dr. George Earl Low (1885–1935)

George Earl Low (aka "G. Earl" Low) was born on June 23, 1886 in Lowville, Murray, Minnesota, to Bartlett Marshall Low (1839–1893) and Lora Zoe McCann (1849–1889). Lowville was named after his father and uncle, who had settled in the area in the 1860s. G. Earl was the youngest of four siblings.

Ad from the *Coquille Herald* September 14, 1915 page 3.

In 1900, G. Earl was living in Montana, and in 1910 he moved to Salem, Oregon, where he received his medical education from the Willamette University Medical School. In 1914, he married Ethel May Templeton in Helena, Montana.

Limited information was found for Dr. Low's medical practice. The *Coquille Sentinel* posted an article on August 17, 1917 about Dr. Low and Dr. S. J. Mann as driving to Portland to enlist in the medical service in the U.S. Army. As a captain, he worked as a surgeon in the Meuse-Argonne campaign in Europe. Dr. Low and family also appear in the 1920 and 1930 federal census as living in Coquille, Oregon, where he was listed as a physician.

While the information about Dr. Low is limited, we do know from local newspaper reports that he was an active member and drillmaster of the "Coquille Coosonians," a group of men who performed intricate drill formations at community events. It was the first marching club to be organized in Coos County. The majority of the members were men from Coquille.[180]

Several other random and somewhat colorful stories about him, all of which appeared in the *Coos Bay Times,* are worthwhile summarizing. They're as follows.

DR. LOW SELLS COOS MAPLE ON TRIP EAST [SEPTEMBER 1926]

... Dr. Low, who has been interested in shipping maple burl east to factories where it is used as a veneer, put in several days visiting plants [on a medical trip to Ohio] which can use that wood, and lined up sufficient orders to keep the men getting it out busy until the first of the year ... [181]

DR. EARL LOW VISITS SITE OF MUSKRAT FARM [JULY 1927]

... Dr. G. Earl Low left yesterday for Grants Pass [Oregon] where [he] will secure titles for the land where he is locating his muskrat farm. Dr. Low has already secured the rats from J. A. Smith, muskrat rancher ... [182]

ESCAPE IN AIR CRASH "MYSTERY" [MAY 1929]

... It is a mystery how Dr. G. Earl Low and William Richardson escaped from the wreck of their airplane without serious injury ... The Eckholms, who live at

Coaledo [a community about 10 miles southwest of Coos Bay] were the first to reach the aviators as they were coming out from the wreck [near Beaver Slough]. Nearly three hours were spent in locating the plane, which is hanging by its tail in a large alder tree, nearly two miles from the highway.

The wreckage of the plane is scattered around for several hundred feet. It lands with its nose down and swings back and forth in the wind. It appears that what is left of the plane is likely at any time to drop from the tree and roll into the canyon below, the drop being at least 100 feet.

Though the nose of the plane is only about 30 feet from the base of the tree in which it hangs, the occupants would have fallen three times that distance, the tree being rooted at the very edge of a canyon ... [183]

No explanation was given for the crash landing.

DR. LOW TO ENTER BUSINESS IN MEXICO [SEPTEMBER 1930]

... Dr. G. Earl Low will leave the latter part of September for Mexico. He will look after logging operations of the timber holdings, which he and Hal Baxter took over last year. Dr. James Wheeler, who has been practicing in Gold Beach for the past eight years, bought Dr. Low's practice [in Coquille]. Dr. Low expects to remain in Mexico ... [184]

Dr. George Earl Low died in 1935 at Grants Pass, Oregon. He was forty-nine years old.

Dr. Ellsworth Francis Lucas (1897–1970)

Ellsworth F. Lucas was born on June 19, 1897 in Spangle, Washington to Elmer Ellsworth Lucas (1868–1944) and Frances E. Almsquist (1876–1967). He was a graduate of Oregon State University and received his medical degree from the University of Oregon Medical School in Portland, Oregon in 1925; that same year he married Mary M. Pike (1900–1979). No children were born to the couple.

After graduation from medical school, Dr. Lucas stayed in Portland for several years, working with Dr. Sternberg, a noted surgeon in that city. In 1932

Ellsworth Lucas was not of conscription age when he graduated from high school, but hailing from a military family, he was able to enlist in the hospital corps of the U.S. Navy, and served during WWI. He undertook training at the U.S. Naval Training School. He said he always wanted to be a doctor, and his time in the military gave him real-world practical experience that started his career in medicine. Once discharged from the navy, Ellsworth enrolled at the University of Oregon Medical College (OMC) in Portland, and received his medical degree in 1925. After graduation from medical school, he interned at both the Multnomah County Hospital as well as the Shriners Hospital in Portland.[185] Photo courtesy of *Hardware World* magazine.

Dr. Lucas moved to Bandon, Oregon, and took over the practice started by Dr. J. D. Rankin, and he continued to care for patients in the area for another thirty-eight years. For part of his career, Dr. Lucas rented space in the back of the Otto Shindler Drug Store in Bandon.[186]

Dr. Lucas was a member of the Masonic Lodge, Lions Club, American Medical Association, American Legion, and Coos County Medical Society.[188]

In the mid-1930s, Dr. Lucas, along with Dr. W. A. Cartwright from Gold Beach, opened an office in Port Orford, in the McIntyre house located north of town. It was known as the Port Orford Hospital Association; Helen Pearson, a trained nurse, managed the facility.

Dr. Ellsworth Lucas died in Portland, Oregon on June 14, 1970. He was seventy-three years old.

Dr. Ellsworth Lucas and Mary M. (nee Pike) Lucas, and dog Spike. Photos courtesy of Mary Schamehorn.

Dr. Lucas shares a slice of cake with Margaret Norton at an event celebrating his 25th year of being a physician in Bandon, Oregon. Seen also is Claude E. "Eddie" Waldrop, mayor of Bandon from 1956–1971. Photo courtesy of Mary Schamehorn.

As a physician in a coastal area, Dr. Lucas saw his fair share of cases that had to do people's interactions with water—and the creatures that live in it.

MUSSELS TO BE EYED AS DEATH CAUSE

… Inquiries concerning the death of a 58-year-old woman from Four Mile who succumbed last Sunday from poisoned mussels eaten a few hours before are being received from the local physicians. The mussels were thought to come from the rocks south of Port Orford; mussels taken from the rocks which are not continually washed by the sea water are declared unfit for consumption.

Dr. Lucas sent samples of the mussels to the state health department in Portland who forwarded them to the University of California for final analysis. The deadly symptoms make themselves apparent only a few minutes after the mussels are eaten. Dr. Lucas explained as proof of its quick action, it is pointed out that a cat that had been eating the leftovers from the mussel dinner was found dead with portions of the food still in its mouth.

Dr. Lucas declared that in his opinion the fatal poison was germinated within the mussels themselves, and was neither the result of copper deposits on the rocks nor the presence of the phosphorescent micro-organisms in the water that have kept the Pacific Ocean continually aglow at night for the past three weeks … [187]

Dr. Reuben "Bucky" Harrison Mast II (1895–1939)

The Mast name is a well-known throughout Coos County and is composed of a large diversified group, many of them involved in farming. In April 1872, William Penn Mast, eventually the Coos County patriarch of the family, was living in North Carolina—but he turned westward with his family and headed for Oregon. In June of that year they arrived in Douglas County, where they spent a year farming. But Mast had acquired 160 acres of land in Coos County, and in October 1873, his family settled upon the property and built a successful farming operation. (William Penn Mast was the grandfather of Dr. Reuben Harrison Mast II, the main subject of this section.)

Reuben Harrison Mast II (aka "Bucky") was born in Portland, Oregon, on August 24, 1895 to Reuben Harrison Mast (1858–1949) and Lola M. Leabo (1872–1942).

His father, Reuben Harrison Mast, who was born in Watauga County, North Carolina, was one of the founders and organizers of the Farmers and Merchants Bank of Coquille, and for years worked at the bank. His family, led by the aforementioned William Penn Mast, came west by train from North Carolina first to Red Bluff, California, where they hired teams of horses and wagons for the trip to Roseburg, Oregon. They stayed in Roseburg about a year, and then came to the Coquille valley in 1873. Young Reuben's mother's family came west from Tennessee in 1846 and settled in the Willamette Valley.

The Reuben Harrison Mast Sr. family, ca. 1900–1905. Reuben Harrison Mast II, or "Bucky," is seen at the far left. Left to right: Reuben, Lola (Leabo) Mast, Leta Mae, Reuben Mast Sr., James. Photo courtesy of the Coquille Valley Museum.

Dr. Reuben Mast at medical school graduation in 1924. Photo courtesy of Patricia Mast Carlson.

Bucky's Schooling, Military, and Medical Practice

Reuben Harrison Mast II attended Coquille High School, and upon graduation, "Bucky" enrolled at the University of Oregon in Eugene where he played football. As a sophomore, he left the university and enrolled in the medical corps of the U.S. Army during WWI. After being discharged, he returned to the University of Oregon to complete his undergraduate degree. He then took up his medical training in Portland, graduating in 1924. After a year of residency in a Portland hospital he moved to Myrtle Point, started his medical practice and built a small hospital in town. His original partners were Drs. H. H. Thomas and Kuffel.[189]

Dr. Mast was an active member in the Coquille Masonic Lodge, as well as the American Legion. When the infamous Bandon Fire broke out in 1936, Dr. Mast personally attended hundreds of injured patients.

Dr. Mast married three times: first to Verna Phillips (1895–?) in 1914 in Eureka, California; then to Florence Cox (1898–?) in 1918 in Vancouver, Washington; and finally to Hilda Mae Hoffman (1907–1998) in 1926 in Coquille, Oregon.

Dr. Mast died on October 9, 1939 from a fall from the eighth floor of the Congress Hotel in Portland. The coroner's inquest concluded that death was accidental, and had occurred when Dr. Mast tried to open the outside window.

Reuben H. Mast II in military uniform, ca. 1918. Photo courtesy of Patricia Mast Carlson.

MANY CASES OF DIPHTHERIA APPEAR AT MYRTLE POINT [1926]

… Dr. R. H. Mast announced today that five new cases of diphtheria had been reported making a total of over forty in Myrtle Point now. Four of the cases are in a rather critical condition. This does not include some cases reported in Bridge and elsewhere in the country. Everything possible is being done to prevent further spread of the contagion. Public meetings are being curtailed and a special effort is being made to keep the children from congregating … [190]

TONSILS REMOVED AT POWERS SCHOOL

… On October 29, 1932, the school nurse at the Powers Elementary School arranged for a tonsil clinic at the school. Dr. Mast of Myrtle Point assisted by two nurses performed 16 operations. The nurse's office in the Little building was the operating room and the kindergarten was equipped with cots and served as a recovery room … [191]

Dr. James Thomas McCormac (1857–1925)

James Thomas McCormac was born at Oregon City, Oregon, on April 29, 1857 to Johnston McCormac (1825–1907) and Maratha Mason (1832–1905). He was the oldest of three children born to the couple in Oregon. Johnston McCormac had been born in Ireland, and was an Episcopal minister—he was one of the pioneers of that church in Oregon. He was a minister in Eugene, Oregon, from 1858–1870, but the church also sent him, family in tow, to other parts of the country—Nevada, Iowa, Kentucky, Colorado as needed.

Thus James T. McCormac attended public schools in Cresco, Iowa. In 1873, James attended the Iowa State Agricultural College for one year, followed by a year of study at the Kentucky University. In 1877, James returned to Oregon, landed in Coos Bay and taught school for three and one-half years at the Marshfield Academy. On December 18, 1878, he married Harriett Bay (1861–1933), the step-daughter of well-known local practitioner Dr. C. B. Golden; three children were born to the couple.

In 1879, James McCormac apprenticed under his father-in-law, Dr. C. B. Golden in Marshfield, and took one lecture course at the University of California medical school, followed by another course in medical science at the Medical Department of the Willamette University (WMD) in Portland, Oregon. He received his medical degree from Willamette University in April 1882. While in college, James roomed with William T. Hornaday, who became a prominent ornithologist and director of the New York Zoological Park. The continued friendship undoubtedly had an influence on McCormac's oldest daughter Annie Grace, who also became a noted ornithologist.

James T. McCormac.
Photos courtesy of the Coos History Museum

Activities Outside of Medicine

There's little information about James McCormac's medical pratice (beyond some local ads for it); perhaps that was because Dr. McCormac himself had many other business interests besides medicine, mainly owning extensive log booms on the Coquille River that later were sold to the C. A. Smith Lumber and Manufacturing Company of Marshfield. It is said that the efforts of Dr. McCormac convinced Smith to build his big mills at Bunker Hill in south Marshfield in 1905.[192]

DR. J. T. McCORMAC,
Physician and Surgeon
Marshfield, Oregon.
Office: Lockhart Building,
                opposite Post Office.
Phone 105-J

Ad from the September 4, 1911 *Coos Bay Times*. While Dr. McCormac was a trained physician, it seemed that he spent a great deal of time on matters that improved the city of Marshfield. One must wonder whether he actually provided much medical support to the community or simply devoted his talents to growing the community.

From 1882 to 1886, Dr. McCormac served as Coos County superintendent of schools, as well as served on the Marshfield school board. In 1911, he was elected as one of the Coos County supervisors (aka commissioners). From 1907 to 1912, he served as president of the Marshfield Chamber of Commerce—

and in that capacity was active in working to get the Southern Pacific Railroad to build the line from Drain, Oregon, into the Coos Bay region. Along with representatives from local industries, he was instrumental in getting the Coos Bay bar and channel dredged as well. In 1907, McCormac started an effort to consolidate the towns of Marshfield and North Bend into one community called Coos Bay, but it never happened.

Dr. McCormac was also given much credit for the construction of the new Marshfield High School in 1912 at a total cost of $65,000. He seemed to be involved in anything that hastened the development of Coos Bay, and for many years gave most of his time and energy to this effort. At one point in 1909, several influential Coos Bay-area citizens wanted Dr. McCormac to run for governor of Oregon, but nothing much happened with that effort.[193-197]

Dr. McCormac's interests were quite wide, as indicated by the following article in the January 14, 1902 *Coquille City Herald*:

> **Dr. McCormac involved in Marshfield Land Company (Coos Bay Times March 30, 1907)**
>
> ... The Marshfield Land Company with paid up capital stock of $20,000 has been organized [March 30, 1907]. The purpose of the organization is the handling of a tract of land which will be placed on the market. It is located just above the site of the new C. A. Smith mill and has fine water frontage. It is what is known as the McCormac tract. The following officers were elected: president, F. A. Golden; vice-president, Dr. J. T. McCormac; secretary, G. W. Leslie; and treasurer, Alva Doll. The officers along with I. S. Kaufman make up the board of directors ...

... A deal was consummated Monday whereby Dr. J. T. McCormac bought 1½ miles of water frontage on the Coquille River at Cedar Point. The purchase of this frontage by Dr. McCormac is part of plans which he has had for some time the carrying out of which will have an important bearing on the development of the timber resources of Coos County.

Dr. McCormac already owns the Eagle Point boom on this side just above the Bay City mill, where the logs brought from the Coquille by rail are dumped into tidewater, this boom having a capacity of about 7,000,000 feet.

The intention is to establish a system whereby for a reasonable price the logs will be taken from the Coquille River and delivered to the mill here, the charges for boomage on the Coquille, loading on cars [rail], freight, boomage on this side and rafting to the mill all being included in one fixed charge which will be low enough to enable Coquille loggers to sell their logs to the mills here at a profit ... [198]

To further expand his log raft towing business in Coos Bay, in 1907 Dr. McCormac contracted with Max Timmerman to build a large gasoline-powered boat called *Dixie*. At the time, it was the largest boat operating on Coos Bay, with a gross tonnage of 14.4; it was 45 feet 9 inches long with an 11-foot beam. It was powered by a 30-horsepowered Standard engine. It was distinctly a Coos Bay product, made throughout with white cedar—a local conifer species common to Coos County. Dr. McCormac also owned a smaller log raft towing boat called *Aloha*.

In early 1909, the executives of the North Bend and Marshfield Chamber of Commerce gathered to take the first steps in the creation of the Port of Coos Bay, and to recommend to the governor of Oregon the appointment of five commissioners: two from North Bend and three from Marshfield. Dr. McCormac was elected chairman

Marshfield's new high school building. Aside from Dr. McCormac's interest in the community at large, he was passionate about the education of young people. At the dedication ceremony for the Marshfield High School building in 1909, he received many accolades for his personal effort to build the finest school possible. In a short speech given at the dedication, he said, "People differ on subjects of religion, politics, etc., but when it comes to education, they are unanimous in desiring the best that can be afforded." He went on to express the hope that it would not be long until the cities on the bay could be consolidated, and an elegant central high school be erected for the benefit of all. Indeed, part of his vision was accomplished when another new Marshfield high school was built, and this building became an elementary school. After some 111 years, this building still stands.[199] Photo courtesy of the *Coos Bay Times*, February 27, 1909.

United Brotherhood of Carpenters and Joiners Union on parade in Marshfield; ca. 1905. Note the signs on the left side of the street for Doctors B. M. Richardson, J. T. McCormac, E. Mingus, and B. E. Schoonmaker (dentist), with offices in the First National Bank building; on the right side of the street is a sign for A. B. Prentiss (dentist). Photo courtesy of the Coos History Museum.

of the committee, being the president of the Marshfield chamber. The group discussed the boundaries of the port, and it was unanimously passed that a committee of four was appointed to recommend the initial boundaries as well as recommending names for the governor to consider appointing. That committee included Dr. Everett Mingus and Henry Sengstacken.

The following is a description told by local Addison Bennett about the location of Dr. McCormac's summer cottage. Bennett had gone there on a boat ride he took up the Coos River with Dr. McCormac one day back in March 1909.[201]

… After you get up the Coos some two or three miles above the forks, you come to the summer homes of the residents of the people on the bay. Our objective point was the bungalow of my host, Dr. McCormac.

In 1916, Dr. McCormac was listed as president of the Coos Bay Land Company, and as such he offered the Chamber of Commerce of Marshfield a factory site adjacent to the Southern Pacific Railroad tracks and on the waterfront. (The Marshfield Land Company and the Coos Bay Land Company may have been one and the same.)[200]

In 1912, Dr. McCormac moved to Berkeley, California where he eventually retired and lived until his death on July 25, 1925 following complications from an operation. He was sixty-eight years old.[202]

Myrtle wood was yet another industry Dr. McCormac was involved in.

MYRTLE MILL WANTED[200]

… Dr. J. T. McCormac of Berkeley has submitted to the Marshfield Chamber of Commerce a report upon the supply, commercial manufacture and probable cost of myrtle wood, delivered at sawmills or at stations on the Southern Pacific Railroad. The main conclusion of Dr. McCormac is that the distribution and growth of Myrtle is such that there is sufficient supply to maintain a mill and manufacturing plant for a number of years and that the manufacture would be possible.

For some years, furniture made from myrtle became wormy, but treatment by dry or moist heat eliminated that trouble and it is now controlled. It is estimated that the myrtle logs delivered in Marshfield would cost the manufacturer $28 per thousand [board feet] …

Dr. McCormac's summer place was about eighteen miles (or possibly ten miles as the story has both measurements) from the city [Marshfield], and it was in the immediate neighborhood of dozens of cabins and tenting floors showing that in the season there was quite a population up there. Some of the structures were quite elaborate, one pointed out to me that it cost some $6,000, and others were very handsome and commodious. There was a boat landing place at each one, and of course each renter or house owner had his own launch, or in some cases more than one, the doctor having had three.
Photo courtesy of the *Oregon Daily Journal*, March 22, 1909.

Dr. Raymond Meril McKeown (1902–1990)

Raymond Meril McKeown was born in Hibbing, Minnesota in 1902 to Harry McKeown (1874–1935) and Alberta Smith (1877–1946). He came to Coos Bay with his parents on Christmas Day in 1907, when his father became manager of the Chandler Hotel, which opened in 1908. They arrived via the steamer *Breakwater*. The McKeowns lived on the second floor of the hotel for about seventeen years. As Dr. McKeown reflected in a talk in 1946 to the local Lions Club: "When the hotel was opened, it set [sic] in the middle of a swamp. But gradually the land was filled in and other business houses appeared alongside. I remember listening to many tales of loggers and longshoremen as I played along the waterfront and Blossom Gulch."

Raymond graduated from Marshfield High School in 1920. He received his bachelor's degree in literature, the arts and science from the University of Oregon in 1924. While at the U of O,

Right: Dr. Raymond M. McKeown as seen in the 1991 yearbook of the Marshfield High School, called the "Mahiscan." Mahiscan is not the name of a local Indian tribe. It's a word made up by Raymond McKeown back in 1920 while a senior at the high school. A contest to name the Marshfield High School yearbook was held that year, and McKeown submitted the winning name; it was a conjunction of the words Marshfield-High-School-Annual. The editors of the 1991 Mahiscan decided to dedicate that year's yearbook in memory of Dr. McKeown (he died in 1990), who during his school and post-school years, exemplified academic learning, professional leadership and community service. Photo courtesy of Oregon State Senator Arnie Roblan.[203]

Dr. Raymond M. McKeown, shown here in 1929 with representatives of (and many who wrote articles for) the University of Toronto Medical Journal. Ray McKeown is shown in the front row, fourth from the left. He was the editor-in-chief of the *Journal* that year. Photo courtesy of the *Torontonensis* yearbook, 1929.

he earned a varsity letter playing left tackle on the football team, and served as president of the Beta Theta Pi fraternity.

Medical Training

Raymond began his medical study at the University of Oregon Medical School in 1926, but then left for the University of Toronto in Ontario, Canada, where he received his medical degree in 1929. While at the University of Toronto, he was a member of the Alpha Omega Alpha medical scholastic society. To pay for his education, McKeown worked as a logger around Coos Bay, a fisherman in Alaska, and as boss of a cement crew in Toronto.[204-206]

Dr. Raymond M. McKeown, top row, fourth from the left. McKeown was a member of the Nu Sigma Nu Fraternity, as well as a member of the Alpha Omega Alpha Honor Medical Fraternity, both at the University of Toronto. Photo courtesy of the *Torontonensis*, 1929

PIONEER DOCTORS OF COOS COUNTY OREGON

Following his graduation from the University of Toronto, McKeown took his internship in surgery at the Yale-New Haven Hospital. He became a research fellow at Yale from 1929–1935 and was an instructor in obstetrics and gynecology there from 1933–1935. In 1931, he married Charlotte Elizabeth Van Cleve (1900–1988) in Brookline, Massachusetts. Charlotte had just graduated from the Yale School of Nursing. Two children were born from this union. (One of the children followed in his father's footsteps; Dr. Michael McKeown, a specialist in obstetrics and gynecology, practiced in Coos Bay from 1970–1997.)

Return to Oregon

In 1936, Raymond McKeown returned to Coos Bay with his family and set up a private medical practice, which he ran for 36 years—until his retirement in 1972. His focus was on obstetrics and gynecology.

Dr. McKeown had a lifelong concern with the socioeconomics of medicine. He was a founder and president of the American Medical Association Education and Research Foundation, and served on the Sears Roebuck Foundation board for several years—overseeing funding for physicians in small towns or non-urban areas.

In a 1976 article published in the *Oregonian*, Dr. McKeown commented:

… When I started my practice in Coos Bay in 1936, a hospital room cost $2.50 per day and the cost to deliver a baby at home was $35. I carried a microscope and materials in the trunk of my car so I could do a blood count [when necessary] and there was no X-ray equipment at the Mercy Hospital, so I [often when helping a patient] had to figure out what bone was broken by feel …

Throughout his career, Dr. McKeown published forty-two surgical research papers.[206]

Leadership Roles

Just before the United States was drawn into WWII, Dr. McKeown was appointed the medical examiner to perform physicals on men placed in the 1-A class by the Coos County draft board. Knowing the extent of the work, Dr. McKeown requested that Dr. Alfred J. French and Dr. Melvin Johnson assist in the work. A year earlier Dr. McKeown was appointed to serve on a three-member committee to evaluate medical education and hospitals for the Oregon State Medical Association. In 1938, he was instrumental in getting the University of Oregon to establish a marine biology institute at the old CCC camp in Charleston, Oregon. McKeown was chairman of the advisory committee for the institute.[207-209]

While rejecting earlier pressure to run for mayor of Marshfield, In 1947, Dr. McKeown became the mayor of Coos Bay for one year (1947–1948). Early in his career as a physician and surgeon, Dr. McKeown was appointed a fellow in the American College of Surgeons, the award being the highest recognition in the field. In 1957, he was elected to the nine-member board of trustees of the American Medical Association. At the time, he was one of only five other physicians in Oregon to hold that position; the others all being from Portland. While on the board of the AMA, he was instrumental in shaping the federal legislation resulting in Medicare health coverage for millions of elderly and disabled Americans. He also served on the Oregon Medical Board, and was named the State of Oregon physician of the year in 1973.[210-213]

Dr. McKeown was a Fellow of the American College of Surgeons, a Fellow of the American College of Obstetrics and Gynecology, and a member of the American Academy of General Practice. He was appointed to the board of directors of the Oregon division of the American Cancer Society. Throughout his long career as a doctor and civic leader in the Coos Bay area, Dr. McKeown was often the keynote speaker at many events throughout Oregon. In 1959, he attended a conference of the AMA, and personally met President Dwight D Eisenhower, who impressed upon the delegates the dangers of inflation and reaffirmed his opposition to socialized medicine.

Dr. Raymond M. McKeown died in North Bend on November 1, 1990 at the age of 88.

Dr. Everett Mingus (1867–1937)

Everett Mingus was born in Dixon, California on June 6, 1867 to Conrad Mingus (1822–1900) and Lavina Dollarhide (1841–1914).

Conrad had migrated from North Carolina across the plains in 1850 to California. In 1868, he moved from California to Oregon, and established a home in the Rogue River valley, where he lived with his family on a large farm near Medford. They moved to Ashland, Oregon, in 1888.

Aside from his time away at college, Everett Mingus, the second of four children born to Conrad and Lavina, lived in Oregon since he was two years old. Everett attended public schools in Jackson County. In 1887, he entered the University of Oregon to study civil engineering. He stayed two years at the university, but after a summer illness he changed his focus to medicine. In 1889, he enrolled in the medical college at the University of Pennsylvania in Philadelphia, and graduated with honors in 1892. In 1901, Dr. Mingus married Edna Seeley (1881–1946) in Coos Bay, with Deacon William Horsfall performing the ceremony.

Dr. Everett Mingus. Photo courtesy of the Coos History Museum.

Early Years as a Doctor

As a young physician Everett Mingus took a job in Portland, Oregon, as an instructor in the old Willamette University College of Medicine, which later merged with the University of Oregon Medical School. Dr. Mingus then spent a year in Grants Pass, Oregon, where he followed his interest in mining. But in 1897 he came to Coos Bay to establish a medical practice, and became the physician for the Beaver Hill coal mine. (Before Dr. Mingus started working in the small hospital at the mine, a Dr. Cross was Beaver Hill's physician.) While at the mine around 1902, Dr. Mingus experimented with making glass from the sandstone and sedimentary clay that were intermixed with the coal seams. No further references were found on this curiosity.

Dr. Mingus held his position at the Beaver Hill mine until 1921, when it closed following an explosion there. Dr. Mingus attended to the injured men on site; those less seriously hurt were taken to the Coquille Hospital, and those with serious conditions were taken to Mercy Hospital in North Bend.

Dr. Mingus was also named the division surgeon for the Southern Pacific Railroad around 1912 when they took over the Coos Bay, Roseburg, and Eastern Railroad Company rail line from Marshfield to Myrtle Point. He maintained an office in the railroad depot in Marshfield to attend to the needs of the railroad workers. Aside from the time spent at the mine and railroad, his main office was upstairs in the First National Bank Building, on the northwest corner of Central and Broadway (formerly called the First Trust & Savings Bank Building) in Marshfield. (Today, much modified, that building is the current location of North Point Real Estate.)[214,215]

Writing about the virtues of Coos County in an article in the January 1, 1901 *Morning Oregonian*, Dr. Mingus recites some interesting facts about the medical conditions in the county:

> *… Would not be complete [Dr. Mingus' comments on the other values of Coos County] unless it embodied the greatest of its virtues, viz., health statistics. Although characterized by considerable humidity, the residents have a high grade of freedom from those diseases which usually predominate in damp localities. Last year, [1900] in a given population of 2000, the mortality sheets show a death rate of 9 percent, and most of those from old age and accidents; no deaths from pneumonia, diphtheria, scarlet fever, smallpox, measles, typhoid fever, or malarial fever, while infectious diseases of all kinds are generally mild …* [216]

In 1902, Dr. Mingus was appointed Marshfield's first city health officer, a position he held for twelve years, and in 1903 became the Coos County coroner when Dr. Horsfall resigned.

Other Medical Necessities

Without modern medicines to deal with various diseases, such as smallpox, diphtheria, measles, and the like, the only method early Coos Bay doctors had at their disposal to battle these deadly diseases was to quarantine patients in their homes. (As we know, this can still be the case with some illnesses, as with us in 2020, and COVID-19!) In June 1909, Dr. Mingus was faced with just such an occasion when three men that had been quarantined because of their exposure to smallpox escaped from a boarding house near Mill Slough in Marshfield.

> ... Dr. E. Mingus, city health officer, announced today that he would swear out warrants for three men to be arrested. He proposes to have them severely dealt with and make an example that will eliminate violations of the quarantine in the future. One of the culprits had broken out with the disease for a day or so before a physician had been called; it was feared that all around the place had been exposed and so a general quarantine was declared on the boarding and lodging house ... Dr. Mingus says that the quarantine laws will be rigidly enforced and that anyone violating them will be given the maximum penalty ... [217]

In August 1910, Dr. Mingus went before the Marshfield City Council with a proposal to pass a "fly ordinance." The ordinance called attention to the menace of flies to health. He wrote regulations about the feeding and breeding grounds of flies, in hopes that it would reduce the health hazard. Of particular concern were the restrictions placed on horse and cattle barns where flies bred. The ordinance also provided that all perishable foods, including vegetables, fruits, meats, etc. in stores shall be encased in a fly-proof box made of either glass, wood, or wire netting. In making his argument for the ordinance, Mingus cited several cities in the eastern U. S. that were taking such action. Within the first two months, a dozen local people were cited for non-compliance.[218]

Yet another activity Dr. Mingus undertook as the city of Marshfield's health officer was to address accusations of tainted drinking water from the city water supply in town. To test different sources of the supply, Dr. Mingus took one sample from his own home and one sample from his office. The sample from his office tested fine, but the sample from his personal residence was contaminated. Dr. Bartle got involved and the two doctors expanded their search for the source of contamination, taking action to eradicate the causes.[219]

Life Outside of Medicine

Along with his medical duties, Dr. Mingus served on the board of the First National Bank in Marshfield and was a charter member of the Port of Coos Bay Commission. As the country prepared to join the Allied forces of WWI in 1917, the call to arms by the United States went out for the enlistment of 25,000 doctors under the age of

> As with many of his peers in the medical field at the time, Dr. Mingus was an inventive man.
>
> *... Dr. Everett Mingus, of Marshfield, has invented an anchor projectile and has it patented ... The object of the invention is to provide a device to be shot from a cannon the same as projectiles are commonly shot from shore or on board a ship, to carry a line to any given point*
>
> *... As the projectile strikes with conical end foremost, it becomes embedded in the soil or other matter (assuming that it does not strike rock) ...*

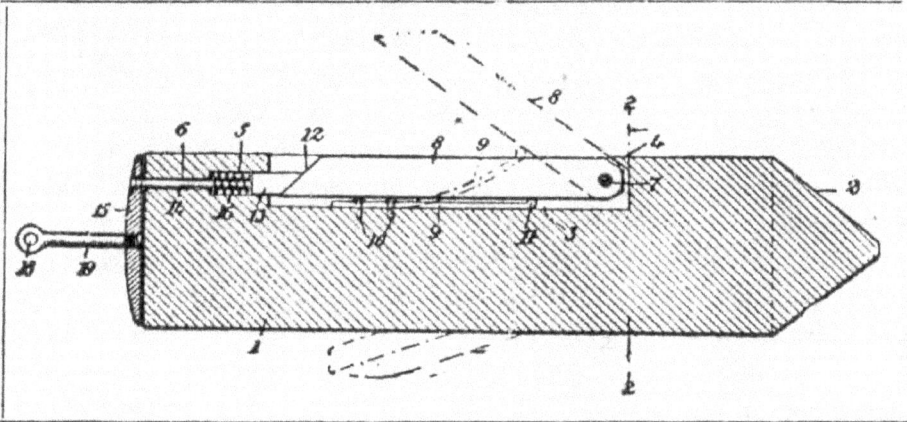

Dr. Mingus' patented anchor projectile

forty-five. Dr. Mingus enlisted in the medical corps as a captain, and at the time of his discharge in 1918 he was a major. In 1924, he was appointed the federal marine doctor for the Coos Bay area, a position he held for many years.[214-216]

In 1911, Dr. Mingus and H. C. Diers (a local civil engineer from North Bend) sent samples of Coos County coal to a New York firm to see if they could use the local product to make briquettes. According to an article in *The Timberman*, the initial reports were encouraging. Dr. Mingus and Mr. Diers, had invented a new fuel made from combining waste wood from the local sawmills with local coal.

The report from a factory in New York that had been experimenting with their process indicated that briquettes made from a blend of Coos County coal and waste sawmill sawdust in equal parts and compressed would make a good fuel. Claims were made that the combination could be made in different grades for domestic, industrial and naval uses. Claims were further made that other products, such as tar, pitch, alcohol, oil, creosote, acid and gas could be extracted during the manufacturing process. Plans were put forth to build a briquetting plant on the shore of Coos Bay, but the timing was wrong, as the lucrative California market was quickly converting from coal to oil—and no production facility was ever built.[220-222]

The following was written by Dr. Mingus in 1930 as a humorous treatise on Paul Bunyan and an "adventure" he might have had off the coast of Oregon:[225]

AN INTERVIEW WITH PAUL BUNYAN

"The stories of my adventures on Coos Bay would not be complete unless I related the manner of my arrival," said Paul Bunyan.

"I was standing on the shores of San Francisco Bay when a horde of natives swept down on me with menacing gestures. I had no means of escape except jumping into the bay; a mammoth whale came up for a yawn and I dropped squarely into his mouth. He seemed to understand the situation and bade me sit still. He informed me that he was just starting for a cruise up the coast and would take me along. Did not like the idea, but he seemed a friendly fellow, so I took a chance. He assured me there was enough air in his mouth to last an hour. His huge jaws closed and everything was in darkness. I could hear the powerful contractions of his body and knew we were travelling at a high rate of speed; harrowing thoughts shot through my mind in rapid confusion, then came a lull; light came and I beheld a beautiful coast covered with evergreens and scenic grandeur. My benefactor was maneuvering to get closer to the shore when he spoke. 'You will have to land; I am going out for breakfast.' I said: 'How far have we come?' He replied, 'Five hundred miles in one hour, that is my usual cruising speed; step out and lie flat across my blow-hole and I will lift you ashore.' Gosh! That was some flight, but I landed with ease where L. J. Simpson now lives ... "

Creating a Park

In January 1928, the Marshfield Parks Commission was established, and Dr. Mingus served as its first president. After a four-year fundraising campaign and a final celebration, Paul Bunyan Park was created in Marshfield in 1934. Apparently, Dr. Mingus had envisioned a park there long before it became a reality. Some local neighbors didn't like the original name, however, and lobbied for it to be changed. When Dr. Mingus died in 1937, the city renamed the park Mingus Park in honor of his efforts.[223,224]

One Final Act of Aid

When fire broke out in the town of Bandon in 1936, the *Coos Bay Times* reported that Dr. Mingus joined the fight to bring comfort to the people of that town during and after the fire:

> *When the Bandon fires struck in 1936, Dr. Mingus, as head of the local Red Cross chapter labored night and day stepped into gaps where his previously carefully worked-out organization had failed him, keeping that organization together and going beyond duties expected of his position to aid sufferers. Probably he never quite recovered from the strain of that labor.[226]*

Dr. Everett Mingus died in Coos County April 22, 1937; he was sixty-nine years old.

Dr. Alfred Bertram Peacock (1892–1966)

Alfred B. Peacock was born in England in 1892 and immigrated with his family to the United States in 1893. The family settled in Brownsville, Oregon, before moving to Portland in 1910, where Alfred attended public schools. Shortly thereafter, his parents both died, and it wasn't until 1940 that Alfred discovered he was still a subject of Britain. Apparently, his parents didn't file the proper papers before they died, and so, at the age of forty-eight, Dr. Peacock became a U.S. citizen!

He attended the University of Oregon and graduated in 1916; he then went on to the University of Oregon Medical School in Portland. After graduating in 1921, Dr. Peacock came to Marshfield to set up his medical practice. He was especially known throughout the medical community as an expert in thyroidectomies. In 1925, he and Dr. Peery performed the first surgical operation in the new Wesley Hospital (later known as McAuley Hospital). In 1928, he headed east for additional training at the Mayo Brothers Institute in Rochester, Minnesota. Dr. Peacock left Coos Bay for Eugene, Oregon, in 1944 and practiced medicine there for several years.[227]

Honors and Other Roles

During WWI, Dr. Peacock served in the navy, and was a medical corps captain in the Oregon National Guard from 1926–1938. He was elected to the American College of

As mentioned in the biographies of other doctors in Coos County, Dr. Peacock, as the city of Marshfield's health officer, was tasked with instituting quarantines. In 1927, he set a broad quarantine in an effort to stop the spread of infantile paralysis. It stated:

RIGID QUARANTINE IMPOSED ON ALL COOS BAY HOMES
Children Under 16 Must Be Confined to Their Own Homes
SCHOOLS CLOSED FOR TWO WEEKS BY ORDER
All Persons Under 21 Prohibited From Public Gatherings in Entire Area

… Dr. Peacock, in announcing the decision reached at the meeting of the city council, said that the county authorities had agreed to impose similar regulations in the surrounding territory including Bunker Hill, Bay Park, Millington, Eastside, Englewood, Cooston, Midway, and other points. Mayor L. L. Thomas has requested that Mayor H. E. Burmester of North Bend take similar action … [228]

On a lighter note, but carried in an adjacent column on the same page in the November 14, 1927 edition of the *Coos Bay Times* was the following:

BRUIN CONTINUES VISITS TO CITY

BLACK BEAR INVADED DR. PEACOCK YARD SUNDAY

… a large black bear which is now known to be inhabiting Nob Hill in Marshfield had his second visit to the homes on the east shoulder of the hill about 1 am. He was seen fighting with a pack of dogs in the yard of Dr. A. B. Peacock. Mrs. Peacock was awakened between midnight and 1 am by the barking of dogs in her yard. She could see the animal in the center of the circle of yelping growling dogs. Each time that a dog came too near, the bear would slap it down with a heavy paw and the dog would retire to the outskirts of the circle, yelping …

SACRED HEART HOSPITAL HAS FIRST TRIPLETS; DOCTOR HAS THIRD TRIO

... Dr. Peacock has not been taking obstetrical cases, but because of the acquaintance with the parents, made an exception. He felt himself rewarded when the triplets appeared. Dr. Peacock officiated at the birth of the Bush triplets, a boy and two girls, who were a well-known attraction in Coos County. Another couple were overtaken by the stork en route north and the mother was delivered of triplets by Dr. Peacock. 'I always sort of hoped I'd get that third set of triplets,' the doctor said, 'but I thought I'd have to put aside the hope when I retired from obstetrical practice. Now I have rounded out my record and not many doctors can equal it—triple triplets' ...

Surgeons in 1928, and was also a member of the Oregon State and Medical Association and Sigma Chi Fraternity He was mayor of Marshfield from 1933–1934, was the first president of the Marshfield Lions Club, and for years served on the board of the West Coast Savings and Loan Association. He was a member of the Oregon State Game Commission from 1937 to 1942.

Also in 1942, Dr. Peacock was named a fellow of the International College of Surgeons. The organization was started in Geneva, Switzerland, in 1935 and the honor of being elected a fellow of the international organization was very special. At the time of his induction, there were only 1,000 doctors named as such within the organization, which drew members from all over the world.

In 1943, he was recorded as being the chief of staff at the McAuley Hospital in Marshfield.[78,229,230]

Dr. Alfred B. Peacock died on December 10, 1966 in Eugene, Oregon. He was seventy-four years old.[231]

Dr. John Deloss Rankin (1897–1985)

John "Jack" Deloss Rankin Jr. was born in Glastonbury, Connecticut, on June 8, 1897 to John Deloss Rankin (1854–1900) and Sarah Hardy (1870–1960). Around 1910, the family moved to Meadow Grove, Madison County, Nebraska, where John grew up with two brothers and one sister, and attended public schools. When World War I broke out, he enlisted in the U.S. Navy.

Move to Oregon and Medical Studies

By 1920 John D. Rankin Jr. had moved to Oregon, and was found working in the Beaver Hill coal mine, some ten miles south of Marshfield, Oregon. Later, he found a rooming house in Eugene, Oregon, and enrolled in pre-med at the University of Oregon. He carried a heavy load of academics while at the university, and worked as a lab assistant during the school year. In the summers he took odd jobs to fund his education.[232,233]

In 1927, Dr. Rankin graduated from the University of Oregon

Dr. John D. Rankin; ca. 1952. He was the first physician from southwestern Oregon to be elected president of the Oregon State Medical Society. Photo courtesy of the Northwest Medical Society.

Medical School in Portland, and then interned at Eastern Oregon State Mental Hospital at Pendleton. In September 1929 he returned to Coos County where he worked with Dr. Lucas and purchased the hospital and office equipment of Dr. Roland V. Leep of Bandon, Oregon, who had passed away in July of that year.[232]

In August 1932, Dr. Rankin moved from Bandon to Marshfield, where he became associated with Dr. William Chisholm. They had been designated by the state industrial accident commission to take care of all employees in the region covered by the Wesley Hospital contract in Marshfield. In 1933, Dr. Rankin opened a medical clinic located in the Coos Bay National Bank building.[234,235]

In 1936, Dr. Rankin who lived in Coquille, was elected its mayor, a position for which he was re-elected for another two-year term before turning the gavel over to Dr. R. F. Milne.

Hospital Ownership

In June 1940, Dr. Rankin became the sole owner of a hospital in Coquille when his partner, Dr. M. Earl Wilson, died. The hospital was located at the corner of 2nd and Hall Streets. The two had drafted an agreement when they first acquired the hospital from the estate of Dr. Leep, that should either Dr. Rankin or Dr. Wilson die, the other would purchase through an insurance policy the deceased half interest in the hospital for $25,000. At that time, an audit of the hospital's value was put at $75,000, so Dr. Rankin paid his partner's estate the additional $12,500 in cash to balance the books. (The insurance policy of $25,000 plus cash of $12,500 equaled one-half of the value of the hospital.)[236]

In June 1942 Rankin's Coquille hospital was closed as a general hospital in order to ration medical supplies until World War II was over. Dr. Rankin and his associates did, however, maintain their offices and clinics, and performed minor surgeries. Those patients needing more advanced care at the time were transferred to the hospital in Myrtle Point or McAuley Hospital in Marshfield. In January 1944, the old Leep Hospital in Coquille was sold to Elmer E. Benham. The plans for the old building were to renovate it and make it into storage and office space.[237,238]

Post-WWII Life

When the war ended, the returning GIs got a warm

The 1953 *Northwest Medical Association Journal* carried the following brief biography of Dr. John Rankin as the new president-elect of the organization. It was the first time a physician from southwestern Oregon had been elected to that position.[240]

... John D. Rankin of Coquille represents an active, proud and energetic section of the State of Oregon. More than that, he represents the type of physician who earns the respect of all who know him because of his sincere desire to be helpful to his fellow citizens. He has had much administrative experience. He has served as mayor of the city of Coquille for two years and has held numerous offices in civic organizations. His participation in community affairs is evidenced by the fact that he has been president of the Coquille Lions Club and has served as delegate to annual convention of Lions International. He is past commander of Bandon Post of American Legion. He has held many offices in the Oregon State Medical Society and has served on numerous committees. He has been secretary and president of Coos-Curry Counties Medical Society. During World War I, he served in the navy ... [241]

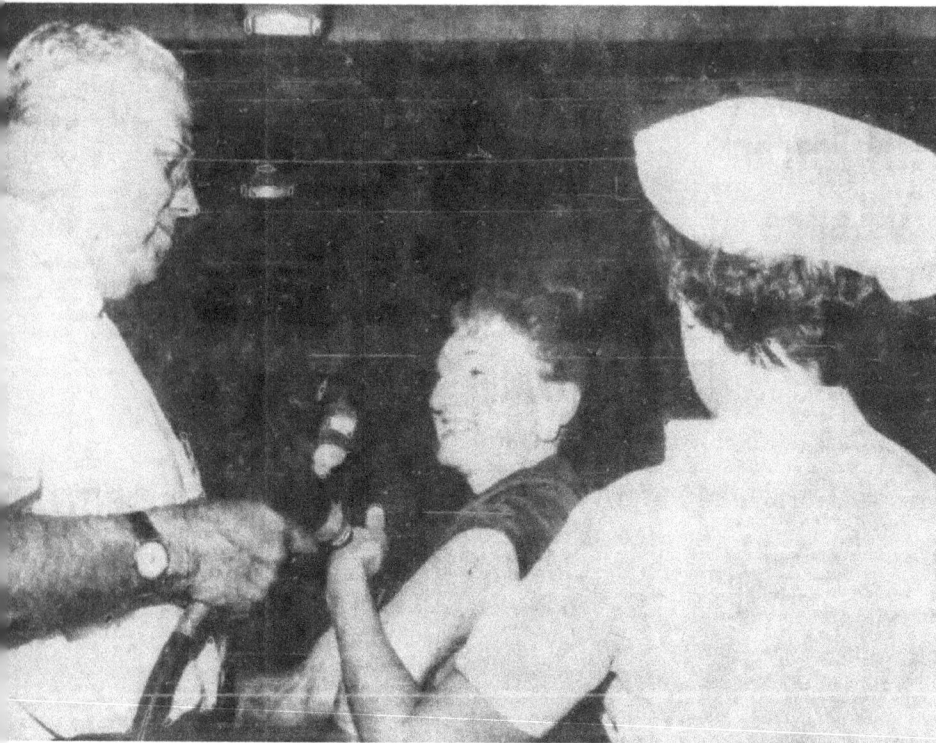

Dr. John Rankin giving a tetanus shot demonstration to his nurses in 1963. Photo courtesy of *The World*.

welcome from a new Coquille nonprofit organization (I never could find its formal name), headed by Dr. Rankin. A group of twenty-five men had assembled all the material to build the first two houses for the returning military men and their families. Dr. Rankin said in an interview at the time that careful records would be kept so that they would know exactly what the houses would cost to build. In total, twenty-three service men signed up to purchase the houses at cost. I could not find any futher information as to whether more houses were built by the group.[239]

Throughout Dr. Rankin's career in Coquille, his family moved around a fair number of times. After moving twice within the town limits, they purchased a small farm near the Coquille River, and dubbed it "El Rankin Rancho." It was here that Rankin and his wife taught their young children to care for farm animals and raise various crops. Later they bought a large ranch on Fat Elk Road, located west of town, and moved there after selling their house on Dean Street in Coquille. Finally, being weary of commuting in and out of town, they sold their farms and moved back into Coquille.[233]

Cold War Preparations

At the beginning of the Cold War with the Soviet Union, America was preparing for survival under an attack with nuclear weapons. Coos County was not without a civil defense coordination. In the event that an atomic bomb was dropped on Portland, Oregon, the direction of the wind would determine how long Coos County residents would have to reach fallout shelters. According to the local newspaper at the time, the area had obtained a 200-bed temporary hospital, which would be used in case of an attack. Dr. Rankin led the civil defense medical department in Coos County, with the assistance of Dr. James Hauschildt of Myrtle Point. Considerable effort and planning went into the fallout bunkers for each of the larger cities in the county—Coos Bay/North Bend, Coquille, Myrtle Point, and Bandon.[242]

Dr. John Rankin died on November 9, 1985 at Coos Bay. He was eighty-eight years old.

Dr. John Mark Simpkin (1894–1962)

John Mark Simpkin was born on September 2, 1894 near Salt Lake City, Utah, to Peter Atherton Simpkin (1866–1930) and Katherine Maria Stryker (1867–1912). John Mark's parents had emigrated to the United States from England in 1887 and settled in Chicago, where his father studied for the ministry. In 1900, the family moved to Salt Lake City, where Peter became the pastor of Phillips Congregational Church.

Throughout his high school years, John was active in the YMCA. He took courses from the University of Utah, but received his undergraduate degree from the University of Chicago in 1916. He immediately enrolled at Rush Medical College in Chicago. In 1919, Dr. Simpkin married Ethel Elizabeth Watkins in Salt Lake City, Utah; Reverend Peter Simpkin performed the ceremony. John and Ethel Simpkin went on to have three children.[243]

Move to Oregon

After John Simpkin completed his public health service as the assistant surgeon at the Sewell's Point Hospital at Norfolk, Virginia, he and Ethel moved their family to Marshfield, Oregon, in 1926, where Dr. Simpkin became associated with Dr. Alfred Peacock. Shortly after moving to Marshfield, Dr. Simpkin spent six weeks taking advanced study at the Mayo Clinic in Rochester, Minnesota, and at the Augustana Hospital in Chicago.

Dr. John Mark Simpkin. Photo courtesy of Ancestry.com.

Ethel Simpkin died in 1933, and in 1937, Dr. Simpkin married Charlotte Zieber (no children were born to this marriage). He served as Marshfield's city health officer until he resigned in 1937 and Dr. Donald M. Long was appointed to take his place. In 1940, Dr. Simpkin left Coos Bay for San Leandro, California where he set up a private medical practice until he died.

Dr. John M. Simpkin, an avid golfer, died on the Alameda Municipal Golf Course in California on January 15, 1962. He was sixty-seven years old.[245]

Even doctors can't always be there to aid family members, as a local paper reported.

… The bright-eyed, black-haired ever-active lad, the ten-year-old son of Dr. John M. Simpkin, who had mastered the intricacies of many a telephone pole and building wall, accidently touched a 220-volt power line as he neared the top of a pole across from his home. Mrs. Arnold Schmitz, a neighbor, saw a flash and then the boy's body as it was hurtled through the air to land on a nearby lawn. When he awoke, Dr. Donald Long was in attendance as Dr. Simpkin was away on a fishing trip on the Rogue River. While suffering from a fractured thigh, and deep burns on his ankle, prognosis is good …[244]

Dr. Ephraim Edwin Straw (1877–1929)

Ephraim Edwin Straw was born in Black Lick, Wythe County, Virginia, on February 28, 1877 to John Brown Straw (1815–1891) and Nancy Margaret Ward (1838–1919). Ephraim was the youngest of twelve siblings. His family originally hailed from Lancaster, Pennsylvania, and his great grandfather, Leonard Straw (Stroh), migrated to Wythe County Virginia sometime in the early 1800s. While Ephraim's father was a farmer, his grandfather, John Frederick Shaw, was a physician in Wythe County. Of the twelve Straw siblings, three became physicians.

Moving West

After graduation from medical school, Dr. Ephraim Straw first practiced his profession for a couple of years in Virginia, and then moved west to Ashland, Wisconsin—but he only stayed there for one year. In 1900, he headed further west, setting up a medical practice in Klamath Falls, Oregon, where he stayed for another two years. He finally came to Coos Bay in 1901–1902, where he served the medical needs of the community until his death in 1929.

Dr. Straw's medical specialty was the care of the eyes, ears, nose, and throat. In 1907, he married Sara C. Lakeman (1883–unknown), who had lived in Marshfield for several years, and owned and operated the Marshfield General Hospital. The wedding occurred in Santa Rosa, California, but the couple were divorced in 1916.

No children were born to this marriage. In 1918, Dr. Straw married Gertrude B. Fluehr in Ogle, Illinois. No children were born to this marriage either. Sara Lakeman married Dr. George Dix.

The Doctor as Mayor Too

Within four years of arriving in Coos Bay, Ephraim Straw was elected mayor of Marshfield.[246] Later, his obituary in the local newspaper claimed that he had served as the mayor of Marshfield longer than any other person up to that time (1905–1913), and when first elected in 1905, he was the

Portrait of Dr. Straw, ca. 1916. Photo courtesy of the Coos History Museum.

After he graduated from the Virginia Agricultural College, Ephraim Straw (see inset close up) went to the medical school at Vanderbilt University in Nashville, Tennessee, graduating in 1898 at the age of twenty-one.

youngest elected mayor of any city in the state of Oregon.

We're all familiar with various lapel pins and buttons worn in support of some cause or political candidate, but Dr. Straw's pin was unique. It was called a "Straw Badge." It was a little bunch of straw, tied with baby ribbon to be attached to the lapel of a coat. He passed them out during his campaign for reelection as mayor of Marshfield in 1909.

When the 1911 campaign for mayor heated up, the *Coos Bay Times* carried on a running forum against electing Dr. Straw for another term. Apparently, the editor of the paper and Dr. Straw had little in common as far as what they believed the community needed, and how to get it done. Dr. Straw was known for his frank and outspoken way, which may not have curried favor with the *Coos Bay Times'* editor, but must have stood him well with the citizens of Marshfield.[247-249]

In appreciation for his years as mayor and his continued efforts put forth for the betterment of the community, in 1915, the citizens of Marshfield built and gave to Dr. Straw an eight-room house-for free. The cost of the house at the time was put at $2,500.

Caricature of Dr. Edwin Straw from the December 13, 1913 edition of the *Coos Bay Times,* while he was mayor of Marshfield.

After his years as mayor were done, Dr. Straw remained popular with many citizens, as evidenced by the following story.

DR. E. E. STRAW PRESENTED WITH RESIDENCE [1915]

ADMIRING FRIENDS OF THE EX-MAYOR MAKE HIM A MAGNIFICIENT PRESENT AS A TOKEN OF THEIR ESTEEM AND APPRECIATION

... At a few minutes past 3:00 p.m., Dr. George Dix took down his telephone receiver and called up Dr. E. E. Straw in the Flanagan and Bennett building. 'I need your help in an important operation right away at the Chandler,' he said and Dr. Straw came hurrying. Bell hops directed him to the Grill Room and once inside the door a host of friends greeted him and presented him with a large myrtlewood key, 'to unlock the home we present to you in appreciation of your efficient work for the city during the eight years you were mayor of Marshfield.'

When he stepped into the mayor's seat, he said: ' We've got to have paving.' And paving they did. Mayor Straw went to Eureka, California to inspect a [road] paving job that city had done and brought back a man by the name of McCann who "citified" Marshfield by paving many streets. Later, Straw put in a sewer system in south Marshfield and in 1909 and 1910 closed the cesspools forever. A water-level road was put in from Marshfield to North Bend and streetlights were placed in darkened corners of the town.

Toward the close of 1914, Dr. Straw put down the official reins of the government but not for a minute has he ceased to be a booster ...[250]

An ad in the February 2, 1907
edition of the *Coos Bay Times*.

Political Wranglings

During Dr. Straw's time as mayor of Marshfield, more specifically in the summer of 1913, a political issue reached its apex with the deportation of Dr. Baily Kay Leach from Bandon and Coos County. Dr. Leach was a chiropractor in Bandon, but his trouble involved his opinions expressed in a local newspaper called *Justice*. During this time frame, the International Wood Workers of America or "Wobblies," were trying to gain a foothold in the logging business around Coos County. The organization expressed strong views about the need for America to become a socialist country. At the forefront of this exportation of Dr. Leach was Al Powers, manager of the huge Smith-Powers Logging Company.

In an effort to get at the story behind the deportation of Dr. Leach, Mr. Fred Lockley (a reporter for the *Oregon Journal*) conducted multiple interviews of local citizens, and posted a detailed article on the front page of the July 27, 1913 edition of the *Oregon Journal* in which Al Powers is quoted as follows:[251]

"... We make no distinction in our camps as to whom we hire. We don't care what a man's politics or religion is if he will do his work and let others do theirs. I found we were getting a lot of men who were more interested in talking than working, so I fired them. Some of our loyal men who have been without company for 20 years or more told me the I. W. W.s were getting as many of their men on the payroll as possible. W. J. Edgeworth, the I. W. W. secretary, worked for us. He got his foot hurt and was in the hospital seven or eight months. When he got well, he came to work for us again.

In the old days, men tried to see how well they could do their work. It seemed as if our men tried to see how little they would do and how poorly they could do it. Our camps were becoming disorganized. The men were becoming sullen and discontented. We put in a few men in our camps to get at the facts and then in one fell swoop, we fired about 250 men.

I gave notice that I wanted no more I. W. W. workers [International Workers of the World; aka "Wobblies"]. They were disloyal and interfered with the efficiency of the camps. I passed the word around that we would run our own business without interference or we would shut down.

Lumberjacks are not always gentle in their method, but their methods are effective. That I suppose led to the deportation of the I. W. W.s by the citizens of Marshfield ..."

When it came time to interview Dr. Straw, the mayor of Marshfield, the reporter from the *Oregon Journal* got an earful. Dr. Straw is quoted as saying:

"... We are handling our own affairs here without any paper butting in. We run these things to suit ourselves. Put that down in your notebook!"

Straw followed this statement with a string of abuse and profanity about outside papers mixing into something that was none of their business.[251]

The house given to Dr. Straw. Photo courtesy of the *Coos Bay Times,* April 10, 1915.

Life Outside the Mayoral Office

Even after Dr. Straw retired as mayor of Marshfield, he continued to advise the city council about health issues within the city. Buildings with poor ventilation and over-crowded boarding houses needed ordinances to provide air flow; buildings in what was known as the Chinatown district near the corner of Third Street and Market Avenue were a breeding ground for flies and mosquitoes where the buildings had settled below the street level and water stagnated beneath their foundation and crawl spaces.

Dr. Straw's energy level was legendary. For relaxation, he headed to a ranch he owned at Cherry Creek, just beyond Gravelford, Oregon (about 8 miles northeast of Myrtle Point).[250] Dr. Straw was also active in the Coos Bay Fish and Game Protective Association. It was organized in 1914, with Straw elected as vice-president. The main purpose of the organization was the preservation and propagation of wild game and fish in the region. Matching his interest in the work he did as a director of the Coos Bay Fish and Game Protective Association, Dr. Straw started a trout hatchery in 1924 on his ranch at Cherry Creek. A Mr. Clanton, who had experience in such matters, joined Straw in that endeavor.[252]

Straw served four consecutive terms as the health officer of Marshfield, and for fifteen years was involved with the U.S. Public Health Service. In 1916, when word went out from President Woodrow Wilson that should the National Guard be called up and there would be a need for 12,000 medical personnel, Dr. Straw was one of the first to offer his services to Oregon Governor Withycombe. Dr. Straw spent two years in the medical corps during WWI, returning to his practice in town after the war. In 1917, Dr. F. M. White joined Dr. Straw. He was also a specialist in ear, nose, and throat issues.[253,254]

Dr. Edwin Straw died of complications from a heart attack at the Keizer Brothers hospital in North Bend on October 14, 1929. He was fifty-two years old.

Dr. Charles C. Taggart (1863–1915)

Charles C. Taggart was born on September 24, 1863 in Greenwood, South Carolina, to Moses Taggart (1830–1890) and Margaret E. Crafton (1829–1897). Charles' father, Moses, was a doctor in Abbeville, South Carolina, where he lived his entire life.

Charles took a medical course while living in South Carolina, but received his formal medical training in Edinburgh, Scotland, and London, England. He travelled extensively, especially in Palestine.

DR. C. C. TAGGART,
Physician and Surgeon.
Office 209-210 Coke Building.
Phones: Residence 96L; Office 162J

Ad from the *Coos Bay Times,* September 23, 1911, page 6.

Time in Oregon

For five years, beginning around 1905, Dr. Taggart had charge of the Southern Pacific Hospital at the Beaver Hill coal mine, but in 1910, he left to take postgraduate work at the Rotunda Hospital in Dublin, Ireland. Upon his return to the Coos Bay area, he moved into Marshfield and opened his own medical practice in the Coke building with Dr. J. W. Ingram, who was planning to leave the area. Two years later, Taggart moved his office from the Coke building to the Flanagan and Bennett Bank building. For a short time, Dr. Taggart was appointed as the marine surgeon for the Port of Coos Bay.[255]

Dr. Charles Taggart never married. He died at the Mercy Hospital in North Bend, Oregon on September 13, 1915. He had suffered a heart attack. He was fifty-two years old.[256]

Like many other area doctors, Dr. Taggart got involved in the community beyond just offering medical treatment.

DIFFER ABOUT PAVING WORK [1913]

… A discussion of the paving of south Broadway last evening at the city council resulted in a rather spirited discussion between supporters of wood blocks and the hard paving. Dr. Taggart led the fight for hard paving, while Hugh McLain was the representative of the wooden blocks. Taggart claimed the hard paving would be cheaper and last longer and was more sanitary than the wood blocks. He said that if the C. A. Smith Lumber Company wanted to experiment with wood blocks, there were plenty of places for them to do this besides this important street.

McLain spoke in favor of wood blocks, saying that even Portland was putting in wood blocks on Fourth Street in preference to the hard paving. McLain said that he was to put in the wood blocks here for the C. A. Smith Company and the latter was to guarantee the paving for five years. No decision was made …"[257]

… A week later, the Marshfield city council voted unanimously to pave south Broadway with bitumen hard paving … [258]

Dr. Charles Walter Tower (1842–1920)

Charles W. Tower was born on July 14, 1842 in Randolph, Norfolk County, Massachusetts to Isaac Tower (1801–1863) and Minora A. Brackett (1806–1865). Charles was one of seven siblings. He received his classical education at Exeter, New Hampshire, and his initial medical training at Harvard Medical College.

In 1863 Charles dropped out of Harvard and enlisted in the Union Army in Company D, Massachusetts 4th Infantry Regiment, and served one year during the Civil War. At least one of his older brothers (Morton Tower,1840–1914) also fought in the Civil War, enlisting in April 1861 in the Massachusetts 13th Infantry Regiment. Charles was wounded twice, and was captured and confined to Libby Prison in Richmond, Virginia. He was one of the one hundred and nine prisoners to have escaped from the prison by tunneling from the basement, but only fifty-three made it to the Union line, and he was one of the lucky ones. Morton, along with his family, would join Charles in Empire City, Oregon, sometime between 1870 and 1880.

After Charles' military service ended, he returned to Harvard to continue his medical education, but didn't graduate due to health issues; he had contracted pulmonary tuberculosis during the war. He also had Bright's Disease, which affected his kidneys. As a result of his poor health, his sister, Ella Tower (1838–1918), who had settled with her husband, Samuel Stillman Mann, at the Newport coal mine just west of Marshfield, Oregon, encouraged Charles to come to the Pacific coast to recuperate from the trials of war. He decided that the West Coast climate would be better for his medical conditions, plus it had the benefit of being close to his sister.[259,260]

Dr. Charles Walter Tower. Photo courtesy of the Coos History Museum.

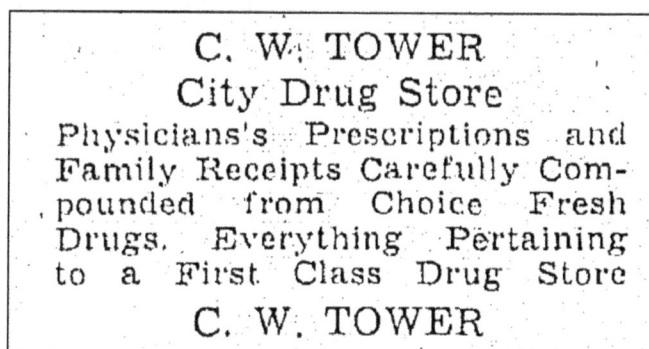

Arrival in Oregon

When Charles arrived at Empire City, Oregon in 1868, his health was so bad from the arduous sea voyage from the east that he had to be carried from the ship. He soon recovered, however, and enrolled at the Willamette Medical College in Salem, Oregon. He graduated with a medical degree in 1870 and returned to Empire City to establish a medical practice.

Over time Dr. Tower's health continued to improve, and he was eventually known as being quite vigorous. His business expanded; from 1874 to 1880 he ran a drug store in conjunction with his medical practice, as well as established the *Coos County Record* (aka *Guide*) in Marshfield—the first edition issued in the spring of 1870.

C. W. TOWER
City Drug Store
Physicians's Prescriptions and Family Receipts Carefully Compounded from Choice Fresh Drugs. Everything Pertaining to a First Class Drug Store
C. W. TOWER

In the bi-weekly newspaper called *The Rustic*, printed in Empire City, the above ad was found.[124]

The main story in the first edition seemed to have been the shooting of a James Aiken by a John Lakin at South Slough.[261-263]

Settling Down

As soon as Dr. Tower arrived in Empire, he began construction of a single-story, gable-roofed building with a lean-to shed as his bachelor's quarters, office, and drug store. On a business trip to San Francisco, however, he became smitten with the daughter of a Dr. Burrell, and persuaded Miss Minora "Minnie" Burrell to come to Coos Bay for a visit.

In 1875, the couple were married, and Dr. Tower began construction of a new and larger house on his property in Empire that was more befitting for his aristocratic wife-to-be. (Dr. Tower himself was not the typical, rugged, picturesque type of western pioneer that was common at the time, but more a gentleman of eastern culture, education, and refinement.) Four children were born to the marriage: Edward Charles (1877–1897), Jay Burrell (1883–1928), Russell Isaac (1885–1971), and Nellie Burrell (1888–1964).

As mentioned earlier, Dr. Tower's older brother Major Morton Tower came to Empire as well. There he built a three-room house that was later expanded in 1892 by Peter Loggie. Both Dr. Tower and Major Tower's houses are on the National Register of Historic Places.[264,265]

For many years, Dr. Tower's office was in Empire, but later he moved his practice to Marshfield. He was the company doctor for the Newport Coal Company mine (which later became known as the Libby mine). Late in the evening of Sunday, February 15, 1898, a fire broke out in the back room of Dr. Tower's office upstairs in the Sengstacken building in Marshfield, resulting in the destruction of most of the upper part of the building. Dr. Tower saved his library and instruments; but the Coke Brother's (local attorneies), lost everything—library, books, papers, typewriters; there was a mail room for the occupants that contained a press, books and material that was located in front of the building and it was only slightly damaged; Dr. O. E. Smith, a dentist, in the building lost everything.[266]

Dr. Tower was chairman of the Republican Party central committee in southwestern Oregon, but while he took an active

Ad in the *Coos Bay Times,* May 8, 1884.

part in political campaigns, he did not aspire to hold public office himself. However, in 1909, Dr. Tower was the campaign chairperson to reelect Dr. Straw as mayor of Marshfield. Dr. Tower was a life-long Mason, was the eminent commander of the Marshfield Knights Templar, and a member of the Shriners organization. He was the first president of the local chamber of commerce.[261]

Dr. Charles W. Tower died in his home on Curtis Avenue, in Marshfield, Oregon, on February 26, 1920 at the age of seventy-eight. The *Coos Bay Times* noted, *"The death of Dr. Tower marks the passing of a good man and a good citizen who left the world better for his having lived."* [261, 268]

Dr. Edward Watson (1868–1937)

Edward Watson was born on August 23, 1868 to William Watson and Elizabeth Myre, immigrants from Germany. When Edward's parents first came to America they settled in Ohio, but after a short time the family moved to Iowa. They were the parents of fourteen children. (It's unclear where Edward was in that lengthy sibling order!)

Edward received his early education in the public schools of Des Moines, Iowa. Upon graduation from high school, he enrolled in the medical department at Drake University in Des Moines. After receiving his medical degree, he practiced medicine in Des Moines for four years, and then went to Bellevue Hospital in New York, where he continued his education for two more years. Upon completing his work at Bellevue, he went west to Michigan and enrolled in the University of Michigan medical department for two more years, and then completed two more years of practical medical training at Rush Medical College in Chicago. From there he headed to Aberdeen, Washington, where he established a medical practice and stayed for eight years.[96,269]

Move to Oregon

In 1900, Dr. Watson met Louis Simpson, a prominent business leader from Coos County. Simpson asked Watson to come to North Bend to set up a medical practice, and the doctor took him up on it. In 1903, Dr. Watson opened the town's the first drug store in the J. R. Robertson building in downtown North Bend. He later sold the store to Charles W. Taylor in order to concentrate on his medical practice—which he continued in North Bend for over twenty-five years.

Over the years, Dr. Watson amassed a considerable fortune. He owned several parcels of land in North Bend, as well as a large timber claim in Lewis County, Washington. In 1930, he moved his office from the Citizen's building in North Bend to his home on McPherson Avenue. Along with his home and office in North Bend, Dr. Watson owned a home and property on North Lake near Lakeside, Oregon.[270,271]

In reflecting on a lifetime of living in North Bend, Emma Spooner (the oldest daughter of Dr. Watson), shared some details with *The World* newspaper in 2000:

> *… Spooner also remembers well a daily trip she often took with her father [Dr. Edward Watson] when she was two- or three-years-old. Milk wasn't delivered then, she said. 'Have you heard of Gordon Ross? Well, his great grandfather used to bring the milk down to the North Bend dock. My father would take me by the hand with a milk bucket in the other hand and we would go down [to the dock]. Mr. Ross would open his can of milk and he would take a big dipper and take the milk out and fill the bucket. We went down [to the dock] very morning, or at least someone did …*
>
> *During the Great Depression, money was scarce. If somebody caught a fish, they would share it with the neighbors. My father wasn't paid in money, but I can remember that groceries came …[271]*

Dr. Edward Watson died at his home on North McPherson Avenue in North Bend, Oregon, January 13, 1937. He was sixty-eight years old.[270]

Dr. Jared D. Wetmore (1858–1914)

Jared D. Wetmore was born on April 8, 1858 in South Creek, Bradfield County, Pennsylvania. His father, George Wetmore, was a lawyer. Jared was the youngest of three brothers and three sisters. At the age of fourteen, Jared's family moved to Sand Lake, Kent County, Michigan, where Jared worked for several years in a sawmill, saving his money for college.

While in Michigan, Jared's interest in medicine was sparked by working with a man named Dr. Willis for four years, after which he took a course of lectures in the medical department at the University of Michigan at Ann Arbor. Having some practical training in the field of medicine, Jared

Dr. Jared Wetmore. Photo courtesy of the *Oregon Daily Journal*, December 20, 1914.[275]

Wetmore opened a practice in Kalkaska, in northern Michigan, but soon he returned to the university for further studies. Jared completed his undergraduate studies at the University of Michigan in the spring of 1879.

He took his medical training at the Hahnemann Medical College in Center City in Philadelphia, graduating in 1882. That spring, Dr. Wetmore moved to Malta, Illinois, to set up his practice, and in 1884, he undertook postgraduate work at the Homeopathic Medical College, in Chicago.[273, 274]

Heading to Oregon

Dr. Wetmore obtained his Oregon license to practice medicine in 1892, when he settled in Toledo, Oregon, where he held the position of the Yaquina Bay health officer, as well as being the physician and surgeon for the Siletz Indian Agency.

Dr. Wetmore. Photos courtesy of the *Oregon Daily Journal,* December 20, 1914.

DR. WETMORE'S
PRIVATE HOSPITAL.

Having Procured the Services of
Dr. Horsfall of Marshfield,
I am now prepared to treat all cases
Medical and Surgical

Special Rates made for Accouchement.

Miss Delia Hoveley Graduated Nurse of San Francisco, Cal., Manager.

For Further Particulars Address
Dr. WETMORE,
Phone 111,   *COQUILLE, OREGON,*

In 1905, Dr. Jared D. Wetmore came to Coquille, Oregon, to operate the Coquille City Hospital and a private hospital in Myrtle Point. In 1907, Dr. Wetmore built an addition to the city hospital in Coquille. Aside from being a successful physician, Dr. Wetmore was an accomplished musician and artist. In 1910, he left Coos County for Portland, where he lived at Wichita Station until the time of his death in 1914. Ad taken from the *Coquille Herald,* October 18, 1905.

Dr. Osmar K. Wolf (1876–1937)

Dr. Osmar Kurt Wolf. Photo courtesy of the *Coos Bay Times*, July 31, 1928.

Osmar Kurt Wolf was born in Glauchau, Saxony, Germany, on July 24, 1876 to Karl Wolf and Eda Tramen. He came to the United States in 1894, making his residence in South Dakota. In 1903, Osmar moved to Salem, Oregon, to attend the medical school at Willamette University (WMD), graduating in 1907. Afterwards, he completed a year's internship at the Minor Hospital in Seattle, Washington.

On August 5, 1912, Osmar married Dorothy Bemis (1883–?) in Chehalis, Lewis County, Washington. He became a naturalized citizen of the United States in November 1916. In 1920, Osmar and Dorothy were living in Castle Rock, Cowlitz County, Washington. In 1921–1922, he took additional graduate work at the Chicago University, and in 1925–1926 did further study in Vienna, Austria.

He came to Marshfield in 1926, where he specialized in eye, ear, nose, and throat issues, practicing in the area until his death. He was a member of the Knights Templar, Royal Arch Masons and the Knights of Pythias.[276]

Dr. Osmar K. Wolf died on May 9, 1937 at Marshfield, Oregon. He was sixty-one years old.

Osmar Wolf was a member of the Glee Club at Willamette University in 1903. He is seen here in the back row, third from the left. Photo courtesy of Willamette University.

PART III

Early Hospitals in Coos County

Once there were more doctors in the area, larger hospitals and clinics followed. I've organized the information on Coos County's first hospitals by town, rather than when they were founded chronologically. However, as noted earlier, the first in the area was the Marshfield General Hospital; it was founded there in 1905, one year before the Mercy Hospital in North Bend was opened. Recall too that there were several "hospitals" connected with the early doctor's offices that contained a few beds and were fairly rudimentary.

North Bend

Mercy Hospital

In 1903, under the watchful eye of Father Edward Donnelly, the Sisters of Mercy started a hospital in North Bend. The building was located on property donated by local businessman Louis J. Simpson, under the stipulation that the Sisters would build a hospital on the site. When completed three years after construction began, the hospital contained forty beds.

> ... Spending her inheritance, Mother Mary Catherine McAuley opened the first House of Mercy on Lower Baggot Street in Dublin, Ireland on September 24, 1827, a place to shelter and educate women and girls. [Mother] Catherine's original intention was to assemble a lay corps of Catholic social workers. Impressed by her good works and the importance of continuity in the ministry, the Archbishop of Dublin advised her to establish a religious congregation. Three years later on December 12, 1831, Catherine and two companions became the first Sisters of Mercy ... [277-279]

Mercy Hospital in North Bend Oregon; ca. 1906. Photo courtesy of the Coos History Museum.

Below: Mercy Hospital and the adjacent Holy Redeemer Catholic Church on Sherman Avenue in North Bend, Oregon. The Mercy Hospital was located just up the hill on the left from where Sherman Avenue meets Highway 101 in North Bend.
Photo courtesy of the Coos History Museum.

The First Sisters

On February 2, 1906, the ship *Alliance* left the port of Portland, Oregon, and headed south, stopping at Coos Bay. On the boat were three nuns from the Sisters of Mercy coming to North Bend to take over the management of Father Donnelly's hospital. They were Sister Mary Genevieve, Sister Mary Ignatius, and Sister Mary Scholastica, and the doors of the new hospital were opened on February 5, 1906. During the first year the hospital was open, 110 patients were admitted. A moderate, reasonable fee was charged to those who could pay for their treatment at Mercy Hospital, but during the first twenty-two years of operation, more than a third of the patients paid nothing.

In 1942, the Lions Club of Marshfield bestowed the title of Outstanding Citizen of the Year on Sister Genevieve. She was lured to the meeting under the ruse that the club wanted an update on the room they sponsored at the hospital. Sister Genevieve was appropriately surprised by the honor.[280]

Nurse Training Too

In September of 1906, a training school for nurses was started at the hospital. Six students enrolled that year, but only two lasted the two years of training to graduation (Misses Elizabeth Gamble and Mary Wall). Applicants admitted into the nurses program were considered on probation during the first two months of training, while the Sisters evaluated their attitude toward patient care. After the first couple of months, the students began their hands-on training in nursing and were paid a salary of $8 per month. As is the situation in today's medical fields, trained nurses were in short supply, and the nursing school at the Mercy Hospital was well received.

The three-story hospital building was described in the July 7, 1907 *Coos Bay Times* as follows:

The Mercy Hospital
AT NORTH BEND

Is now open for the reception of patients. The terms are $10 per week and upwards. For particulars apply to

Sisters of Mercy
NORTH BEND, OREGON

An ad from the March 21, 1906 *Coquille Herald*, page 2. When the hospital opened, there were six doctors practicing in the area: Dr. Mingus, Dr. Ingram, Dr. Gale, Dr. Horsfall, Dr. McCormac, and Dr. Dix. The doctors were then able to separate medical practices and attend to patients at the hospital as well.

> *The basement contained the laundry, the furnace room, kitchen, three refractories, store room, and a large pantry. On the first floor was the office, waiting room, reception room, house doctor's office, priest's dormitory, ten handsomely furnished rooms for medical patients, the pharmacy, a large ward containing nine beds, and accompanying the ward were two large and modern bath rooms. On the second or surgical floor was the operating room, equipped with modern conveniences of the time, a preparatory room, two bath rooms, a small and a large ward, ten single rooms for surgical patients, and a large balcony. On the third floor is the chapel and Sisters' dormitory, nurses' apartments, and two bath rooms. The entire building is lighted by electricity, heated by steam and furnished with hot and cold water.[281]*

Need Outgrows the Site and the Sisters Add Wesley Hospital

By 1921, Mercy Hospital was no longer adequate to meet the demand from the growing community. In 1929, the Sisters acquired an eight-acre parcel of land that overlooked the bay between North Bend and Marshfield; it was known as "Kittyville." The original purpose for the site was to build a new larger hospital, but times were difficult after the war and money was very tight. The Sisters postponed the effort.

Mercy Hospital in North Bend operated until 1939, when the Sisters purchased the Wesley Hospital in Marshfield in July of that year. The Wesley Hospital was built by the Methodists in 1925; after it moved under the direction of the Sisters, the name was changed to the McAuley Hospital to honor the matriarch of the Order. (The Wesley/McAuley Hospital also has its own entry in this book, with more details, in the Marshfield section.) [282]

After the Wesley Hospital was purchased, the old Mercy Hospital in North Bend was changed to a care facility for the elderly and the name was changed to Mercy Home. It operated as such until it was condemned by the fire department in 1955. The old facility was allowed to continue to operate under certain conditions until a new facility could be built on the bluff to the south overlooking the bay at Kittyville. (Kittyville, should readers wonder, had been named after a pioneer lady who had lived on family lands there for ninety years.) The old Mercy Hospital was eventually demolished.

Mercy Home was the forerunner of St. Catherine's convalescent home, which was opened on November 25, 1957. It contained facilities for eighty-eight patients and cost $1,600,000 to construct. Funding for the new building involved contributions from the federal government as well as local fund drives. However, the Sisters still took on a debt of $900,000 to complete the facility. They kept the name of Mercy Home for the new convalescent center until 1963, when the name was officially changed to St. Catherine's Residence and Nursing Center. In 1982, St. Catherine's became a member of Catholic Health Corporation, a national Catholic health system, which merged with two other national Catholic health care systems in 1996 to form Catholic Health Initiatives. In 2003, the facility was sold to the Dover Management and Farmington Center, Inc., two Oregon-based companies with facilities throughout the state.

Mercy Home was the forerunner of St. Catherine's convalescent home. Image courtesy of PostCard.com; ca. 1958.

PIONEER DOCTORS OF COOS COUNTY OREGON

Keizer Brothers Hospital

By the early 1920s, Doctors Philip John (1884–1936) and Russel C. (1886–1929) Keizer determined that if the community of North Bend was to continue growing, it must have a modern, adequately equipped hospital. Marshfield had the new Wesley Hospital, and the Mercy Hospital on Sherman Avenue was thought to be at capacity.

The first section of the Keizer Brothers Hospital was opened in February 1923. It had twenty-five beds, doctors' offices, a dental office, and more. A portion of the nursing staff even lived at the hospital. The second part of the hospital opened in

The Keizer Brothers Hospital, North Bend, Oregon, ca. 1928. Photo courtesy of the *Coos Bay Times*.

August 1926, expanding the number of beds to sixty. And in 1946 the McPherson Street wing was added to the hospital, increasing the number of beds by another twenty-six.

As reported by the *Coos Bay Times* in July 1928:

> … *The hospital [Keizer Brothers Hospital] is a beautiful white concrete structure. In 1922, construction of the first unit of the building was begun. The first unit, completed in February 1923, was large enough to serve the demands made upon the services of the Keizer brothers. Within two years the demand on the facility began to outstrip the need of the community, so an annex was added to the original building. The total investment was over $200,000 … Russel became the hospital's president and Phil John was vice-president. Phil's wife, Laura May (née Rees), a registered nurse, acted as hospital superintendent, and Henry J. Wenderoth (a brother-in-law of the Keizer brothers) was manager …[160]*

More Family Involved

Phil and Russel Keizer's sister, Grace Keizer (1889–1958), who married Henry J. Wenderoth, was the original head nurse and manager at the hospital. Philip died in 1929 and Russel in 1939, but Russel's two sons, Dr. Ennis Keizer and Dr. John Philip Keizer, acquired the property from Russel Keizer's widow and continued to operate it under the original name, Keizer Brothers Hospital. (Dr. John Philip Keizer had graduated from the University of Oregon Medical School in Portland, Oregon in 1937, returning to North Bend, where he worked with his brother Ennis.) Dr. John

KEIZER BROS.
HOSPITAL
of
North Bend

——o——

STAFF

Russell C. Keizer, M. D.

Dean P. Crowell, M. D.

G. Earl Low, M. D.

J. B. Gillis, M. D.

H. C. Eastland, M. D.

Mrs. P. J. Keizer, R. N., Supt.

——o——

Phones: Office, 1781; Hospital, 2371.

Ad documenting the staff at the Keizer Brothers Hospital, from the *Coos Bay Times*, December 21, 1929.

The Keizer Brothers Hospital in North Bend, Oregon, ca. mid-1950s. Photo courtesy of the Coos History Museum.

(as his patients often called him) and his wife Julia (a registered nurse) lived at Keizer Brothers Hospital, often working seven days a week. Julia used to quip that she earned more money than John![7] By 1944 the hospital's capacity was sixty beds.

In 1951, John Keizer sold his interest in the hospital to his brother Ennis, and Dr. John and his wife moved to the University of Oregon Medical School in Portland to take a residency (from 1951 to 1954) in ophthalmology.

More Changes, and Growth

Around 1954, the Keizer Brothers Hospital was purchased from Doctor Ennis Keizer by a community nonprofit organization called the Keizer Brothers Memorial Hospital. Prior to the sale, several appraisals were made of the building, the land, medical equipment, and various receivable and payable accounts. When all was said and done, the sales price totaled $137,584.94. There were several special considerations as to how the funds would be paid over time.

Within the first year under the new ownership, financial problems arose, especially from the lack of funds pledged by some of the local businessmen in town. When bids to start the first rounds of renovation were received, the lowest bid was $208,000—which was far greater than expected by the new nonprofit organization. The project was downsized to $115,000 with most of the savings coming from a reduction in the remodeling of patient rooms.

In 1958, the Keizer Brothers Memorial Hospital received its first approval from the Joint Commission on Accreditation of Hospitals. (Founded in 1951, today, the Joint Commission evaluates and accredits more than 22,000 health care organizations and programs throughout the United States.) It was the first hospital in the area at the time to be so recognized.[283, 284]

The board of directors of the nonprofit Keizer Brothers Memorial Hospital at the time the hospital was purchased consisted of president, James M. Opland, of the North Bend Chamber of Commerce; vice president, Robert Pittam, of the North Bend City Council; secretary, M. L. Burnette, of the Empire City Council; and treasurer, Louis P. Trebalo, of the Empire-Charleston Chamber of Commerce. Other board members were Stella A. Cutlip, Dr. Melvin C. Johnson, Charles F. McCulloch, Dr. Raymond M. McKeown, and Robert Wucherpfennig.[283]

By 1965, there were forty-two doctors on staff at the hospital: twenty on the active staff; seven on the consulting staff; ten on the courtesy staff, and five on the dental staff. Thirty registered nurses worked at the hospital, along with twenty-one licensed practical nurses and seventeen aides. The total employed by the hospital in 1965 was 139, with 87 full-time and 52 part-time. They must have been efficient, though. The average daily cost for a patient's stay at the hospital that year was $19.50—the lowest in the state.[285]

During the late 1950s and into the 1960s, about 50 percent of the surgeries done in the area were performed by local orthopedic surgeons in a room at the hospital affectionately called the "bone room."[285]

The old Keizer Brothers Memorial Hospital building in North Bend became the Coos County Annex in 1974. The cost to the county was $1 to purchase it, compared to the assessed appraisal of $1,500,000. Photo by the Author, 2020.

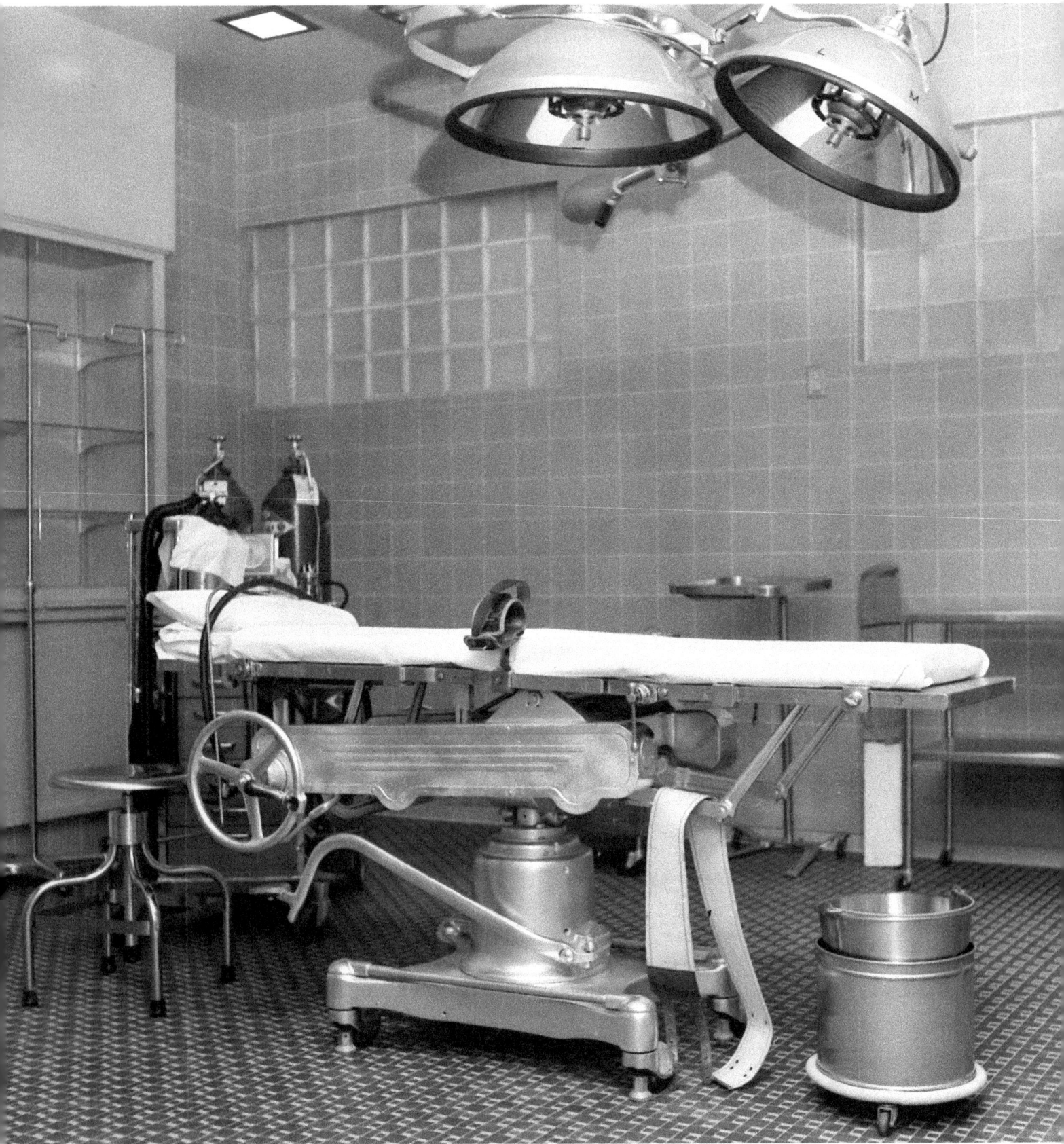

One of the surgical rooms at Keizer Brothers Memorial Hospital, ca. 1954. Photo courtesy of the Coos History Museum.

PIONEER DOCTORS OF COOS COUNTY OREGON

In an interview by the local newspaper during the 50th anniversary of the opening of the Keizer Brothers Hospital, Mrs. Philip John Keizer (nee Bertha Schmid) recalled:

... The hospital opened with 35 beds. Three years later we had people all over each other, so another wing with 25 more beds was built. There weren't many doctors in the Bay Area back then except for the Keizer brothers, [so] Dr. Bartles joined the hospital staff. Coos Bay had five doctors, Reedsport two, and Coquille one or two.

The Keizer brothers worked on the project for a year and a half before it opened. We used to charge $2.50 a day and didn't charge for most drugs, only for excessive dressings. During the Depression, it was a hardship on everyone. McAuley Hospital went into receivership, but Keizer Hospital managed to keep its financial head above water ... [282,286]

Marshfield (aka Coos Bay after 1944)

Marshfield General Hospital

In February 1905, the Marshfield General Hospital was started by Miss S. C. Lakeman, who came to Coos County from Mountain View, California. Miss Lakeman was a trained nurse who was educated in San Francisco. The hospital, the first in Marshfield, Oregon, was located at 562 North 2nd Street and had nine rooms for its patients—but demand for service often outweighed the availability of beds. The hospital was open to all physicians in the region.

In 1907, Miss Lakeman left Marshfield and returned to her home in California. Miss M. Black took over the management of the hospital, and was followed by Mrs. Dillon (Edmunds). The latter retired in the spring of 1910 and the hospital closed. However, local doctors stated that they had hoped to find another competent nurse to take charge of the facility. (Back then, a lot of the local hospitals were run by nurses. The doctors generally simply used the facilities.)

In March 1915, the hospital was once again in operation under the direction of Mrs. M. J. Ostrow, but only as a maternity facility. The hospital closed permanently in April 1920. [287-291]

Wesley Hospital (aka McAuley Hospital)

The Wesley Hospital in Marshfield, Oregon, grew out of local interest to add another hospital in the Coos Bay area, as the Sisters of Mercy facility was at capacity.

Ad for the Marshfield General Hospital from the *Coos Bay Times*, October 16, 1906.

Ad taken from the April 23, 1937 edition of the *Coos Bay Times*, page 5.

Wesley Hospital Memorials

The plans for the new hospital include opportunity for donors to provide living memorials, to commemorate both the living and the dead.

INDIVIDUALS, FAMILIES, CORPORATIONS AND BUSINESS FIRMS RARELY HAVE SUCH AN OPPORTUNITY TO CREATE PERMANENT MEMORIALS AND, AT THE SAME TIME, RENDER A HUMANITARIAN SERVICE OF THE HIGHEST VALUE.

MEMBERS OF A FAMILY MAY UNITE IN A GIFT IN HONOR OF A FATHER, MOTHER OR OTHER RELATIVE.

What more fitting tribute to a beloved member of a family is possible than to name for him or her, a part of the hospital which extends its ministrations to all regardless of creed, race or ability to pay.

This form of gift will certainly appeal to those who realize that hospital service provides one of the most efficient means of helping humanity and rendering vitally important aid in the hour of distress.

What finer thing can be done than to provide a living memorial of service for our boys of the World war?

THE FOLLOWING MEMORIALS ARE AVAILABLE TO DONORS:

$2500 will provide for construction cost and furnishings and memorialize a private room.

$1000 will memorialize and name a private room.
$1500 will memorialize and name a two-bed private room.
$1500 will memorialize and name the babies' nursery.
$1500 will memorialize and name the delivery room.
$2500 will memorialize the X-ray equipment complete.
$10,000 will memorialize the medical department.
$5000 will memorialize the maternity department
$300 will furnish a private room.

Every memorial unit will be marked by a bronze tablet or other proper marking bearing the name of the donor or another, as shall be desired.

GROUP MEMORIAL—All donors of $500 or over will, if desired, be memorialized with names inscribed on a suitable bronze tablet to be erected in a public location in Wesley Hospital.

METHOD OF PAYMENT—All memorial gifts are payable in five equal, semi-annual payments, beginning June 1, 1924. Every gift to create a memorial will be used exclusively for that purpose.

For further information please call at Campaign Headquarters, Chamber of Commerce. Phone 335.

An ad requesting contributions to build the Wesley Hospital, as seen in the May 1, 1924 *Coos Bay Times*, page 2.

First Attempts at Location

The first motion for a new hospital in Marshfield was started by the Kiwanis Club of Coos Bay around 1922. They had asked the Marshfield City Council to donate an old Chinese cemetery property, upon which a new hospital could be built. Apparently, the last burial in the old cemetery was made around 1908, the site had been abandoned, and in 1913 the bodies disinterred and shipped to China (see sidebar). The title to the property belonged to the city of Marshfield.

Jon Littlefield, a retired attorney who wrote about the Chinese community in Marshfield in 2017, suggested that the old Chinese cemetery was located at the west end of Highland Street in Coos Bay, being on the southeastern slope of Telegraph Hill.[292] On August 18, 1943, the *Coos Bay Times* further suggested the first cemetery in Marshfield (indeed also noted to be on the Telegraph Hill spot) was created in 1870, and later called the Chinese cemetery.

The local effort by the Kiwanis fell through, but in July 1923, a local Methodist bishop took the need for a new hospital in Marshfield to the president of the board of hospitals and homes of the Methodist Church, and things then began to take shape. The church had considerable experience in building hospitals across the nation and they undertook the challenge to build one in Marshfield. They also petitioned the Marshfield City Council to give them the old Chinese cemetery site for the Methodist hospital. That, however, was also turned down.[293]

While the exact location of the Chinese cemetery in Marshfield remains somewhat of a mystery, one of the local papers in 1913 makes reference to the "old Chinese burying ground on Knob Hill."

CHINESE WILL SHIP BONES

[*COOS BAY TIMES*, JUNE 6, 1913]

Six Bodies to be Sent From Marshfield to China Soon—Have Long Been Dead

... So that their spirits may be in glory with Joss and their mortal remains may rest in peace, the remains of six Chinamen, who were buried in the old Chinese burying ground on Knob Hill [now Telegraph Hill], have been disinterred and will be shipped back to China for internment there. The bodies were disinterred a few days ago and will be shipped on the next Redondo to San Francisco run from where they will be reshipped with hundreds of others for the Flowery Kingdom ...

[Death Certificates] were secured from Coroner Wilson to show that none of the Chinese had died of contagious diseases ... [Those disinterred] were; Wong Cone, heart disease; G. Fee, heart disease; Jon Youn See, senility; Gee Some, crushed head; and Lee On, heart disease ... [294]

A petition was presented to the Marshfield City Council in June 1924, again requesting the old Chinese cemetery site be donated by the city for the proposed Wesley Hospital. This time, the petition claimed that $60,000 had been pledged towards construction, and the additional $40,000 needed was assured. Again the Marshfield City Council rejected the proposal. (I never could find reasons for this continued rejection.)

Architectural sketch of the Wesley Hospital, as shown in the *Coos Bay Times*, December 16, 1924.

Finally, a Building Site

The Wesley Hospital was finally built on the northeast side of Commercial Avenue and North 8th Street. The property where the Wesley Hospital was built was purchased from M. W. Payne. A building already on the land had been used as a nursing home. The board of the hospital purchased the land and building for $13,000 in August 1924.

The Wesley Hospital, ca. 1930. According to Stan Blackwell, owner of a barbershop nearby, "This hospital was actually three buildings. The far right hand side was the original building and then they built the left, then later they built the middle section to put it all together." Photo courtesy of the Coos History Museum.

Ads taken from the April 23, 1937 edition of the *Coos Bay Times*, page 5.

The nursing home was converted to the nurse's headquarters for the hospital, as well as a training school for nurses. The hospital itself was designed by Lee Thomas, an architect in Portland, Oregon, and had the capacity for sixty beds.[295]

In February 1924, Articles of Incorporation for the Wesley Hospital were filed in the Coos County Clerk's Office. The purpose of the organization, as stated in the articles, was to establish a benevolent and charitable institution to give medical and surgical care, and to form a nurses training school. The officers of the corporation were listed as president, T. H Temple (of the Methodist Church); vice president, Mrs. J. W. McInturff; treasurer, Ben Chandler; and secretary, George C. Huggins.[296]

The July 11, 1925 issue of the *Coos Bay Times* in Marshfield, Oregon, carried a full-page spread on the construction of the Wesley Hospital:

… The equipment of the hospital will be of the best and the interior arrangement of the rooms such that the highest degree of efficiency and comfort can be obtained. Lee Thomas of Portland [Oregon], architect of the building, designed it to correspond with the nurses' home, the former M. W. Payne home which was purchased by the hospital board several months ago at a cost of $13,000 including the property upon which both buildings stand. The Payne home will be used as nurses' headquarters and training school for nurses, which is required by all class A hospitals. I. L. Young was the general contractor and had general supervision of numerous sub-contractors … [297]

The Wesley Hospital was the only Protestant institution of its kind along the Oregon coast, and it cost about $175,000 to build. It was named after John Wesley, who was believed to have started the Methodist faith in England. The hospital operated for about seven years at first, but then had to close its doors for five years because of the impact of the Great Depression on its revenue.

The Wesley Hospital reopened in April 1937 under a lease purchase agreement with the Methodist Church by Mrs. Mary Hunger. After Mrs. Hunger's death in February 1938, her husband, George Hunger, became manager of the hospital, but the arrangement with the church ended before it really got going. The purchase option of the Wesley Hospital

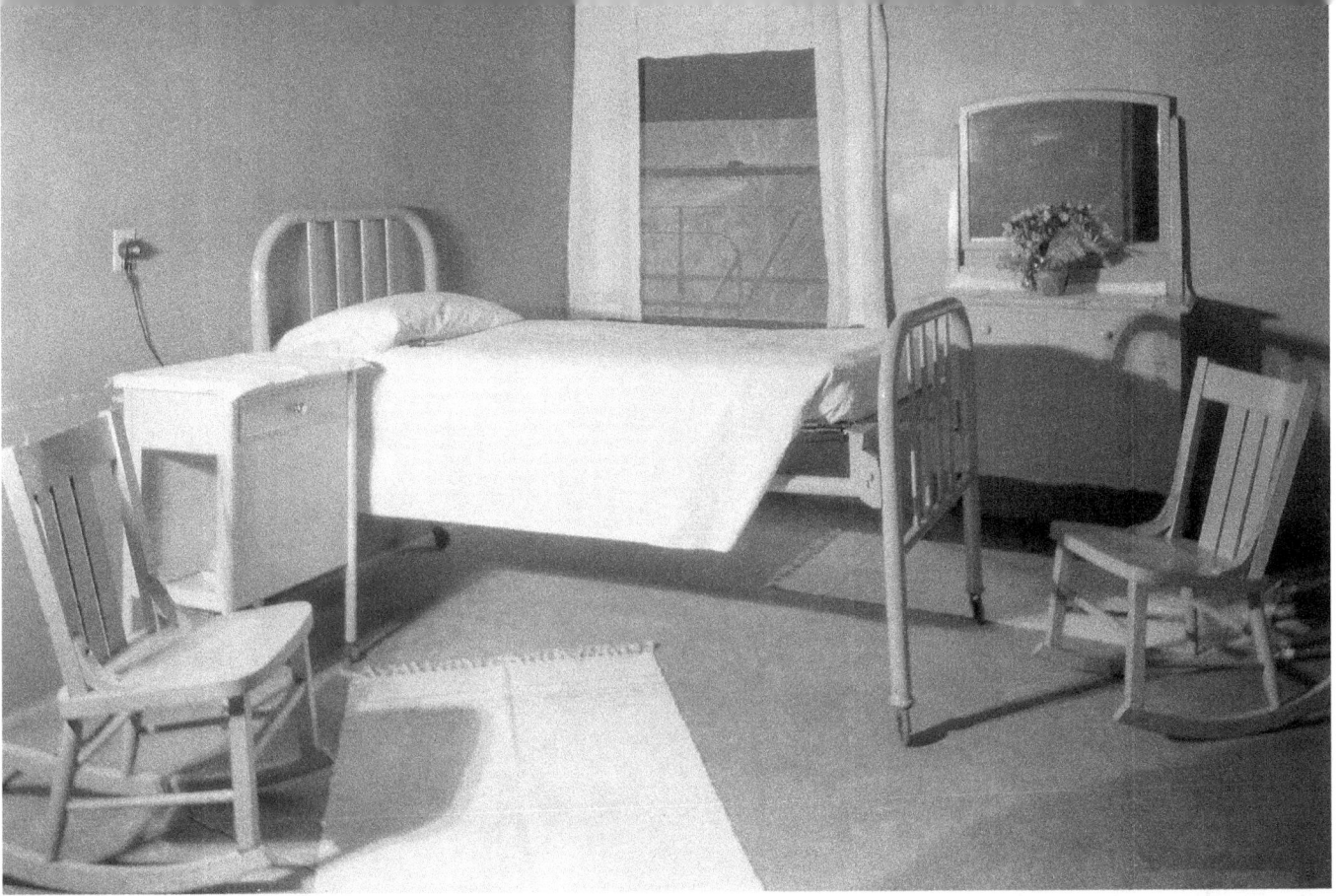

Patient rooms at the Wesley Hospital; ca. 1930. Photos courtesy of the Coos History Museum.

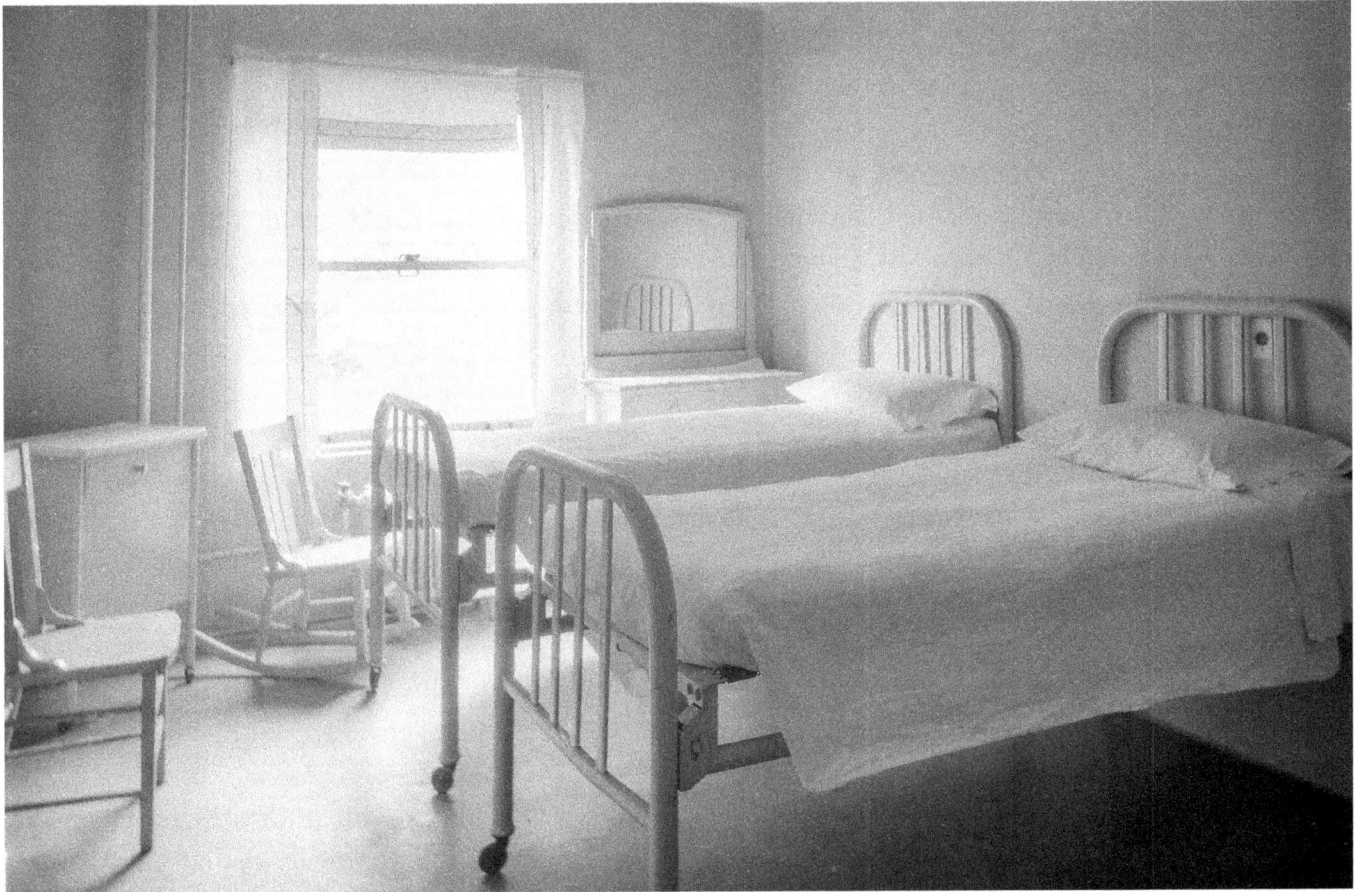

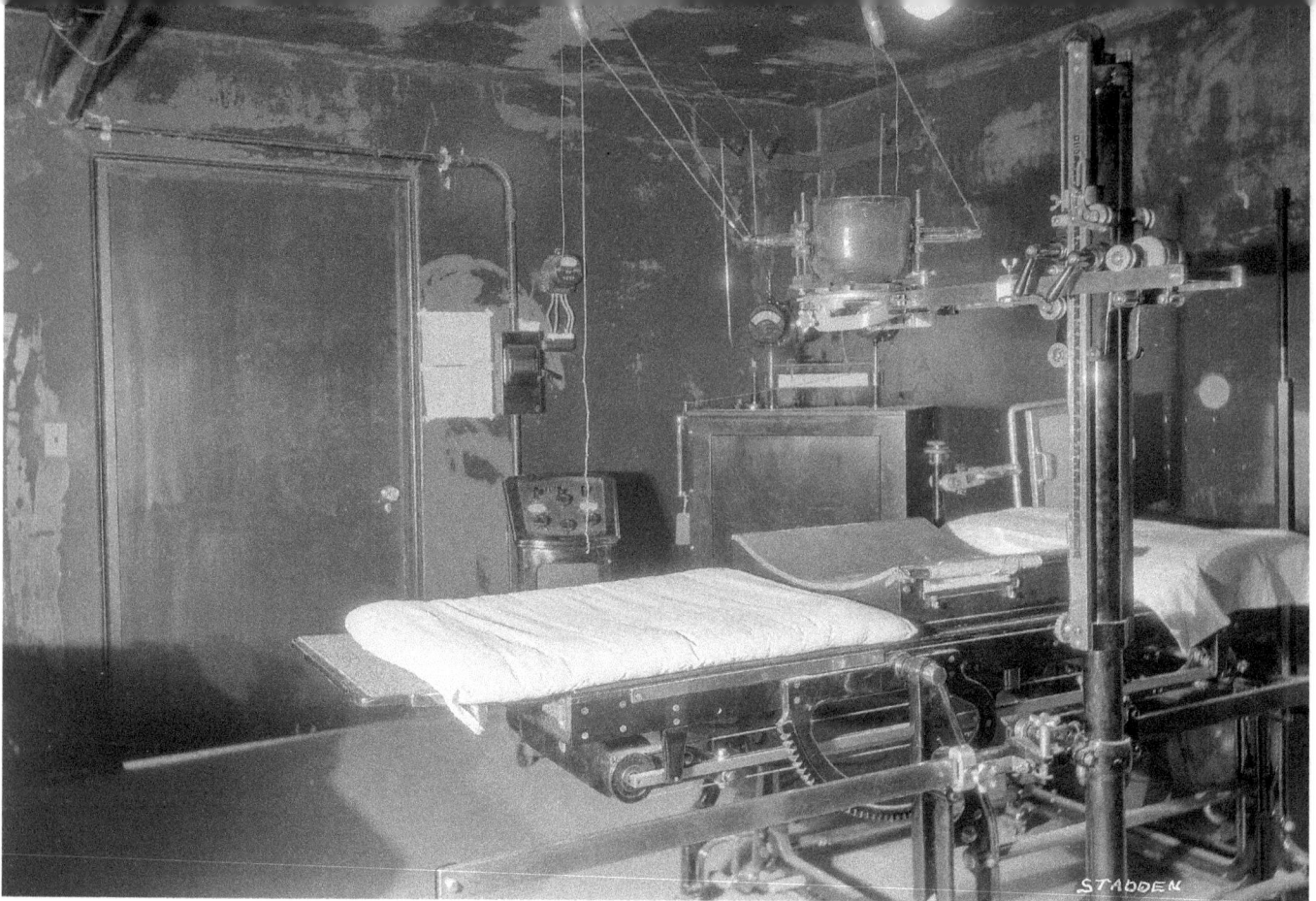

Operating room at the Wesley Hospital; ca. 1930. Photo courtesy of the Coos History Museum.

was immediately picked up by the Catholic Church through the Sisters of Mercy in July 1939. As mentioned, the name was changed to McAuley Hospital to honor the matriarch of the Order—Sister Catherine McAuley, an Catholic laywoman in Ireland.

Enter the Sisters of Mercy

The Sisters negotiated a two-year lease with purchase option with the Methodist Church. At the time the Sisters acquired the Hospital, the staff of doctors announced that they had set a goal to work together to make the hospital conform to standards of the American College of Surgeons. In April 1941, the Sisters purchased the hospital and property for $45,000. Sister M. Genevieve from Mercy Hospital in North Bend was placed in charge of the McAuley Hospital. Dr. Horsfall was elected chief of staff of the new hospital staff, Dr. Leslie G. Johnson elected vice president, and Dr. Alfred French as secretary. Dr. Donald M. Long was appointed chairman of the committee on hospital records.

In 1982, the old McAuley Hospital building was remodeled and became the home of the Ken Keys College. It remained in that use for about ten years. Photo, ca. 1983, courtesy of Ken Keys College.

In 1971, the Sisters of Mercy announced their intention of closing the McAuley

Hospital. Several local doctors were able to keep the hospital going until 1974, when the new Bay Area Hospital opened.[298-301]

Bay Area Hospital, Coos Bay

The opening of the new Bay Area Hospital in 1974 culminated efforts begun much earlier—in the late 1940s—to build a single hospital to serve our area. It's informative to track the project's progress over its two and a half decades of planning.

In 2018, the old McAuley Hospital building was demolished, and as of this writing, the land lies idle with a "For Sale" sign quietly seeking a new owner. Photo courtesy of television station KEZI.

In 1949, an extensive study of the medical needs of the region was undertaken and financed by some of the major industries in the Coos Bay area. The study was triggered when the Oregon state health department pointed out a need for additional hospital facilities in the region. In 1952, voters approved the formation of a hospital district (4,800 in favor, 1,500 opposed) but six months later, voters defeated a $1.5 million bond issue to build a new hospital. The bonds for constructing the new hospital failed by a vote of 5,802 against and 5,432 in favor.

In 1954, an effort began to create a semi-private/public hospital district in place of the original hospital district boundaries established in 1949. Progress toward devising a semi-private/public hospital district was not without naysayers, however. Many of the local industries opposed the new district hospital because industry executives thought they would have to pay a disproportionate share of property taxes. Many in the opposition camp had promised to make substantial contributions to renovate the Keizer Brothers Memorial Hospital, rather than build a new one. Some doctors on the staff of Keizer and McAuley Hospitals also resisted the formation of the new district, presuming more surgeons would be recruited—thus cutting down on the established physicians' personal incomes.

In 1969, a second feasibility study was undertaken by the "Bay Area Hospital Committee" after the Southwestern Oregon Medical Society asked the community how to move forward with a new regional hospital. This study was funded through a loan by the Federal Department of Housing and Urban Development. The urgency of conducting the feasibility study was prompted by the announcement by the Sisters of Mercy that they intended to close the McAuley Hospital on December 31, 1971. As mentioned earlier, local doctors purchased the McAuley Hospital and kept it operational until a new Bay Area Hospital could be built.

In 1974, voters within the hospital district reaffirmed their support of the $6.75 million bond passed by the district voters in 1970 (6,500 in favor, 5,200 opposed), and also defeated a move to dissolve the hospital district.

According to John Whitty, a local attorney who was instrumental in getting the Bay Area Hospital District formed, as well as assisting the effort to fund the construction:

> … The day we opened, all of the patients [at Keizer's and McAuley Hospitals] were brought over here, all of their employees came over here, and we opened on May 19th of '74. On May 18th of '74 those two hospitals were running and by end of the day on May 19th they were closed, and that was all as planned … [302]

Ad in R. L. Polk & Co.'s Coquille directory, about the Coquille City Hospital, ca. 1906.

An ad from the *Coquille City Herald*, March 27, 1900.

Coquille

Early Coquille City Hospital
The following article appeared in the July 4, 1906 *Coquille Herald*:

> … Dr. Wetmore is now located in his new hospital, on second street opposite the Masonic Hall [in Coquille, Oregon] … There are accommodations for twenty patients and eight private rooms, electric lights, with toilets and bath rooms, new Institution iron beds. The Doctor's reception, operatory and office rooms are models of neatness and convenience. The Doctor since location here one year ago has by his success won the confidence of all who have had any business dealings with him since opening the hospital in the Collier building eight months ago, treating numerous patients and has not lost a case, which speaks for itself …[303]

I didn't find much information about Coquille City Hospital, but from what I found, it appears it was at least operational between 1900 and 1906.

Pinkston Maternity Hospital

According to an article written by Dorothy Taylor about her pregnancy and published in the February 11, 2009 *Coquille Valley Sentinel*:

> *By then [I assume this is to mean 1949] Alice and Martin Pinkston were no longer running their hospital. Alice had been a nurse in Belle Knife and Dr. Rankin's hospital for years and later opened her own maternity hospital. No patients other than maternity were taken there.*

Sometime between 1920 and 1930, Martin and Alice Pinkston moved from Buffalo, New York, to Coquille, Oregon. Alice Pinkston was listed in the 1930 Coquille census as being born in 1882 in New York, and was a matron in a hospital. Martin Pinkston was also listed in 1930 as being born in 1883 in Missouri, and was a truck driver in Coquille. In 1940, Marrtin was living in Coquille and working as a janitor in a hospital, but there was no reference to Alice. Someone had written on the back of the photo that I include here that the hospital was located on the 200 block of Dean Street in Coquille. I could find no other information about this hospital.

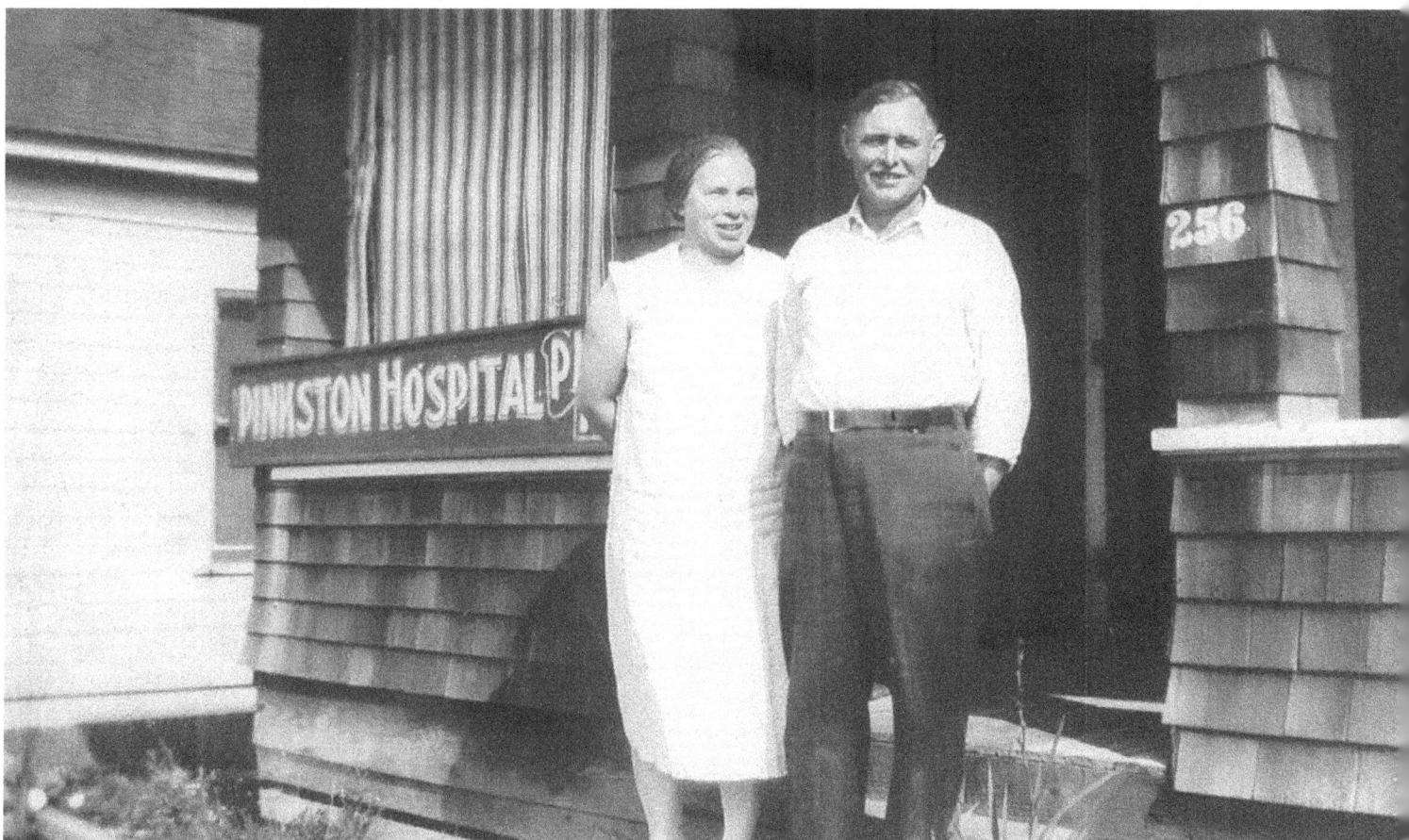

The Pinkston Maternity Hospital in Coquille. Photo of Alice and Martin Pinkston, ca. 1929.

More Coquille Hospitals

Over the years, the city of Coquille had many hospitals, but the information about them is a bit sketchy and confusing. Here's what I learned.

In 1907, a small city hospital was built at the northwest corner of Second Street and Alder in Coquille.

Then around 1911, Dr. Richmond and Dr. Culin also established a hospital; this one was near the southwest corner of Second Street and Folsom. (It was a two-storied building with a footprint of 30 feet by 50 feet; it was later renamed the Grayce Hospital—but it closed in January 1914). Dr. Richmond built a residence for his family on North Folsom between 1st and 2nd Streets, with a walkway that connected the home to the hospital building next door.

A nurse, Ms. Belle Knife, purchased doctor Richmond's small hospital in 1930 and ran it for several years before moving the operations to a much larger hospital in the Richmond-Barker Building, where the Broiler restaurant is located downstairs today. I don't know what happened to the small Richmond hospital after Belle Knive moved. When Belle Knife retired in 1949, she sold her hospital in the Richmond-Barker building to Dr. Rollin M. Falk. [305-307]

A Dr. Stark had a small hospital above what is now the Warp and Woof building in downtown Coquille. His offices were on the ground floor, with the hospital above. Later Stark closed this hospital and worked out of Dr. Falk's (aka the former Belle Knife) hospital (located on the second floor the Richmond-Barker building.

Photo of Coquille Hospital, ca. 1943. Courtesy of the Coquille Valley Museum.[304]

The Farmers and Merchants Bank in Coquille, Oregon, ca. 1912 (aka Dr. Richmond-Barker Building; or, today, the Broiler restaurant). Photo courtesy of the Coquille Historical Society.

BELLE KNIFE

Ms. Belle Knife (aka Aunt Belle, nee Serelda Belle Medlock) was a nurse in Coquille, Oregon, for over forty years. She was born January 12, 1884 in Elston, Missouri, and died in Coquille on October 29, 1977. On December 18, 1901, she married Robert Benjamin Knife (1880–1963) at Elston. In 1974, the local newspaper carried a lengthy article about her:

BELLE KNIFE RECALLS PIONEER DAYS[308]

… *Belle Knife [Serelda Belle Medlock] married R. B. Knife in 1901. The young couple came to Oregon in 1908, traveling by train to Roseburg and then reaching Fishtrap after two days of riding on a wagon over the old Coos Bay Wagon Road. It wasn't long before the nursing experience she had acquired in Missouri came into use and she became associated with Dr. James Richmond, making house calls via horseback, wagon, boat, or even on foot.*

In 1930, Belle purchased the little hospital opened by Dr. [James] Richmond on North Folsom street in Coquille and she operated it until 1937, when Dr. Vern Hamilton became the owner. Dr. Hamilton moved the hospital to what became the old Greyhound Bus depot. Dr. Hamilton moved to Portland in 1939 and it remained the Belle Knife Hospital until it closed in 1949, when Belle finally retired [and sold to Dr. Falk].

The Great Depression wreaked havoc on the Coquille Valley and on several occasions, Belle's hospital was the only one that was in operation. Belle said, 'money was scarce, but Dr. Richmond and I never turned away anyone who needed help. People paid what they could. Much was in the form of fresh meat, chickens, fish, and vegetables. That meant we had plenty of food for our patients.'

'Aunt Belle' assisted at hundreds of births at homes up and down the Coquille River, the valley's roads, and in the hospital. No one knows how many girl babies have been named for her but there are many.' Belle's husband, Benjamin, took care of the maintenance at the hospital and became known as 'Uncle Ben' …

Dr. Rollin M. Falk

Dr. and Mrs. Falk took over ownership of the Belle Knife Hospital and operated it from 1949 to 1955, when he and his family moved to Mapleton, Oregon, to continue his medical practice for two more years until he retired. Dr. Falk was born on January 29, 1898 in Calhoun County, Iowa. He died on February 29, 1964 in Lane County, Oregon. In 1922, he graduated from Union College and taught school for several years before returning to college for a master's degree. In 1936, he received his medical degree from the Loma Linda University in California. He started his first practice in North Hollywood, California, before moving to Coquille in late 1946.

When Dr. Falk purchased the Belle Knife hospital, he took over the practice of Dr. James Richmond, who retired. Mrs. Falk (1898–1990), nee Gladys Leggitt, was a registered nurse and became the manager of the hospital. The couple lived on a 400-acre ranch at Hauser, Oregon, formerly the Pinkerton Ranch, where they had large cranberry holdings.

Dr. Rollin Merton Falk. Photo courtesy of the *Coos Bay Times*, February 14, 1947, page 1.[309, 310]

Coquille Valley Hospital

In 1963, the two major employers (Georgia Pacific and Roseburg Lumber Company) in Coquille determined that the community needed a general hospital, and their executives set about making it happen. However, in 1964, the voters rejected a ballot measure to form a hospital district and float a bond to pay for the facility. Their objection was based on the fact that the Mast Hospital in Myrtle Point (see entry as follows) adequately served the needs of Coquille.

Not to be dissuaded, in 1969, Roseburg Lumber Company, Georgia Pacific, and local plywood pioneer George Ulett each contributed $50,000 as seed money, and the community passed a twenty-five-year bond issue totaling $650,000—and the hospital facility was built. It became licensed for thirty beds. The Coquille Valley Hospital opened its doors in January 1970, and continues to provide care today.

Myrtle Point

Mast Hospital

In 1926, Doctors Reuben H. Mast and M. E. Wilson built a hospital containing fourteen beds at Myrtle Point. It was a two-story affair with a footprint of 75 feet by 33 feet. When completed, the second floor contained the hospital rooms, a fully equipped major surgery room, and other modern features of the day. The bottom floor was divided into the doctors' offices, a dental office, a ladies' restroom, and a minor surgery area.

After running the hospital for a couple of years, however, the partners decided that it took too much of their time, and in 1928 hired Mr. and Mrs. T. V. Johnson to take charge of operating the facility. By 1944, the hospital had grown to accommodate forty beds.

In 1970, the Mast Hospital was closed and its patients were transferred to the new hospital in Coquille. Over its forty-four years in existence up through 1970, the Mast Hospital building had four owners (Drs. Mast-Wilson, Dr. H. H. Thomas, Paul Hammer, and finally, the Western Medical Care Foundation, Inc.). It had been remodeled and improved several times. In 1970, the hospital was sold a fifth time, to Lloyd Emrey of Bandon and Ron Roderick of Salem, and changed from a hospital to the Myrtle Point Convalescent Center, Inc.[7,311-313]

The Mast Hospital, Myrtle Point, Oregon. Photo; ca. 1930s, courtesy of OHSU.

Bandon

Leep Hospital and Leep Memorial Hospital

The original Leep Hospital was built by Dr. Roland V. Leep in Bandon and opened in the spring of 1926, but was destroyed by the catastrophic Bandon fire of 1936. The facility was replaced by a new hospital, named after Dr. Leep, who had died of a gunshot wound while hunting sea lions in 1929.

The Leep Memorial Hospital was built shortly after the disastrous fire that destroyed the town. It was constructed on Front Street, along the Coquille River waterfront between Delaware and Chicago Streets. It was originally occupied by the Red Cross during and after the Bandon fire. Dr. Ellsworth Lucas was instrumental in helping form the hospital association supporting the emergency hospital.

Ready or not, the new memorial hospital was opened on April 13, 1937 with the delivery of a new baby girl, Barbara Jane Norton, who weighed in at five and one-half pounds. The little girl's father was one of the founders and trustees of the new hospital. When in full operation, the hospital had a capacity of ten beds. The Leep Memorial Hospital served the community of Bandon until 1961, when a new hospital was built on the bluffs to the south and overlooking the town.[314]

Southern Coos General Hospital

Over the years, the old Leep Memorial Hospital building was used for various things, including as a residence, after the first "new hospital" was built on the hill overlooking the river and the lighthouse. The new hospital was called the Southern Coos General Hospital.

Leep Memorial Hospital in Bandon, Oregon, ca. 1940s. Photo courtesy of the Oregon Hospital Association.

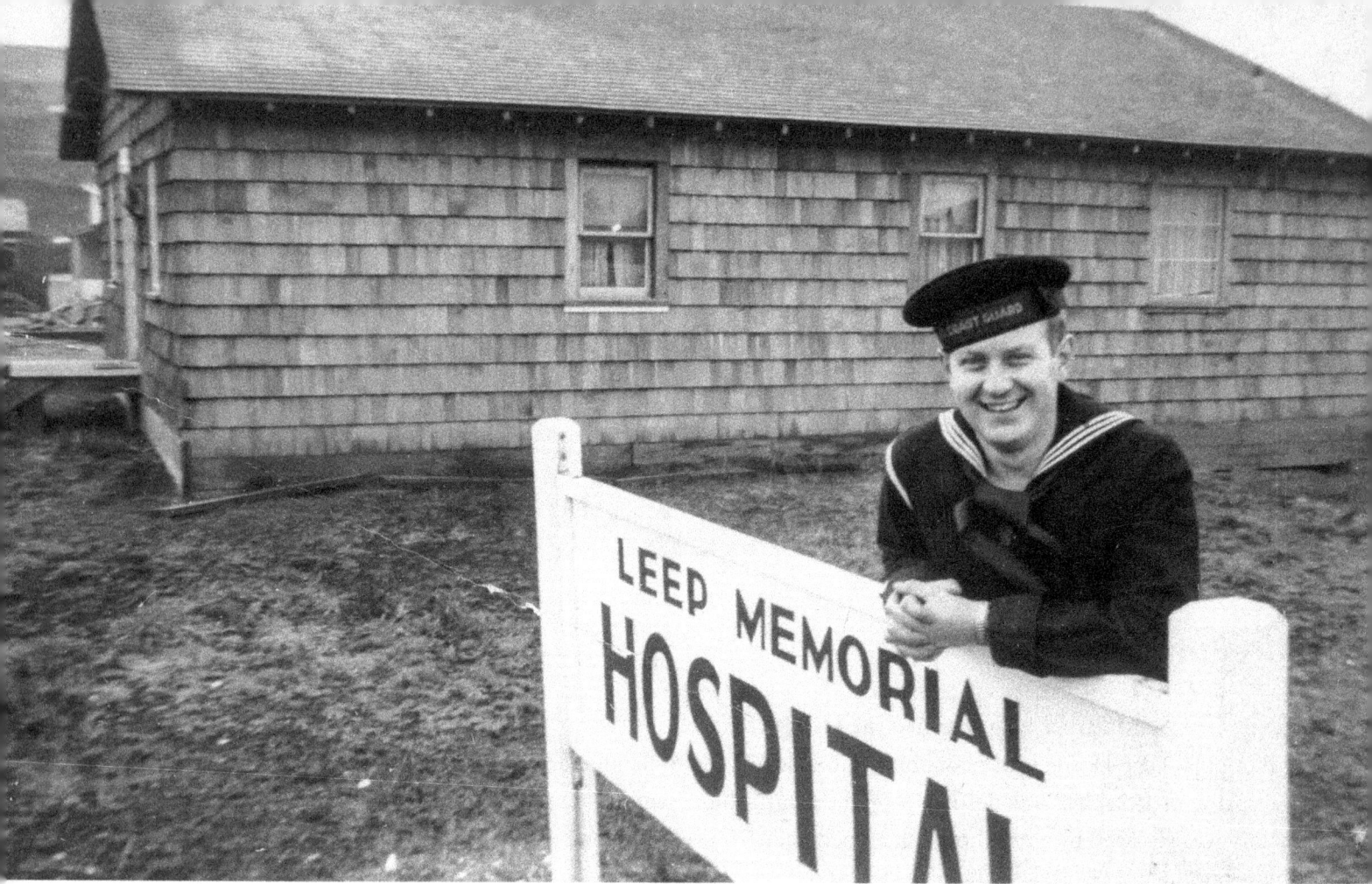

The Leep Memorial Hospital
in Bandon, Oregon, ca. 1945.
Photo courtesy of the Oregon
Hospital Association.

Building the Southern Coos General Hospital on the 4th Street hill, overlooking the town of Bandon, ca. 1960–61. Bandon claimed bragging rights to the construction of the new hospital as one of the finest small hospitals in the nation, by virtue of its efficient layout and low cost per square foot. It cost about $325,000 to build and equip. Photos courtesy of the Bandon History Museum.

PART IV

EARLY DENTISTRY

EARLY DENTAL TOOLS

A toothache—usually caused by an abscess—is a fairly common part of human life. In the olden days, the only solution for a toothache was extraction by someone such as a blacksmith—using crude, unclean tools. While this technique often solved the problem, it was painful, and frequently resulted in broken teeth with bone and secondary infections. Something more was needed!

Anesthetics

In 1884, Karl Koller, an Austrian ophthalmologist, discovered that cocaine produced surface anesthesia. Later that year, a dentist used a 4 percent solution of cocaine in a hypodermic syringe to deliver the first mandibular local anesthetic bloc.

But the dangers of using cocaine led to a search for a substitute. In 1904, Alfred Einhorn discovered procaine (Novocain), which replaced cocaine in dental procedures.[316, 317]

THE DENTIST by WALT MASON[315]

He well deserves a laurel wreath,
the man who tinkers with my teeth,
when they come out of plumb;
he plugs them up with melted lead,
and soothes my swelled and aching head,
and heals the tortured bum.

When his skill your comfort hangs
when you have trouble with your fangs,
and seldom does he fall;
his shining instrument he wags and draws
the old insurgent snags,
then draws his slice of kale.

No more you hear in dentist's room
the shrieks of those who dread their doom,
of those whose souls are sick;
the patient calmly sits and smiles,
the while the dentist with is files
and pinchers does the trick.

How different in olden ways!
The dentist then had painful ways;
he sat upon a bench,
and took your head between his knees,
and, muttering, 'Look pleasant, please,'
he plied his monkey wrench.

It took six men to hold me down
when he adjusted bridge or crown,
or plugged a hollow fang,
and travelers could hear me roar
away upon the distant shore
of Yang-tse-kiang.

But now I like the dentist's chair,
I like to sit and rest me there,
from morning until dusk,
to sit in comfort and to snooze
and have the gentle dentist use
his forceps on my tusk.

Other Basics

A Morton ether gas inhaler used by dentists. It was created by William Morton in 1846 and demonstrated the effective use of the anesthetic for the painless extraction of a tooth. By soaking sponges with ether and placed into the container, patients were able to inhale the gas for its numbing effect. Ether was a pleasant smelling, colorless, but highly flammable liquid that could be vaporized into a gas that numbed pain, but left the patient conscious, long after the procedure was completed. Photo courtesy of *Pioneer Lasers, History of Anesthesia in Dentistry.*

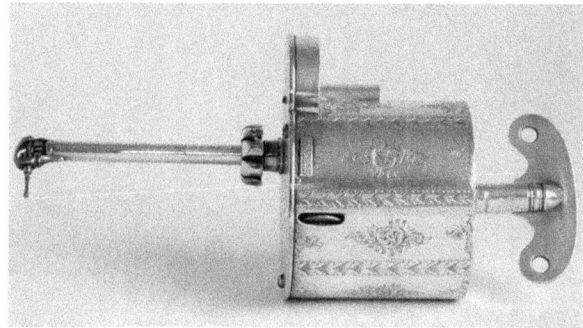

The Harrington clockwork dental drill. Prior to the invention of the clockwork drill by George Fellows Harrington in 1864, it was difficult to prepare a tooth for filling because earlier drills were cumbersome and made it difficult to accurately create a tooth crater. The Harrington drill was a spring-loaded affair that when wound tight would run for about two minutes before needing to be rewound. Photo courtesy of the British Dental Association Museum.

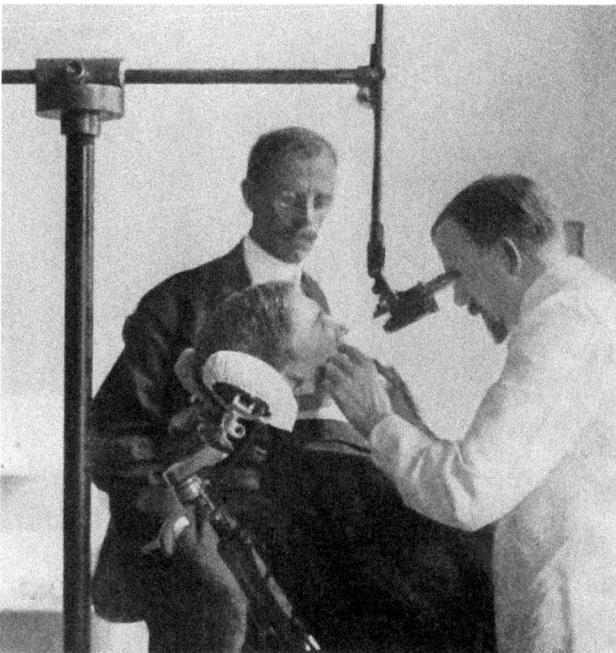

A dental microscope, ca. 1907. Photograph courtesy of Wikipedia.

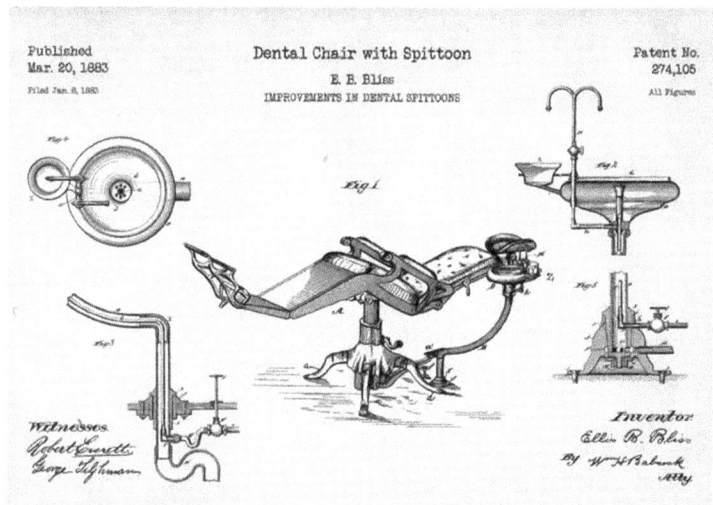

The patent dental chair with spittoon. It was invented by Ellis B. Bliss in 1883.

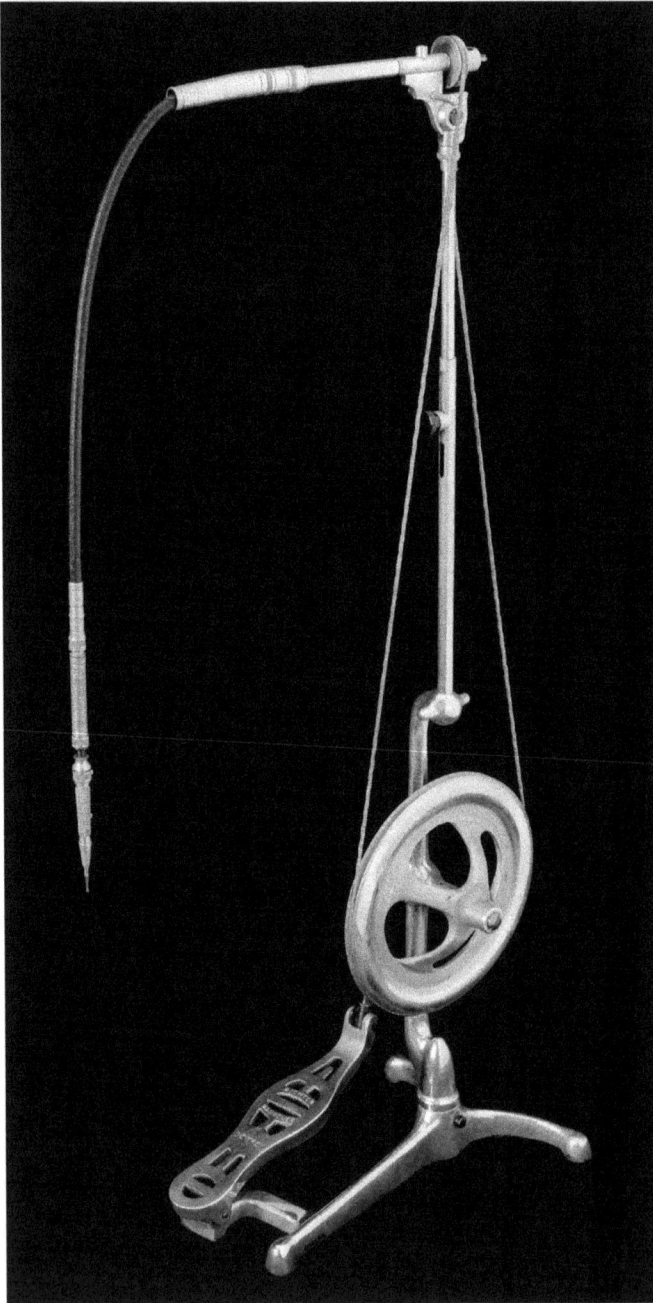

A foot-powered treadle dental drill, ca. 1910–1920. The foot-powered drill was invented in 1872 by James B. Morrison to replace the clockwork drill invented a decade earlier. It could achieve 2,000 rpm and vastly improve the performance of preparing a tooth for repair. Once a crude crater had been excavated in the tooth, the dentist would attempt to fill the area with various materials. Gold was the preferred choice, though it was expensive and took hours to complete. Once the gold filings were in place, the dentist would apply pressure to the material in the form of a metal rod and mallet to drive the gold into the tooth. It must have taken great skill on the part of the dentist—and considerable fortitude on the part of the patient. Photo courtesy of the Jordon History Museum.

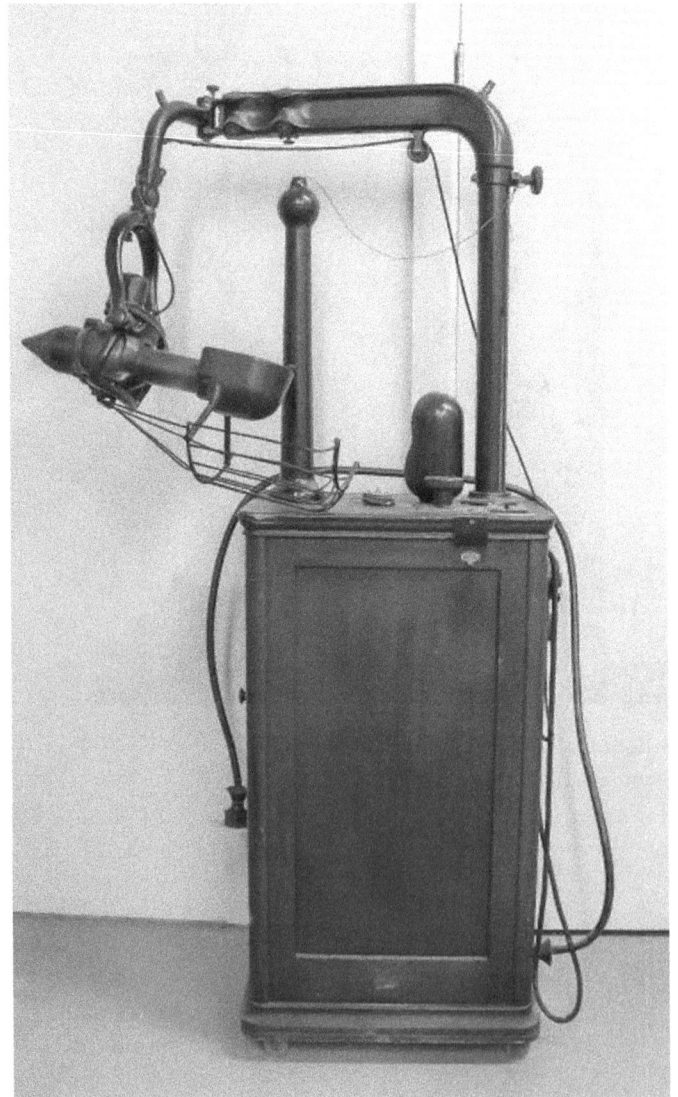

Manufactured by the Ritter Dental Company in 1920, the Model A Dental X-ray was one of the most significant advancements in the history of dentistry. It allowed the dentist to see the bone structure below a patient's gum line. The X-ray machine was stored inside the wooden cabinet and ran at 100/120 volts, 40/140 cycles, 800 watts. Photo and description courtesy of the Edward Hand Medical Museum.

Oregon Dentistry Gets Organized

On March 29, 1873, a group of dentists met in the Portland office of J.H. Hatch to organize a state dental organization that would "permit them to keep pace with and reap the same benefits as their eastern brethren." The first Oregon State Dental Society lasted only six years. A few years later, on June 14, 1893, the Oregon State Dental Association was formed; it survives today as the Oregon Dental Association.[317]

In Oregon, the legislature passed the Oregon Dental Practice Act on February 23, 1887 and created an Oregon State Board of Dental Examiners to enforce it. The act required that a dentist be a graduate of a "reputable" dental college and extended authority to the board to examine applicants' qualifications.[317]

PIONEER DENTISTS OF COOS COUNTY

Dr. Clarence Frederick Chapin (1893–1944)

Clarence F. Chapin was born in Loomis, Nebraska, in 1893 to Julius C. Chapin (1852–1922) and Ellen Amelia Swanson (1864–1938). His father was born in France, and his mother in Sweden. Clarence had nine siblings—and sometime before 1910, the family moved to Payette, Idaho.

In 1913, Clarence enrolled in the Northwest Dental College in Portland, Oregon, and upon graduation, he returned to Payette to begin his practice. But in 1918, Dr. Chapin again moved—to Marshfield, Oregon, where he established a dental office in the Bank of Southwestern Oregon building. By 1924 he had moved his practice to the second floor of the Coos Bay National Bank building, where he practiced for many years.

Dr. Clarence F. Chapin died in Coos County in 1944. He was fifty years old.

His obituary ran on page 1 of *The World* newspaper on August 28, 1944:

… The body of Dr. C. F. Chapin, 51, former Marshfield dentist was recovered today from the North Coos river, about 50 feet above Knight's landing, by Harold Ott, pilot of the river boat Welcome [on its regular run back to Marshfield]. Dr. Chapin had been missing from the Roland C. Beattie ranch on the North Coos.

Chapin was missed about one hour after he had gone to work in the separator house of the Beattie ranch, where he was employed. The separator house is located about 15 feet from the bank of the river and it is believed that he slipped from the river dock at this point …

Dr. Charles William Endicott (1885–1970)

Charles Endicott was born August 10, 1885 on his parents' ranch in Coos County, Oregon, located on the Middle Fork of the Coquille River. His father was Solomon Endicott (1848–1933) and his mother was Delila Crawford (1847–1927). Charles was the last of nine children born to that marriage. The Endicott family line in Coos County dates back to Jacob Endicott, who settled with his large family in the Myrtle Point area in 1866.

Charles attended the University of California at Los Angeles, and graduated with a medical degree in dentistry in 1909 from the North Pacific Dental College in Portland, Oregon. In June 1912, he married Celestia Johanna Walker, then was married a second time in 1923 to Clara Isabel Muren. He practiced his profession in Coquille as well as Coos Bay, until his retirement in 1964.

Charles' older brother, Solomon C. Endicott, was also a dentist—in Eugene, Oregon for twenty-seven years. His son, Stewart C. Endicott (as follows), also became a dentist.

Dr. Charles W. Endicott died in Coos County on May 4, 1970. He was eighty-four.

Charles W. Endicott. Photo copied from the *Coos Bay Times,* July 31, 1928.

Dr. Stewart Crawford Endicott (1916–1994)

Stewart C. Endicott was born on January 7, 1916 in Coquille, Oregon, to Dr. Charles W. Endicott (also a dentist) and Celestia J. Walker. He graduated from Marshfield High School in 1934. He served in the U.S. Army during WWII and was wounded in New Guinea. In 1941, he married Mary Lorraine Callicrate.

Stewart graduated from the University of Oregon Dental School in 1946. He practiced his profession in Lakeview, Oregon, as well as with his father (Charles Endicott) in Coquille, until Stewart's war injuries forced him into retirement.

Dr. Stewart Endicott died at his home in Gold Beach on October 1, 1994 at the age of seventy-eight.[318]

Dr. Thomas Farrar Montgomery (1884–1956)

Thomas F. Montgomery was born in Lake Providence, Carroll County, Louisiana, on April 10, 1884 to Thomas Farrar Montgomery (1845–1903) and Emilie Terrell Ransdell (1848–1944). He spent his youth around Lake Providence, and after graduating from the local high school, enrolled in Emory University in Atlanta, Georgia.

Thomas graduated in 1914 and came to North Bend, Oregon, to practice his profession. In 1928, after having an office in the Odd Fellows building in North Bend, he shared space with Dr. Clarence L. Brown (1893–1957) in an office over the Hub building in Marshfield.

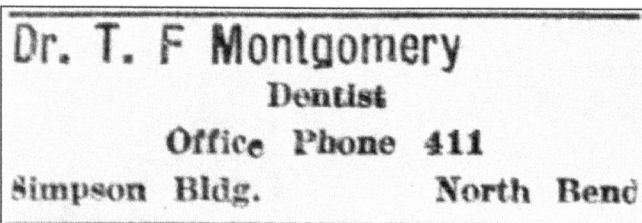

An ad that appeared in the April 16, 1917 *Coos Bay Times,* page 2.

In 1939, Dr. Montgomery was elected president of the North Bend-Coos Bay Rotary Club. He was a past grand knight of the Knights of Columbus, and a member of the American Legion and Elks Lodge. Dr. Montgomery served in WWI, and in July 1942, while serving in the medical reserves, was called up to active duty to work again for the army as a dentist.

Dr. Thomas F. Montgomery died at the Veterans Hospital in Portland, Oregon on May 11, 1956 at the age of seventy-two.

Dr. Augustus Brandegee Prentis (1862–1910)

Augustus B. Prentis was born on February 8, 1862 in New London, Connecticut, to Edward Prentis (1813–1892) and Caroline Lee Mulford (1822–1870). In the 1870 federal census he was listed as living in New London with his father and five siblings. At that time, one of his older brothers, Edward, age nineteen, was listed as a dentist.

In 1880 Augustus Prentis was still living in New London, and at the age of eighteen was also listed as a dentist. He came to Marshfield, Oregon, around 1890 from Crescent City, California, to practice dentistry. He remained in Marshfield for about seventeen years. He moved to Bandon, Oregon, in 1907, but poor health plagued him, and he moved to Stockton, California.

Dr. Augustus B. Prentis died on February 24, 1910 in Portland, Oregon. He was forty-eight years old.

Dr. Oscar Elliot Smith (1846–1909)

Oscar E. Smith was born in Milford, Knox County, Ohio, on November 13, 1846 to Preserve Smith (1800–1871) and Amelia Knowles (1804–1872). He was the youngest of eleven children—some born in Connecticut, but most born in Ohio.

Oscar Smith came to Oregon on the first train that made a through-trip on the transcontinental railroad, in 1869. He settled in Empire City, Coos County, Oregon, about 1870, and set up a dental practice. (It's unclear where and when he went to dental school.)

In 1879, Smith married Sarah Amelia West (1853–?) and the couple had four children, all born in Marshfield, Oregon. Over the years, Oscar acquired several parcels of land in Marshfield, and he became known not only for his dental work, but also for keeping accurate records of the rainfall in town!

Dr. Oscar E. Smith. Photo courtesy of Ancestry.com.

O. E. SMITH,
SURGICAL AND MECHANICAL
DENTIST.

Rooms: Over Kenyon's store, opposite
Whitney's market, Front street,
MARSHFIELD, OREGON.

Dr. Oscar E. Smith provided dental care to the residents of Marshfield for thirty years. Ad from the March 6, 1884 *Coast Mail*.[319]

Below: Dr. William A. Toye's dental office. Photo courtesy of the Coos History Museum.

In 1902, Dr. Smith moved to Eugene, Oregon, and opened a dental office in the Eugene Loan and Savings Bank building. In 1903, he was appointed to a three-year term on the Oregon state board of dental examiners by then Governor George E. Chamberlain.

Oscar E. Smith died of cancer on May 1, 1909 in Eugene, Lane County, Oregon. He was sixty-two years old.

Dr. William Albert Toye (1868–1923)

William A. Toye was born in Amprior, Ontario, Canada, on August 8, 1868 to Thomas Toye (1829–1901) and Catherine O'Meara (1832–1897). In 1879, William immigrated with his parents to Portland, Oregon.

He graduated from the Portland Dental College. After graduation, he stayed in Portland and worked with Dr. Cox, a pioneer dentist there. In 1895, Dr. Toye moved to Marshfield and set up his dental practice in the El Dorado building, where he kept his office for over twenty years. In 1904, Dr. Toye married Olive Rose Pearch, and to that union one child was born.[320]

Dr. Toye was a prominent musician, having been a member of the famous Portland Marine Band before moving to Coos Bay. He was able to share his love of music with others around the bay by joining local bands and orchestras around Marshfield. He was a member of the Knights of Columbus, the Elks Lodge, and the Rotary Club.

Dr. William A. Toye died on August 15, 1923. He was fifty-five years old.

DR. W. A. TOYE

Caricature of Dr. William Albert Toye, as seen in the December 12, 1915 edition of the *Coos Bay Times*, page 6.

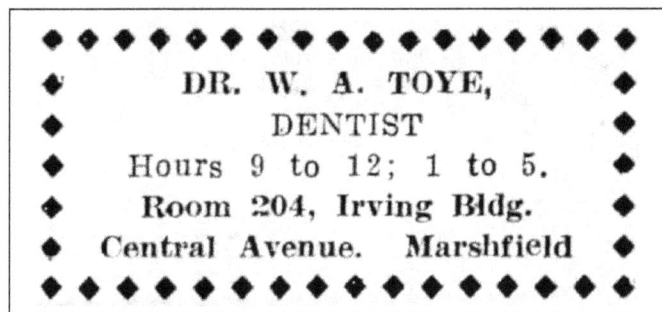

DR. W. A. TOYE,
DENTIST
Hours 9 to 12; 1 to 5.
Room 204, Irving Bldg.
Central Avenue. Marshfield

An ad in the *Coos Bay Times,* November 5, 1915.

> … *In the days when the First Regimental Band was the pride and glory of all Portlanders, Dr. Toye was one of the most prominent figures in the organization—prominent because of his towering bulk, for he stood head and shoulders above his fellow musicians and only the drum major with the big bearskin cap loomed higher …*

Dr. Toye's office was upstairs in this building, ca. 1925. Photo courtesy of the Coos History Museum.

The following editorial was found in the November 9, 1907 edition of the *Washington Post*, I find it apropos to many people's feelings about visiting the dentist today:

A PRIVATE DENTIST

ONE LUXURY THIS MAN WILL HAVE WHEN HE GETS RICH

If ever I get really rich, said the man with a toothache, I shall have a private dentist. What do I want of a private "dentist", well I'll tell you?

It's bad enough anyway to suffer from your teeth, but to me this suffering is made doubly distressing by the circumstances attendant upon my visit to the dentist's office.

I arrive there to fine the dentist working away upon the teeth of some patient in his chair, and that always sort of disturbs me-to find somebody else being worked over and cared for while I wait in distress. I think I am entitled to all the care and sympathy. And maybe I find somebody else waiting, perhaps a friend of the person in the chair, or somebody waiting his turn, come ahead of time, and that disturbs me, for I like to wait with my pain in solitude.

But the dentist gets through with the patient in the chair on time for me, and I take my place under his hands. And I don't doubt that I get his concentrated and complete attention and skill while he is operating upon me, but I can't get away from the idea that he is working as rapidly as he can so as to be ready for the next patient.

And then, with all my pain, I can't forget either that person in the waiting room waiting his turn after me, and waiting without a particle of sympathy for me, and, in face, rather impatient of my presence and thinking of himself alone. This is rather wounding to my self-esteem.

In fact, however I regard it, a visit to the dentist office is always a jarring experience. My dentist is a man of the highest professional skill, and, as I said, I am sure I get his best care, but still all these familiar things that I have mentioned to your jar me, and I would avoid them all if I could. So when I get real rich I shall certainly have a private dentist.[321]

PART V

Early Drug Stores in Coos County

Initially known as "apothecaries," early community pharmacies where druggists prepared and dispensed remedies while also offering front-line medical advice to their customers. Pharmacists often took on the title of doctor, even if they didn't have any formal training or a medical degree. And frequently, as was the case during the western migration across the plains, a doctor might have set up a small hospital and drug store while they established themselves in a rural community.

There were many various drug stores in the Coos Bay area, without a lot of information about each, beyond advertisements for them. So, rather than being able to present a feature on each, for many I've simply included their ad, and what I could find out about the store.

Hudson Drug Store, Coquille, Oregon, ca. 1920s.
Photo courtesy of the Coos History Museum.

Hudson Drug Store ad, *Coquille Valley Sentinel*, April 14, 1922.

Preuss Drug store (aka Red Cross Drug Store) in the Eldorado building Marshfield, Oregon, ca. 1905. The Preuss Drug store was one of the pioneer stores in Marshfield. The store had its real beginning in October 1896, when John Preuss and William Neissl became partners and owners of the Deutche Apotheke. In 1897, Preuss bought out his partner. In 1909, the store was sold to the Preuss Drug Company of which John Preuss, Rosa Preuss and Dr. Franklin C. Birch were officers. When John Preuss died in that same year, Dr. Birch took over managing the operation. In 1913, Birch purchased the interest held by Rosa Preuss. Photo courtesy of the Coos History Museum.

THE

COQUILLE
PHARMACY

COQUILLE CITY, OR.,

Corner Second and Taylor Streets,

Is the Coming Drug Store.

——o——

IF WE HAVEN'T GOT

WHAT YOU WANT,

Will Supply It For You.

——o——

Don't fail to call at the Pharmacy. You will find a full stock of Stationary, Tablets and School Supplies on hand.

Prescriptions Scientifically "Filled."

DR. J. BURT MOORE, Proprietor.

Ad for the Dr. J. Burt Moore pharmacy in Coquille, Oregon, found in the *Coquille City Herald,* March 8, 1897.

New Drug Store,
GEO- A- CHURCHMAN, PROP

GENERAL LINE OF CHEMICALS, DRUGS, PATENT MEDICINES, DRUGGISTS' SUPPLIES TOILET ARTICLES, ETC.

Prescriptions
A Specialty.

Having had many years of experience in this line we are prepared to give all the best of satisfaction.

Golden Building - - - **Coquille, Oregon.**

Ad for the George A. Churchman Drug Store from the *Coquille City Herald*, October 6, 1903.

Knowlton's DRUG STORE
Coquille City, Oregon,

Drugs and Druggists Sundries,
Schoolbooks, Blankbooks. Fine Stationery

A Specialty.

Ad for the R. S. Knowlton's Drug Store in Coquille City from the *Coquille City Herald*, October 27, 1903. Rudolphus S. Knowlton was born on a farm in Tennessee. He was one of nine children. Following the Civil War, Rudolphus began training in drug stores in his home state, as well as in Arkansas. After several years learning the pharmacy trade, he moved to San Francisco. Then in 1888 he moved to Empire, Oregon, where he was a clerk in a drug store. Finally, in 1890, he acquired his own drug store in Coquille—but the fire of 1892 destroyed the store and all of its contents. Rudolphus rebuilt the store and continued to own it until his death in 1925. His son, Owen H. Knowlton, was the manager.

MYRTLE DRUG STORE.
Myrtle Point, Ogn.

W. L. DIXON . . . . Proprietor.

DEALER IN

Drugs, Medicins, Paints, Oils, Candies, Cigars, Tobaco, Fancy Articles, Stationery and the finest quality of School Books. Agent for the leading sewing Machines, Mason & Hamlin organs, &c. Old Wines and Liquors of the best quailty. Prescriptions carefully compounded

LIVE and LET LIVE. v1n3 tf

Ad for the W. L. Dixon Drug Store from the *Coquille City Herald*, October 28, 1884.

160   PIONEER DOCTORS OF COOS COUNTY OREGON

HENRY SENGSTACKEN!

Founder and Proprietor of the Coos Bay Drug-Store,

MARSHFIELD, OREGON,
WHOLESALE AND RETAIL DRUGGIST;

Prescription Pharmacist and Pharmaceutical Chemist.

Scrupulous attention given to compounding prescriptions and family recipes by the most skilled pharmacists. We buy only the best and purest drugs and are careful to see that they are fresh and kept in good condition. Patients never kept waiting as several physicians have their cards at our store. We have in stock all the standard patent medicines; have agencies for all the leading proprietary medicines. If you see a medicine advertised and want it we will gladly get it for you if we do not have it in stock. We have a large and well selected stock of druggist sundries, sponges, chamois skins, trusses, supporters, anklets, shoulder braces, package dyes, dye woods, dye stuffs, etc. etc.

PERFUMERY!

Colognes, Bay rum, Oils, essential extracts for the handkerchief and Florida Water. Our stock comprises all of the popular odors from the most famous manufacturers.

TOILET AND FANCY GOODS.

Fine soaps, Tooth powders, Infant and face powders, Satchel powders, etc. etc. Plush toilet cases, Infants cases, shaving and manicure sets etc.

BRUSHES.

HAIR BRUSHES, CLOTH BRUSHES, TOOTH BRUSHES, BATH AND FLESH BRUSHES, NAIL BRUSHES, CAMELS HAIR PENCILS AND DUST BRUSHES.

Stationery.

Writing paper and envelopes, plain and fancy boxed stationery, writing tablets, mucilage, inks, erasers, paper knives, fine gold pens and holders, gold pencils, bill, note, and memorandum books, blank books in sets, receipt, to-do order journal, ledger to sets, etc. etc., autograph albums, scrap book, pictures books, agency for Lovell Library. Complete stock of that famous library will be found at our place. Mail orders a specialty. School books we carry all. Wholesale orders are receiving special discounts and prompt attention. Prices of colged and plain, standard sets of authors at very reasonable prices. Your orders solicited. Birthday cards, the latest patterns.

CUTLERY.

Fine pocket knives, guaranteed razors, scissors, curtains, etc. etc.

Musical Merchandise.

Agencies for pianos and organs. Keep on hand a full stock of violins, accordions, harmonicas, Jews harps, music boxes, and strings. A full line of sheet music and instruction. Sole agency for Coos and Curry counties of Dr. Organ Electric Vigorosus, a new patent on improved home electric belts. The therapeutical value of electricity when scientifically applied is recognized by all schools of medicine. Best female regulator known as Organ Electric Vigorosus. Orders solicited, filled and forwarded by mail.

GRASS AND GARDEN SEEDS.

The largest and best selected stock at the Coos Bay Drug Store.

JEWELRY.

We are the only wholesale dealer on the bay. Our stock of gold, nickel and plated ware differs no comparison. Gold and diamond rings, lockets, charms, necklaces, tie and hair pin clasps, emblems, watches, silver and gold are only a few articles of our mammoth stock. Everything sold under binding guaranty. If not as represented money refunded.

SMOKERS ARTICLES.

You will find the best equipped stock. Smokers headquarters. CONFECTIONERIES.—Premiums for the choicest are unanimously awarded to the Coos Bay Drug Store.

When at the bay call and see us. Your patronage, irrespective of quantity of purchase, is appreciated. We aim to give our customers the best of goods at the most reasonable prices.

Branch Store of Drugs and General Merchandise at Empire City.

AGENT FOR WELLS, FARGO & CO'S. EXPRESS FOR MARSHFIELD AND EMPIRE CITY.

Ad for the Henry Sengstacken Drug Store in Marshfield and Empire, Oregon, in the *Coquille City Herald*, October 30, 1888.

Henry Sengstacken was born in Hanover, Germany, in 1851 and spent his early years living in Germany, until at the age of 15 when he emigrated to the United States, landing in San Francisco. While in the city, he took business courses at the Heald's Business College and worked at various enterprises. In 1874, he moved to Coos County, Oregon. Over the years, Mr. Sengstacken acquired thousands of acres of land as well property in Marshfield, North Bend, Empire, Coquille and Bandon. He married twice; first to Lillie Lockhart, and after she died in 1892, he married her sister, Agnes Lockhart (in 1894). Henry Sengstacken died in Marshfield in 1922.

In September 1907, the Sengstacken Drug Store and Pharmacy was sold to E. D. McArthur. McArthur was an experienced druggist who came from Idaho.[322]

Ad for the Winkler Pharmacy in Marshfield, Oregon, from the *Coos Bay Times*, May 16, 1913.

Ad for the J. Lee Brown Drug Store in Marshfield, Oregon, from the *Coos Bay Times*, April 5, 1909.

In December 1914, J. Lee Brown purchased the stock held in the L. Platt Pharmacy on Virginia Street in North Bend. The Platt store had been taken over by a creditor's committee for the benefit of the store's creditors.[323]

Ad for the Louis Munroe drug store from the *Coast Mail*, Marshfield, Oregon, October 18, 1879.

Ad for the Henry Sengstacken Pharmacy in Marshfield, from the *Oregon Weekly Coast Mail*, August 1, 1903.

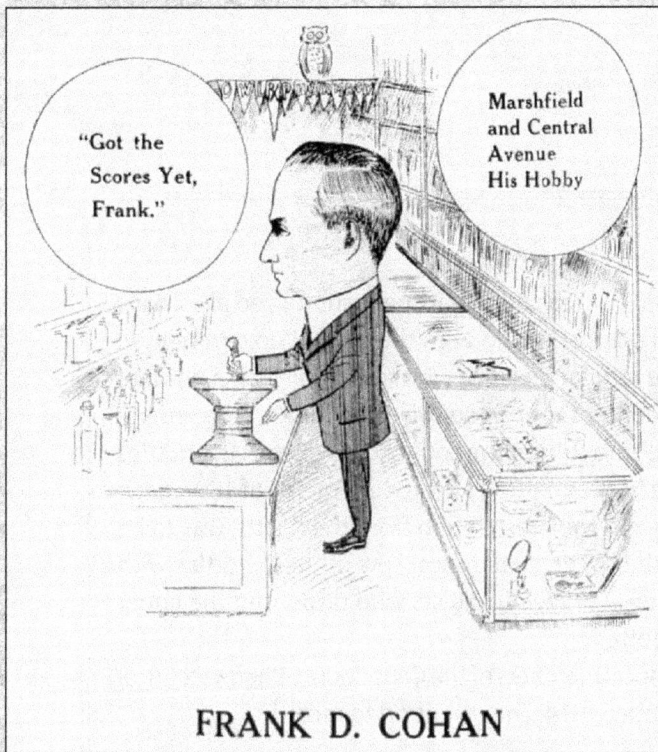

"Got the Scores Yet, Frank."

Marshfield and Central Avenue His Hobby

FRANK D. COHAN

Ad for Owl Pharmacy from the *Coos Bay Times,* December 2, 1912.

Caricature of Frank D. Cohan (dba Owl Pharmacy) in Marshfield, Oregon, in the May 9, 1913 *Coos Bay Times.*

A MESSAGE TO THE PEOPLE

Today—at 7 A. M. the writer took his place as a merchant in Marshfield—in his own store—conducted under his own name—having completed negotiations for the purchase of the McArthur Pharmacy.

The greetings and good wishes of a host of friends are encouraging.

I hope to deserve success.

Success will not come unless I deserve it.

I shall strive very hard to please you.

The store is small, but at present the only available.

But then you know large oaks from little acorns grow.

One of the dominating features of this store will be courtesy.

Courtesy to my patrons.

Courtesy to the public.

Courtesy to everyone.

Much, yes, nearly everything else is of small consequence where there is courtesy—a smile, a respectful attitude to everyone.

This store will be conducted to serve all the people.

My guarantee to buy back anything at the price I sold it for, is only fair dealing—nothing more.

This principle will form the keystone of my future business.

And as to my capital, I may not have as much money as some of my friends, not nearly as much, but I have sufficient for my business—that is enough.

I am not exclusive agent for anything—this is not an exclusive store.

Phone all your wants to 74-J.

When you want prompt service in case of accident or emergency, call 74-J.

If you need medicine of any kind, call 74-J.

If you want a doctor quickly, phone 74-J.

In fact, if you want anything from my store, call 74-J, and it will be quickly delivered.

My object is to serve you promptly.

All 'phones lead to this store—74-J.

If what you want is not in stock I will be earnest in my endeavor to get it. If I have it, you may buy it safely—under my guarantee.

Now I have told my story briefly—A rather plain, matter of fact tale. This is probably the most I will have to say for many a day.

MY HAT IS IN THE RING—NOW FOR RESULTS.

I will sincerely appreciate the opportunity for meeting any service or other test to which you might subject me.

Many thanks for your attention,
        FRANK D. COHAN.

P. S.—To all the friends of my predecessor, Mr. McArthur, I desire to say, I shall strive to merit a continuance of their patronage by earnest and conscientious endeavor to serve faithfully and well as he has. My appeal to prospective patrons is based on my business platform of principles printed above.

Courtesy and Prompt Attention to Your Every Want Always

The above message from Frank Cohan was taken from the *Coos Bay Times,* June 1, 1912. In 1912 Frank D. Cohan purchased the McArthur Pharmacy in Marshfield. Mr. Cohan was a registered pharmacist with several years of experience in the profession. He started his career as a pharmacist in Portland, Oregon, before coming to Marshfield.

PHARMACISTS AND ALCOHOL

As discussed earlier, during Prohibition (1920–1933), the U.S. Treasury Department authorized physicians to write prescriptions for medicinal alcohol. Licensed doctors, along with the special government-issued prescription forms, advised their patients to take regular doses of whiskey to ward off a number of ailments—cancer, indigestion, and depression among others. To supply the whiskey, the federal government gave out licenses to six whiskey distilleries throughout the country. To be legal, the bottles containing 100-proof liquor were stamped to meet the Bottled-in-Bond act requirements of 1897. Each person was allowed one pint of liquor every ten days, and the prescription from the doctor was to be applied to and required to remain on the outside of the bottle at all times. Few of these bottles with the prescriptions attached survived the ravages of time—or few druggists who dispensed the liquor even took the time to glue them on the bottles—or both.

When prohibition laws were being contemplated, the local members of the Coos County Pharmaceutical Association gathered together for a meeting in December 1914. They went on to record:

> … We realize that alcoholic stimulants are not a necessity in modern material medicine, there being many other drugs that are safer and better and which are free from the objectionable properties of intoxicating liquors. We know the great harm the use of intoxicants causes, and the difficulty of judging whether by physician or pharmacist, when in any instance their use would be justifiable. We desire to free ourselves from the necessity of holding a license from the U.S. Internal Revenue Department, thus avoiding the odium of being classed as retail liquor dealers.
>
> In accordance, therefore, with modern advancement, and in order to avoid even the suspicion of catering to the 'booze' business, and desiring to uphold in the highest degree the honor and integrity of our profession, we, the members of the Coos County Pharmaceutical Association, hereby RESOLVE that we will refuse henceforth to sell or offer for sale for any purpose whatsoever, whether on the prescription of a physician or otherwise, any spiritous, vinous, or malt liquors.
>
> Signed:

Brown Drug Co., Marshfield	Lockhart-Parsons Drug Co., Marshfield
Preuss Drug Co., Marshfield	R. S. Knowlton, Coquille
Winkler's Pharmacy, Marshfield	Fuhrman's Pharmacy, Coquille
Owl Prescription Pharmacy, Marshfield	Pacific Drug Co., Myrtle Point
The Everitt Pharmacy, Marshfield	Perkins Pharmacy, Myrtle Point … [324]
Platt's Pharmacy, North Bend	

PART VI

Tonics, Elixirs and Quackery

Unfortuntely, for many early Oregonians, "quack" physicians were their first exposure to medical services. These "quacks" understood the powerful combination of ignorance and desperation exploited the public's wariness of medical treatment, by soliciting testimonials from "patients" who claimed to have benefited from the advertised treatment. Advertisements of cures flooded the newspapers throughout the country. The wondrous cures and improved health and well-being made by self-proclaimed medicine men peddling tonics, elixirs, and snake oil were often no more than mixtures of water, opium, cocaine, or alcohol. Since the therapeutic treatments of most quack physicians were never endorsed by reputable medical journals, "patient" testimonials became the route by which quacks gained their reputations as well as access to markets.[325]

Testimonial about a cure for consumption (tuberculosis) published in the *Coquille City Herald*, February 22, 1887.

One of the most common techniques to advertise these questionable products was to have testimonials by someone who had received a miraculous cure after taking a certain elixir or pill. Since there was no oversight of these claims by the government until Teddy Roosevelt was president, assertions of miraculous cures were commonplace.

Resistance to limiting regulation of these questionable "cures" came from an organization formed in 1881 called the "Proprietary Association" (now known as the Consumer Healthcare Products Association). The trade group was aided by the press, who relied on the organization's advertising revenue.[326]

At a time when doctors and medical clinics were less common, especially in rural areas, patent medicines promised relief from pain and chronic conditions when few other options existed. The term "patent medicine" referred to ingredients that had been granted a government patent—though ironically, many purveyors of patent medicine did not register their concoctions with the government! Some had trademarks on their bottles, while many simply mixed their potions in their huckster wagons as they traveled between towns. As a result, many competitors offered similar formulas, and they all freely imitated each other's products.[327]

Patent medicines were supposedly able to cure just about everything. Nostrums were openly sold that claimed to cure or prevent venereal diseases, tuberculosis, and cancer. Bonnore's Electro Magnetic Bathing Fluid claimed to cure cholera, neuralgia, epilepsy, scarlet fever, necrosis, mercurial eruptions, paralysis, hip diseases, chronic abscesses, and "female complaints." Essentially every manufacturer of patented drugs published long lists of testimonials that described their product as having the ability to cure all sorts of human ailments.

During the June 1913 meeting of the American Medical Association (AMA) in Minneapolis, Minnesota, the board of trustees of the association announced: "The patent medicine business and quackery have become so serious and widespread that a world wide effort is being made to curtail it."[328]

Drug stores throughout Coos County were not immune from advertising these cure-alls in the local newspapers. A few examples follow.

An ad in the *Coast Mail*, November 12, 1885 claiming great restorative powers to the Hall's Vegetable Sicilian Hair Renewer.

Snake oil was advertised as a cure-all for arthritis, bursitis, and other types of inflammation. One such salesman who claimed to have learned medicine from ancient Hopi rituals performed a demonstration of his art at the Chicago World's Fair in Chicago in 1893. He reached into a bag, pulled out a live rattlesnake, cut it open, and squeezed out some fluid. He labeled his product "Snake Oil" and soon thereafter, salesmen began travelling the west with this product. What is especially intriguing about snake oil is the fact that if you boiled a specific Chinese water snake and skimmed off the fatty oil, it indeed had beneficial properties to treat inflammation and was high in omega-3 fatty acids. Clark Stanley's Snake Oil liniment actually contained no snake oil; it was made of mineral oil, beef fat, red pepper, and turpentine!

With strong support from President Theodore Roosevelt, the Pure Food and Drug Act was

SIMPLE MEDICINES [1906]
Remedies that may be Found in Nature's Drug Stores

If chemists and druggists disappeared from the face of the earth humanity could still worry along with the simple remedies which nature yields practically ready-made. There is nothing to beat rhubarb juice as a cure for gout or rheumatism except water from medicinal springs. All kinds of scurvy and blood poisoning yield to the juice of lemons or of limes, which are the greatest blood purifiers in existence. Even doctors acknowledge that natural, fresh cream of cows' milk can give points to cod liver oil and similar nasty liquids in treating consumption. Common mustard used as a plaster or poultice is the best cure for a cold on the chest, and the white of an egg with sugar is the finest medicine for hoarseness. To cure a burn an application of the white skin that lines the shell of an egg is unbeatable, while the raw yolk is a capital conic. In fact, gardens and roadsides are full of herbs of which the juice or leaves afford remedies or palliatives for almost every disease to which humanity is heir.[331]

One common elixir peddled by unscrupulous salesmen and doctors was "Snake Oil." Photo courtesy of Brynn Holland.[329, 330]

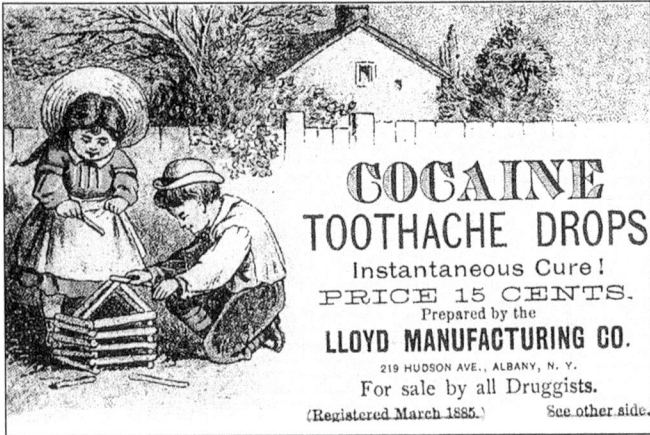

Around the mid-1880s, the active ingredient of the coca leaf was isolated. It was a fast-acting, relatively inexpensive stimulant marketed for the treatment of various ailments such as toothaches, depression, sinusitis, lethargy, alcoholism, etc.—and you didn't need a doctor's prescription to purchase it.[329] Courtesy of the American Medical Association archives.

passed by Congress in 1906 (and went into effect January 1, 1907). It imposed regulations on the labeling of products containing alcohol, morphine, opium, cocaine, heroin, chloroform, Cannabis Indica, chloral hydrate, or acetanilide. It required that products containing any of those substances be labeled with the substance and quantity on the label. Use of the word "cure" for most medicines was nominally prohibited, though there were few teeth in the law, and enforcement was rare. In 1912, the act was amended—it prohibited the labeling of medicines with false therapeutic claims intended to defraud the purchaser. This paved the way for public health action against unlabeled or unsafe ingredients, misleading advertising, the practice of quackery, and similar rackets.[332]

Shopping online is something we in the twenty-first century take for granted as a process that evolved with our generation. While we are mostly protected from unscrupulous medicines by the regulations of the Food and Drug Administration, 100 years ago shopping via the local newspaper was common practice. I have collected a random set of advertisements for various medical remedies that appeared in local papers from the late 1870s to the 1920s.

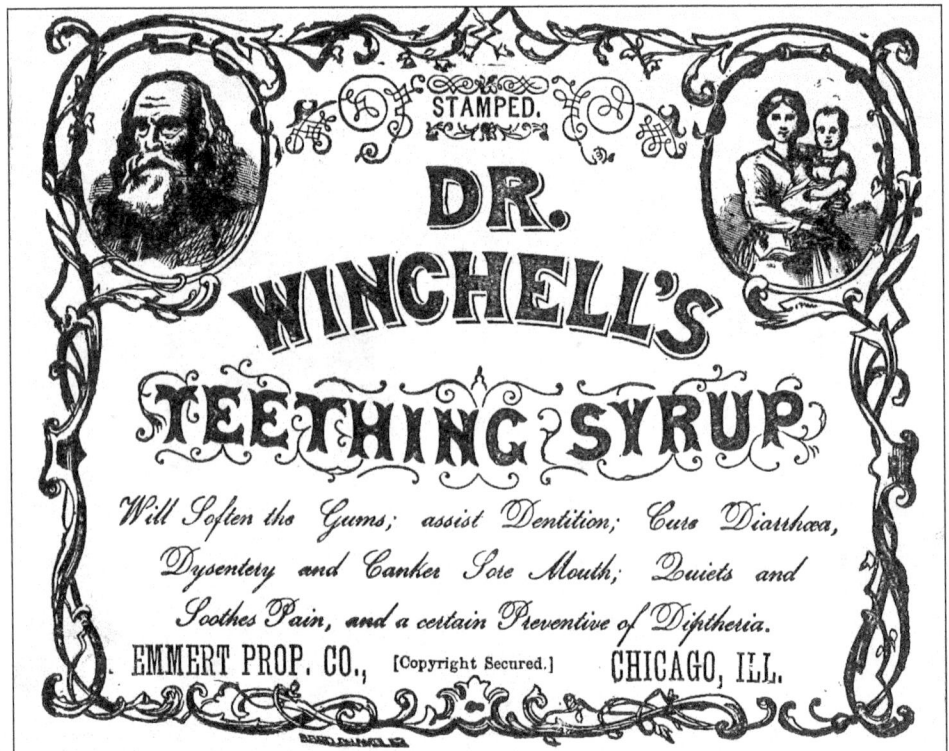

Courtesy of the American Medical Association archives.

An Example of Fraud Being Caught

During a 1912 hearing before the postal service, an expert witness testified as to the content of Toxo-Absorbent-Cancer Cure No. 8: *"A mixture of sand and clay 97.25% and animal charcoal 2.75%."* [333]

In summing up the case in the 1912 hearing on the validity of these advertisements the assistant attorney general said:

> *I am convinced from the evidence that the business of this person in the treatment of patients at their homes for cancer under the representations made, is a scheme to obtain money through the mails by means of false and fraudulent pretenses, representations and promises. I am satisfied that this business in not conducted in good faith, but merely as a scheme to fraudulently extort money without intending to return therefore the services promised and without any belief that patients with cancer can be cured as represented. The analysis of the preparations proves conclusively, I think, the spuriousness of the practice of this advertiser.*
>
> *I find that this is a scheme for obtaining money through the mails by means of false and fraudulent pretenses, representations and promises and I therefore recommend that a fraud order be issued against this concern.* [333]

A fraud order was issued by the postal service to F. W. Warner, of Rochester, New York, the manufacturer of Toxo-Absorbent. Apparently Mr. Warner was neither a physician nor a graduate chemist but claimed to have "discovered" what he called "Toxo-Absorbent packs," which were advertised as a cure for many diseases.

Toxo-Absorbent—Cancer Cure
No. 8.

Price $5.00. Six for $25.00.

This is the most successful cure for Cancers ever discovered. It has the chemical affinity for the poisons and microbes which cause the disease. It dislodges them and draws them out through the pores. Absorbs the growth and builds up the wasted tissues.

It cures **Tumors** by the same process. Cancers and Tumors, whether external or internal, are cured by **Toxo-Absorbents**.

HOSTETTER'S

CELEBRATED

STOMACH BITTERS

The bitters invariably remedy yellowness of the complexion and whites of the eyes, pains in the right side and under the right shoulder-blade, furred tongue, high-colored urine, nausea, vertigo, dyspepsia, constipation, heaviness of the head, mental despondency, and every other manifestation or accompaniment of a disordered condition of the liver. The stomach, bowels and kidneys also experience their regulating and tonic influence.

For sale by all Druggists and Dealers
v2-6-1y   generally.

From the *Coast Mail* on March 6, 1880.

Rich Red

Blood is absolutely essential to health. It is secured easily and naturally by taking Hood's Sarsaparilla, but is impossible to get it from so-called "nerve tonics," and opiate compounds, absurdly advertised as "blood purifiers." They have temporary, sleeping effect, but do not CURE. To have pure

Blood

And good health, take Hood's Sarsaparilla, which has first, last, and all the time, been advertised as just what it is — the best medicine for the blood ever produced. Its success in curing Scrofula, Salt Rheum, Rheumatism, Catarrh, Dyspepsia, Nervous Prostration and That Tired Feeling, have made

Hood's
Sarsaparilla

The One True Blood Purifier. All druggists. $1.

Hood's Pills are purely vegetable, reliable and beneficial. 25c.

From the *Coquille City Herald*, Dec. 22, 1896.

To Regulate

THE FAVORITE HOME REMEDY is warranted not to contain a single particle of Mercury or any injurious substance, but is purely vegetable.

It will Cure all Diseases caused by Derangement of the Liver, Kidneys and Stomach.

If your Liver is out of order, then your whole system is deranged. The blood is impure, the breath offensive; you have headache, feel languid, dispirited and nervous. To prevent a more serious condition, take at once Simmons

LIVER REGULATOR. If you lead a sedentary life, or suffer with Kidney Affections, avoid stimulants and take Simmons Liver Regulator. Sure to relieve.

If you have eaten anything hard of digestion, or feel heavy after meals or sleepless at night, take a dose and you will feel relieved and sleep pleasantly.

If you are a miserable sufferer with Constipation, Dyspepsia and Biliousness, seek relief at once in Simmons Liver Regulator. It does not require continual dosing, and costs but a trifle. It will cure you.

If you wake up in the morning with a bitter, bad taste in your mouth,

TAKE Simmons Liver Regulator. It corrects the Bilious Stomach, sweetens the Breath, and cleanses the Furred Tongue. Children often need some safe Cathartic and Tonic to avert approaching sickness. Simmons Liver Regulator will relieve Colic, Headache, Sick Stomach, Indigestion, Dysentery, and the Complaints incident to Childhood.

At any time you feel your system needs cleansing, toning, regulating without violent purging, or stimulating without intoxicating, take

Simmons Liver Regulator.

PREPARED BY
J. H. ZEILIN & CO., Philadelphia, Pa.
PRICE $1.00.

From the *Coast Mail* November 12, 1885..

DR. WOOD'S LIVER REGULATOR

A VEGETABLE PANACEA

PREPARED FROM
ROOTS & HERBS,
FOR THE CURE OF

- DYSPEPSIA · JAUNDICE ·
- CHILLS & FEVER ·
- DISORDERED DIGESTION ·
- SICK HEADACHE ·
- GENERAL DEBILITY ·

AND ALL OTHER DISEASES
ARISING FROM A
DISORDERED STATE OF THE STOMACH
OR AN
INACTIVE LIVER.

FOR SALE BY ALL
DRUGGISTS & GENERAL DEALERS

From the *Coquille City Herald*, Sept. 19, 1890.

The Aceme Electric Belt leads the van in perfection and price. Remember it is warranted to give full satisfaction. It equalizes the circulation, gives instant relief from pain and nervousness, and Speedily Cures wakefulness, spasms and all nervous diseases, disorders of the liver, kidneys, stomach, bowels; neuralgia, lumbago, incipient paralysis, colic, coldness of hands and feet, backache, spinal weakness, male infirmities, female complaints and general debility.

Single circuit belt, $5; double circuit belt, $8.

J. E. HAGENBUCH,

Agent,

At Blanco Drug Store, Marshfield.
n6 3m

From the *Coquille City Herald*, Dec. 29, 1885.

Delicate women will never become strong, happy, hearty, free from pain, until you build up your system with the nerve refreshing, blood-making tonic, Hollister's Rocky Mountain Tea. Tea or Tablets, 35 cents. John Preuss.

From the *Coos Bay Times*, August 11, 1908

From the *Coquille City Herald*, March 27, 1890.

COSTIVENESS

affects seriously all the digestive and assimilative organs, including the Kidneys. When these organs are so affected, they fail to extract from the blood the uric acid, which, carried through the circulation, causes Rheumatism and Neuralgia.

The functions of the Liver are also affected by costiveness, causing

Bilious Disorders.

Among the warning symptoms of Biliousness are Nausea, Dizziness, Headache, Weakness, Fever, Dimness of Vision, Yellowness of Skin, Pains in the Side, Back and Shoulders, Foul Mouth, Furred Tongue, Irregularity in the action of the Bowels, Vomiting, etc.

The Stomach suffers when the bowels are constipated, and Indigestion or

Dyspepsia,

follows. Fetid Breath, Gastric Pains, Headache, Acidity of the Stomach, Waterbrash, Nervousness, and Depression, are all evidences of the presence of this distressing malady. A Sure Relief for irregularities of the stomach and all consequent diseases, will be found in the use of

AYER'S PILLS.

They stimulate the stomach, free the bowels, healthfully invigorate the torpid liver and kidneys, and by their cleansing, healing and tonic properties, strengthen and purify the whole system, and restore it to a salutary and normal condition.

PREPARED BY

Dr. J. C. Ayer & Co., Lowell, Mass.
Sold by all Druggists.

From the *Coquille City Herald*, March 15, 1886.

The Great **Cure** for Dyspepsia, Indigestion, Bilious Headache, Liver Complaint, Fever and Ague, General Debility, and all complaints of Stomach, Liver & Spleen on the newly discovered principle of

DR. FISHER'S Medicated BELTS.

ABSORPTION.

No Drugs, No Doctor Bills. Send for Circulars, describing the Absorption Cure and the revolution it is causing in the science of medicine.

Dyspepsia Belt, $2.
Fever and Ague Belt, $2.
Tonic Belt, $2, and Infants Belt, $1.

These Belts will be sent to any address free of postage on receipt of $2.00 each, or $1.00 for Infant's Belt.

AGENTS wanted in every county in the United States.

Address, FISHER MEDICATED BELT CO. 232 Illinois St., Chicago.

From the *Coast Mail* October 18, 1879.

NO COLD FEET!

Send one dollar in currency, with size of shoe usually worn, and try a pair of our Magnetic Insoles for rheumatism, cold feet and bad circulation. They are the most powerful made in the world. The wearer feels the warmth, life and revitalization in three minutes after putting them on. Sent by return mail upon receipt of price. Send your address for the "New Departure in Medical Treatment Without Medicine," with thousands of testimonials. Write us full particulars of difficulties.

Our Magnetic Kidney Belts for gentlemen will positively cure the following diseases without medicine: Pain in the back, head or limbs, nervous debility, lumbago, general debility, rheumatism, paralysis, neuralgia, sciatica, diseases of the kidneys, torpid liver, seminal emissions, impotency, heart disease, dyspepsia, indigestion, hernia or rupture, piles, etc. Consultation free. Price of Belt, with Magnetic Insoles, $10. Sent by express C. O. D. or by return mail upon receipt of price. Send measure of waist and size of shoe worn. Send for circulars. Order direct.

NOTE—The above described Belt with Insoles is warranted to positively cure chronic cases of seminal emissions and impotency or money refunded even after one year's trial.

THE MAGNETIC APPLIANCE CO., 134 Dearborn St., Chicago, Ill.

From the *Coquille City Herald* March 15, 1887.

Catarrh Cannot be Cured

With LOCAL APPLICATIONS, as they cannot reach the seat of the disease. Catarrh is a blood or constitutional disease, and in order to cure it you must take internal remedies. Hall's Catarrh Cure is taken internally, and acts directly on the blood and mucus surfaces. Hall's Catarrh Cure is not a quack medicine. It was prescribed by one of the best physicians in this country for years, and is a regular prescription. It is composed of the best tonics known, combined with the best blood purifiers, acting directly on the mucous surfaces. The perfect combination of the two ingredients is what produces such wonderful results in curing Catarrh. Send for testimonials free.

F. J. CHENEY & CO., Props., Toledo, O. Sold by druggists, price 75c.

From the *Coquille City Herald*, February 2, 1897.

From the *Coos Bay Times,* March 12, 1910

An ad for a process that cures just about everything, including cancer.

From the Coquille City Herald, March 27, 1890.

From the Coos Bay Times, March 12, 1910.

EPILOGUE

Much has changed in the medical profession over these past 120 years, not only in our local area, but also across the nation and the world. At one time, doctors traveled by horse or boat to their patients, often miles from town, armed with whatever was in their marginally equipped medicine bags in order to offer treatment. Hospitals were typically simply rooms attached to a physician's clinic. Surgeons often got their training directly from the necessity of conducting on-the-field operations during various wars—without, of course, the opportunity to see inside the patient, as is standard with our modern multitude of non-invasive diagnostic tools. In the old days, the quality of surgery was based upon the speed of the surgeon—as anesthetics were yet in their infancy, and whiskey was looked to as the universal numbing agent. Infections often took the life of the patients, rather than the operations themselves.

Today, patients travel to clinics where multiple medical specialties are assembled to provide an entire range of services. The modern physician has a wide range of diagnostic tests that help with treatment plans, whereas the old family doctor often simply relied on a "best guess" practice from experience.

Early dentists used crude and unsanitary methods to extract a tooth—without anesthesia—while today with our modern anesthetics, the most traumatic part of tooth extraction is the healing process after the numbing agent wears off—and even that's minimized with powerful drugs.

Years ago, payment for services rendered by a physician was often a chicken, a sack of potatoes, a pig, or a cord of firewood, while today the bureaucracy of government oversight, medical insurance paperwork, and the financial burden of educating a doctor has changed the dynamic of how medicine has evolved and is paid for.

Sadly, the equality of medicine is not uniform around the globe. This has become abundantly clear as the world fights the COVID-19 virus. Even with all the modern medical information we've gained from scientific research since humanity's horrific losses from the Spanish flu in 1918, (where more than 500,000 Americans died), the new virus is still wreaking havoc on both a U.S. and world population.

On positive note, modern medicine has extended our average life span in America by a factor of two. In the middle of the nineteenth century, the average man's life was 37 years long; today it's approaching 80 years. Along with the evolution of medical science was a change in where Americans lived. Initial dispersal into rural areas changed to a migration to the cities and suburbs. These changes allowed more people to have access to care, which in turn allowed for the application of modern science to cure ailments—and hopefully extend a person's quality and quantity of life.

Modern clinics and hospitals are really a thing of wonder. Not only do most have fully equipped diagnostic and treatment tools, and a plethora of trained medical professionals, technology also more readily allows the family doctor to keep close tabs on their patients.

But let's not forget the supporting industries that evolved along with medical science. For instance, working in the pharmaceutical industry was often how early physicians got started. They made their own patented drugs—and through their everyday use on patients, doctors learned what worked and what didn't. Several of our local pioneer medics started out distributing homemade drugs, and then evolved into becoming a "doctor"—even though they may not have been university trained or licensed to practice medicine.

Growing up in a rural area of Northern California as I did 60 to 70 years ago, I can still remember the smell of the waiting room in our family doctor's office. When I needed to see him, I remember that as my father would pull our family car to the curb outside the doctor's clinic (attached to his house), I'd check out the garage where he typically parked his Cadillac car. While my mother had probably called ahead for an appointment, there was always the possibility that the doctor may have been pulled away for an emergency. Seeing his car parked in the garage indicated the doctor was in! While I may not have enjoyed that notion then, today, as an adult that's lived a full life, I sincerely appreciate whenever my doctor is "in."

APPENDIX

Physicians and Surgeons: Coos County, Oregon

The following is a list of those doctors who advertised in the local newspapers from 1870–1915, with their brief ad copy, and the dates and paper included for reference. (Bracketed material is where I added content that was incorrect or missing, but seemed important.) I found many of the brief notations included—such as services offered, locations and other small information bits—interesting, and for some, even a bit humorous!

W. C. Angel, M.D.

PHYSICIAN AND SURGEON

Coquille City, Oregon

From the *Coast Mail,* May 31, 1879

B. P. Baumbaugh

PHYSICIAN AND SURGEON

Diseases of Women and Children

Office Rooms 209–10 Coos Building

From the *Coos Bay Times,* April 11, 1908

D. M. Brower, M.D.

PHYSICIAN AND SURGEON

Myrtle Point, Oregon

Calls promptly attended day or night

From the *Coquille City Herald,* July 8, 1890

Dr. A. C. Burroughs

HOMEOPATHIC PHYSICIAN

Chronic diseases a specialty

Residence and office corner of "C" and Second Streets, Marshfield

From the *Coos Bay Times,* July 15, 1908

J. G. Cook, M.D.

PHYSICIAN AND SURGEON

Office in Sengstacken's building, Empire City, Coos County, Oregon

From the *Coast Mail,* August 7, 1890

W. Culin, M.D.

PHYSICIAN AND SURGEON

Office and Residence

Coquille City, Oregon

From the *Coquille City Herald,* July 30, 1895

Dr. George E. Dix

PHYSICIAN AND SURGEON

Office: First National Bank Building

Phone 1681

From the *Coos Bay Times,* February 26, 1908

S. N. A. Downing, M.D.

PHYSICIAN AND SURGEON

Coquille City, Oregon

Calls day or night promptly attended

From the *Coquille City Herald,* March 1, 1887

Dr. H. E. Dunham

HOMEOPATHIC PHYSICIAN AND SURGEON

Office over Lando's store, opposite Blanco Hotel

Marshfield, Oregon

Can be found in office at nights

From the *Coast Mail,* August 7, 1890

J. P. Easter, M.D.

PHYSICIAN, SURGEON AND OBSTETRICIAN

Special attention given to diseases of women and children, and all chronic forms of disease

Cases of Obstetrics $10.

Teeth extracted for 50 cents each.

Special treatment for rheumatism and neuralgia for the medicated vapor bath

Office at residence on Cunningham Creek

From the *Coquille City Herald,* March 1, 1887

M. Evans, M.D.

PHYSICIAN AND SURGEON

Offices in the west end of Holland building

Front Street, Marshfield, Oregon

Inquire at Golden Drug Store

From the *Coast Mail,* August 7, 1890

H. Flentge, M.D.
PHYSICIAN AND SURGEON
Myrtle Point, Oregon
From the *Coquille City Herald,* May 17, 1887

Dr. Arthur Gale
PHYSICIAN AND SURGEON
Office over Orange Pharmacy
Bandon, Oregon
From the *Bandon Recorder,* December 5, 1913

Dr. C. B. Golden, M.D.
PHYSICIAN AND SURGEON
Marshfield, Oregon
From the *Coast Mail,* May 31, 1879

Dr. R. E. Golden
PHYSICIAN AND SURGEON
202-03 Coos Building
Office hours 10 am to 12 noon, 2 to 5 pm, 7 to 8 pm
Office 1051 Residence 165
From the *Coos Bay Times,* November 18, 1908

A. G. Gross, M.D.
PHYSICIAN AND SURGEON
Office, Nasburg Building
Phone 423
Marshfield, Oregon
From the *Coast Mail,* August 30, 1902

J. J. Gussenhoven
PHYSICIAN AND SURGEON
Bandon, Oregon
From the *Coquille City Herald,* July 8, 1890

Dr. W. Hayden M.D.
PHYSICIAN AND SURGEON
Office opposite Union Furniture Store
Hours 10 to 12 and 3 to 5
Special attention paid to disease of skin, urinary, and
digestive organs
U.S. Pension Examiner
Marshfield, Oregon
From the *Coast Mail,* June 11, 1904

R. B. Hoag, M.D.
PHYSICIAN AND SURGEON
Richmond-Barker Building
From the *Coquille City Herald,* July 18, 1912

Wm. Horsfal, M.D.
PHYSICIAN AND SURGEON
Holland Building
Marshfield, Oregon
From the *Coast Mail,* June 11, 1904

Dr. H. L. Houston
PHYSICIAN AND SURGEON
Office in Pacific Hotel.
Hours: 9 to 12 am, 1:30 to 4 pm, and 7 to 8 pm
From the *Bandon Recorder,* May 4, 1905

Dr. A. L. Houseworth
PHYSICIAN AND SURGEON
Office over First National Bank
Residence, two blocks north of Crystal Theater
Office phone 1431 residence 1656
From the *Coos Bay Times,* January 11, 1908

R. C. Hunter, M.D.

PHYSICIAN AND SURGEON

Office-In the Holland Building, opposite the Blanco hotel

Residence, W. G. Webster's late residence

Pine street Near A.

From the *Coast Mail,* May 15, 1884

J. W. Ingram, M.D.

PHYSICIAN AND SURGEON

Office over Sengstacken's Drug Store

Phone: Office 1621; residence 783

From the *Coos Bay Times,* May 10, 1907

J. H. Jessen, M.D.

PHYSICIAN AND SURGEON

Surgery and Diseases of Women a specialty

Office, 307 Coke Building

From the *Coos Bay Times,* January 1, 1915

Dr. A. W. Kime, M.D.

PHYSICIAN AND SURGEON

Bandon, Oregon

Calls to all parts of town and county

Promptly answered day or night

Office on corner of Lower Main and Atwater Streets

From the *Bandon Recorder,* March 28, 1901

L. B. Lawrence, M.D.

PHYSICIAN AND SURGEON

Coquille City, Oregon

From the *Coquille City Herald,* July 8, 1890

Dr. R. V. Leep

PHYSICIAN AND SURGEON

Bandon, Oregon

From the *Bandon Recorder,* December 5, 1913

George W. Leslie

OSTEOPATHIC PHYSICIAN

Graduate of American School of Osteopathy

Kirkville, Missouri

Office hours: 9:00 a.m. to 4 p. m.

Office in Nasburg block

Marshfield, Oregon

From the *Coos Bay Times,* April 11, 1908

G. Earl Low, M.D.

PHYSICIAN AND SURGEON

Office over Farmers & Merchant Bank

Coquille, Oregon

From the *Coquille Herald,* May 15, 1917

Dr. Milla Svance Lund

PHYSICIAN AND SURGEON

Graduate From Woman's Medical

College, Chicago, Illinois

Empire City, Oregon

Residence at I Hacker's

From the *Coast Mail,* December 10, 1885

J. T. McCormac, M.D., C. B. Golden, M.D.

PHYSICIANS AND SURGEONS

Offices at the Marshfield Drug Store, opposite the Central Hotel

Front Street, Marshfield, Oregon

Dr. McCormac is the United States examining surgeon for the district of southern Oregon.

From the *Coast Mail,* May 15, 1884

T. C. MacKay, M.D.

PHYSICIAN AND SURGEON

Empire City, Oregon

From the *Coast Mail,* May 31, 1879

Dr. Smith J. Mann

PHYSICIAN AND SURGEON

Office in Panter Building

Bandon, Oregon

From the *Bandon Recorder,* December 5, 1913

Dr. C. Minnis

PHYSICIAN AND SURGEON

Office in O'Connell's building, Front Street

Marshfield, Oregon

Office hours: 8 to 11 am, 1 to 4 pm, and 6 to 8 pm

From the *Coast Mail,* October 4, 1890

J. Burt Moore, M.D.

SURGEON AND PHYSICIAN

Coquille City, Oregon

From the *Coquille City Herald,* December 3, 1895

M. M. Murphy, M.D.

PHYSICIAN AND SURGEON

Office over Dr. Leneve's Drugstore

Coquille City, Oregon

From the *Coquille City Herald,* March 1, 1887

W. C. Owen, M.D.

PHYSICIAN AND SURGEON

Office over New Drugstore

Coquille City, Oregon

Office hours: 10 am to 12 pm, 2 to 4 pm, 7 to 9 pm

From the *Coquille City Herald,* July 8, 1890

S. L. Perkins

PHYSICIAN AND SURGEON

Bandon, Oregon

Office over Wm. Gallier's Store

Office hours: 6 to 9 am

Call at residence at other hours

From the *Bandon Recorder,* May 4, 1905

Dr. B. M. Richardson

PHYSICIAN AND SURGEON

Diseases of eye, ear, nose, and throat a specialty

Office in Eldorado Block

From the *Coos Bay Times,* May 19, 1907

Dr. Jas. A. Richmond

PHYSICIAN AND SURGEON

Office at Slocum's Drug Store

Coquille, Oregon

From the *Coquille City Herald,* June 5, 1907

S. L. Roberts, M.D.

PHYSICIAN AND SURGEON

Office in Residence

Coquille City, Oregon

From the *Coquille City Herald,* April 22, 1902

Geo. Russell, M.D.

PHYSICIAN AND SURGEON

Office upstairs in Martin Building

Calls promptly answered day or night.

From the *Coquille City Herald,* July 28, 1903

H. M. Shaw, M.D.

PHYSICIAN AND SURGEON

EYE, EAR, NOSE, AND THROAT SPECIALIST

Office: Room 330–J Irving Block

Marshfield, Oregon

From the *Bandon Recorder,* September 11, 1914

J. D. Sponogle, M.D.

PHYSICIAN AND SURGEON

Office in Webster's brick building (upstairs)

Marshfield, Oregon

From the *Coast Mail,* August 7, 1890

Charles C. Taggart, M.D.

PHYSICIAN AND SURGEON
Office 209–210 Coke Building
Marshfield, Oregon
From the *Coos Bay Times*, September 23, 1911

C. W. Tower, M.D.

PHYSICIAN AND SURGEON
Office in the Holland Building opposite the Blanco
Hotel
Front Street, Marshfield, Oregon.
From the *Coast Mail*, May 31, 1879

J. M. Volkmar, M.D.

PHYSICIAN AND SURGEON
Bandon, Oregon
From the *Coquille City Herald*, March 1, 1887

F. M. White, M.D.

PHYSICIAN AND SURGEON
EYE, EAR, NOSE, AND THROAT SPECIALIST
Flanagan and Bennett Bank Bldg.
Eyes tested – Glasses Fitted
Office hours: 10–12, 2–3, 7–8
From the *Coos Bay Times*, June 26, 1918

Dentists: Coos County, Oregon

The following is a list of those dentists who advertised in the local newspapers from 1880–1920. Their ad content, as well as the name and date of the paper where the ad ran, is included.

Dr. C. R. Bennett

DENTIST

217–218 Coos Building

Marshfield, Oregon

From the *Coos Bay Times*, October 2, 1909

Dr. F. G. Bunch

DENTIST

Farmers and Merchant Bank Building

Coquille, Oregon

From the *Coquille Valley Sentinel,* July 2, 1920

Dr. Henry Ernest Burmester

DENTIST

North Bend, Oregon

From the *Coos Bay Times*, December 7, 1916

Dr. G. H. Carter

DENTIST

Coquille City, Oregon

Office in Gray Building, opposite the Depot.

Nothing but first-class work; charges reasonable

From the *Coquille City Herald*, November 3, 1896

Dr. C. F. Chapin

DENTIST

Second Floor Bank of Southwestern Oregon Bldg.

From the *Coos Bay Times,* March 21, 1919

Dr. S. C. Endicott

DENTIST

Bandon, Oregon

From the *Bandon Recorder,* December 1, 1913

Dr. A. J. Hendry

DENTIST

Modern Dental Parlors

We are equipped to do high class work on short notice
at the very lowest prices.

Examination free. Lady attendant.

Coke Building, Opposite Chandler Hotel

From the *Coos Bay Times*, January 3, 1913

J. Z. Holcomb

SURGICAL AND MECHANICAL DENTIST

Offices above Sengstacken's Drug Store in the Holland
Building

Front street, Marshfield, Oregon

From the *Coast Mail*, May 15, 1884

Dr. T. J. Holden

DENTIST

Office in Olive Hotel, Coquille City

Practices Dentistry in all its branches

Fine, solid, reliable, operations guaranteed.

Families visited at their residences if desired.

From the *Coquille City Herald*, October 28, 1890

Dr. A. F. Kirshman

DENTIST

Office two doors south of post office

Coquille, Oregon

From the *Coquille Herald*, June 5, 1907

Dr. R. W. Morrow

DENTIST

171 Grimes Building over Grand Theater

From the *Coos Bay Times*, November 15, 1912

Dr. F. H. Nickerson

DENTIST

Office in Holland building in rooms formerly occupied
by Dr. D. L. Steele
Marshfield, Oregon
From the *Coast Mail*, August 7, 1890

Dr. W. J. Phillips

DENTIST

First National Bank Bldg.
North Bend, Oregon
From the *Coos Bay Times*, June 26, 1918

Dr. A. B. Prentis

DENTIST

Holland Block
Marshfield, Oregon
From the *Daily Coast Mail*, January 7, 1904

Dr. C. A. Rietman

DENTIST

First National Bank Building
Coquille, Oregon
From the *Coquille Valley Sentinel* June 3, 1921

Dr. Fred Sasman

DENTIST

204 Coke Bldg.
From the *Coos Bay Times* June 26, 1918

Dr. Bert E. Schoonmaker

DENTIST

Crown, Bridge and Gold Work a Specialty
All work guaranteed
Douglas Building, Marshfield, Oregon
From the *Coos Bay Times* September 11, 1906

Dr. I. L. Scofield

DENTIST

Office in Fahy and Morrison Building
Next to Emergency Hospital
From the *Bandon Recorder* June 23, 1914

Dr Fred Seaman

DENTIST

204 Coke Building, Marshfield, Oregon
From the *Coos Bay Times* October 19, 1916

O. E. Smith

SURGICAL AND MECHANICAL DENTIST

Rooms: Over Kenyon's store, opposite
Whitney's market, Front street, Marshfield, Oregon.
From the *Coast Mail* May 15, 1884

E. A. Smith

DENTIST

401 Hall Building
Marshfield, Oregon
From the *Coos Bay Times* May 9, 1928

J. Curtis Snook, D.D.S.

DENTIST

Office over Johnson, Dean and Co's
Market, Coquille, Oregon
From the *Coquille City Herald* August 19, 1902

Dr. L. P. Sorenson

DENTIST

Office over Vienna Café
Bandon, Oregon
From the *Bandon Recorder* December 5, 1913

Dr. D. L. Steele, M.D.

DENTIST

Marshfield, Oregon

Office Holland building, opposite Blanco Hotel.

Laughing gas and other anesthetics administered for
the painless extraction of teeth

From the *Coquille City Herald* March 1, 1887

Daniel L. Steele, Dentist, is in town and can be found
for the coming two weeks at the Central Hotel-Werden
Bros. Proprietors. His room is over the dining hall,
where after having your teeth extracted with the greatest pains, you can go downstairs and get a good square
meal. (*Coast Mail*, April 3, 1880.)

[Dr. Steele was an early pioneer Dentist in Coos
County. He was born in Ontario, Canada, and came to
Coquille in 1878, where he practiced for 30 years until
his death in January 1908.]

R. H. Walter, D.D.S.

DENTAL SURGEON AND MECHANICAL DENTIST

Office Nasburg Bldg. A. St., Phone 26

Marshfield, Oregon

From the *Coast Mail* August 30, 1902

SOURCES

1. Mann S. S. Nearly Thirty Years Old. *The Coos Bay Times (successor to the Coast Mail)*. February 24, 1907, 1879: 2.

2. First Officials. *The Coos Bay Times*. August 24, 1916: 32.

3. Larsell O. *The Doctor in Oregon*. Portland, Oregon: Oregon Historical Society; 1947.

4. Stories of Frontier Settlement Doctors. OHSU. https://www.ohsu.edu/historical-collections-archives/stories-frontier-settlement-doctors. Published 2019.

5. Doctor's Life Span. *The Coos Bay Times*. March 5, 1909: 2.

6. Editors History.com. Ether and Chloroform. URL https://www.history.com/topics/inventions/ether-and-chloroform. Published 2010.

7. Larsell Olaf. *The Doctor in Oregon: A Medical History*. Portland, Oregon: Binfords and Mort for the Oregon Historical Society; 1947.

8. Among the First Settlers A. H. Thrift tells of Old-time Events in Coos. *Coquille Herald*. November 18, 1913: 1.

9. Peterson Emil R. and Alfred Powers. *A century of Coos and Curry History of Southwest Oregon*. Coquille, Oregon: Coos-Curry Pioneer and Historical Association; 1977.

10. Dr. Cook, of Empire, Dead. *Coquille Herald*. November 15, 1904: 3.

11. Cameron Frank. Heal the Sick the development of European medical care and healing and its introduction to the Northwest coast and the Columbia river basin 1760-1865. http://www.oregonpioneers.com/Heal_the_Sick_by_FrankCameron.pdf. Published 2018.

12. *Roseburg review*. July 29, 1887: 3.

13. A Persistent Vision. https://www.ohsu.edu/historical-collections-archives/persistent-vision. Published 2020.

14. Larson Olaf, PhD. Medical Education in the Pacific Northwest. In. Vol 28 No. 4: Bulletin of the Medical Library Association 1940:173.

15. Holman Charles N. , M.D. University of Oregon Medical School a history of the years 1904-1909. In. Oregon Health Sciences University1977:27.

16. University of Oregon Medical School Faculty minutes, 01903-1969. Archives West. http://archiveswest.orbiscascade.org/ark. Published 2012.

17. Hunter Alan J., M.D. The Portraits...and a little More...A History of the Department of Medicine: A Sampler. Department of Medicine Grand Rounds. https://www.ohsu.edu/sites/default/files/2019-04/dom-history-grand-rounds-pdf.pdf. Published 2001..

18. Willamette University Medical Courses. *Evening capital journal*. July 2, 1890: 4.

19. Willamette University medical department. *The Dalles weekly chronicle*. September 25, 1895: 2.

20. McCormack Joseph N., M.D. Oregon Practically an Unorganized State. American Medical Association. 1905;42 No. 15-26:1818-1819.

21. How did Oregon Pass Medical Licensing Laws? https://dailyhistory.org/How_did_Oregon_pass_Medical_Licensing_Laws%3F. Published 2019.

22. How did Oregon pass Medical Licensing Laws. https://dailyhistory.org/How_did_Oregon_pass_Medical_Licensing_Laws. Published 2020.

23. Board History. https://www.oregon.gov/omb/board/about/Pages/Board-History.aspx. Published 2019.

24. A Handbook for Oregon Medical Board Licensees. https://www.oregon.gov/omb/licensing/Documents/licensee-handbook.pdf. Published 2019.

25. Wikipedia. Rene'Laennec. https://en.wikipedia.org/wiki/Ren%C3%A9_Laennec. Published 2019.

26. Nelson Chris. A Little Defibrillator History and Its Potential Future. http://www.aed.com/blog/a-little-defibrillator-history-and-its-potential-future/. Published 2013.

27. Klein Roger L., M.D. and Angela Kendrick, M.D. The History of Anesthesia in Oregon. Portland, Oregon: The Oregon Trail Publishing Company; 2004.

28. Diphtheria Epidemic. *The World*. November 27, 1968: 10.

29. Diphtheria. *The Coos Bay News*. July 28, 1880.

30. Gaston Joseph. *The Centennial History of Oregon*. Vol 4: S. J. Clark Publishing Co.; 1912.

31. Ira Bartle. http://genealogytrails.com/ore/coos/biography/bios.html. Published 2019..

32. Eugene Man Is Promoted. *Oregonian*. June 18, 1918: 18.

33. Human Ostrich At North Bend - Large Amount of Junk Removed From ------ at Mercy Hospital. *The Coos Bay Times*. July 1, 1908: 1.

34. Colon Bacilli in City Water. *The Coos Bay Times*. April 25, 1911: 1.

35. Buehner Company Plant at Allegany Declared Quite Sanitary. *Oregonian*. October 31, 1916: 7.

36. To Leave but Two. *Coquille Herald*. August 28, 1917: 3.

37. How long can germs live. In. Vol 73 No 2: H. H. Windsor, Jr.; 1940:238.

38. *The Coos Bay Times*. February 11, 1937: 4.

39. Bacteria Retain Life in Ice Cube. *The Bakersfield Californian*. January 18, 1938: 2.

40. Dr. Franklin C. Birch. *The Coos Bay Times*. July 31, 1928: 50.

41. Dr. Franklin C. Birch. *The Coos Bay Times*. December 31, 1929: 99.

42. Dr. Franklin C. Birch. *The Coos Bay Times*. December 30, 1937: 56.

43. Announcing. *The Coos Bay Times*. July 23, 1938: 6.

44. Albany Doctor Tells Rotarians The Peace Angle. *Corvallis Gazette-Times*. August 1, 1929: 1.

45. Road Project Is Discussed. *The Coos Bay Times*. February 16, 1932: 2.

46. Dr. Crowell New C. of C. Leader. *The Coos Bay Times*. January 5, 1933: 1.

47. North Bend Men Buy Plane for use in School. *The Coos Bay Times*. October 23, 1935: 3.

48. Empire Mill Will Reopen November 1. *The Coos Bay times*. October 16, 1940: 1.

49. Lansing William. *The Mills That Built Coos Bay and the Men Who Made It Happen*. Vol 1. Coos Bay, Oregon: Self; 2020.

50. Dr. Crowell Is Deferred: Stays at Bay Office. *The Coos Bay Times*. January 26, 1943: 2.

51. Dr. Crowell To Enter Navy. *The Coos Bay Times*. May 14, 1945: 1.

52. Dr. Crowell Home on Navy Leave. *The Coos Bay Times*. April 4, 1946: 5.

53. Doc's Order: Lots of Air, Up in The Air. *Daily Independent Journal*. May 1, 1954: 4.

54. *Portrait and Biological Record of Western Oregon*. Vol https://books.google.com4.

55. Walter Culin. http://genealogytrails.com. Published 2019.

56. *Portrait and Biographical Record of Western Oregon Containing Original Sketches of Many Well Known Citizens of the Past and Present*. Chicago, Illinois: Chapman Publishing Company; 1904.

57. *Portrait and Biographical Record of Western Oregon*. Chicago, Illinois: Chapman Publishing Company; 1904.

58. Simmons George H. The Journal of the American Medical Association. In. Chicago, Illinois: American Medical Association; 1912:1078.

59. Mingus Everett. The Journal of American Medical Association. In. Vol XLIV. Chicago, Illinois: American Medical Association; 1905:5547.

60. Dodge Orvil. *Pioneer History of Coos and Curry Counties, Or*. Salem, Oregon: Capital Printing Company; 1898.

61. Dr. Culin. *Semi-weekly herald*. February 17, 1905.

62. Culin Walter, M.D. A Motor Pioneer. In. Vol 581912:1078.

63. *Medical Sentinel*. 1907;XV No. 6:146 and 249.

64. Smallpox Is Getting Worse. *The Coos Bay Times*. May 6, 1914: 2.

65. Will Fill Spring to Stop Typhoid. *The Coos Bay Times*. March 4, 1915: 4.

66. May Post Guards. *The Coos Bay Times*. October 7, 1915: 3.

67. Has Fine Cherries. *The Coos Bay Times*. March 5, 1915: 5.

68. Dodge Edward N. *Encyclopedia of American Biography*. Vol XXXII. New York West Palm Beach: The American Historical Company, Inc; 1963.

69. Plan to Protect Wild Game Here. *The Coos Bay times*. December 1, 1914: 5.

70. Lou Blanc Building Sold To Doctor Dix. *The World*. January 28, 1959: 1.

71. Evans Kenneth R. Producing and Processing Safe Milk at Brookmead Dairy Found to Have Many Individual Factors. *The Coos Bay Times*. December 27, 1938: 3-5.

72. Saw Mills and Logging Camps of Coos Bay anda Coquille River Section. In. XII ed. Portland, Oregon: Cornwall, George M.; 1911:45.

73. A History Tioga Hotel Once Sold By Coos County for $500. *The World*. May 26, 1959: 2.

74. In:1911.

75. Lansing William A. *Can't you Hear the Whistle Blowin'.* 0-9767649-1-1: 117-127; 2007.

76. In:1922:420.

77. Dr. George E. Dix. *The Coos Bay Times.* March 23, 1912: 43.

78. McLain Lucile. Exploits of Pioneer Doctors Recalled; Coos Bay Enjoys Rare Medical Protection. *The Coos Bay Times.* October 22, 1943: 1 & 6.

79. Millhands Arrange for Medical Aid. *The Coos Bay times.* November 5, 1907: 1.

80. Dr. Robert J. Dixon. *The Coos Bay Times.* July 31, 1928: 72.

81. Dr. Dixon Dies in Coos Bay. *The Coos Bay Times.* May 2, 1963: 1.

82. Committee For Hospital Named. *The Coos Bay Times.* Marsh 29, 1924: 1.

83. Doctors to Enter Spitting Meet. *The Coos Bay Times.* July 31, 1941: 1 and 8.

84. Dr. Easter Gives His Life History. *The Coos Bay Times.* July 16, 1927: 4.

85. Dr. J. P. Easter Funeral Is Held. *The Coos Bay Times.* July 21, 1932: 6.

86. Aged Couple Wed on Unlucky Date. *The Coos Bay Times.* November 16, 1925: 2.

87. Walling A. G. . *History of Southern Oregon comprising Jackson, Josephine, Douglas, Curry and Coos Counties.* Portland, Oregon: House of A. G. Walling; 1884.

88. Elgin Arrives. *The Coos Bay times.* May 24, 1939: 20.

89. *The World.* November 27, 1968: 10.

90. Schroeder Elton. Letter to Elton Schroeder from George D. Elgin April 28, 1888. In:1959.

91. Dr. Geo. Elgin of Sixes Succumbs in Missouri. *The Port Orford Tribune.* June 12, 1916.

92. French Head Unit Staff. *The World.* December 16, 1957: 10.

93. Dr. Alfred J. French. *The World.* February 22, 2001: 3.

94. Rescue Efforts Fruitless After Wave Pounds USS Gilligan. *The Coos Bay Times.* September 25, 1950: 1.

95. Loving care and empathy. *The World.* July 9, 1985: 4.

96. Gaston Joseph and George H. Himes. *The Centennial History of Oregon 1811-1912.* Vol III. Chicago, Illinois: The S. J. Clarke Publishing Company; 1912.

97. Dr. Arthur Gale Called By Death. *The Coos Bay Times.* December 1, 1936: 1.

98. Dr. Arthur Gale Obituary. *The Western World.* December 31, 1936.

99. Takes Over Practice of Late Dr. Gale. *The Coos Bay Times.* January 9, 1937: 2.

100. History National Museum of American. National Prohibition Act Prescription Form for Medicinal Liquor. https://americanhistory.si.edu. Published 2019.

101. Family of Doctors. *The Coos Bay Times.* March 15, 1920: 3.

102. Cullings of Coquille. *The Coos Bay Times.* August 29, 1914: 11.

103. Aids in Work. *The Coos Bay Times.* September 12, 1914: 7.

104. Dr. Hamilton to Go to the Dalles. *The Coos Bay Times.* December 4, 1922: 2.

105. Powered Scooter Gets 120 Miles Per Gallon. *The Coos Bay Times.* December 17, 1936: 2.

106. Alka-Algae. In. Vol 450-No. 11935.

107. Two Coquille Physicians to Build $50,000 Hospital

Coos Bay times. September 1, 1936: 6.

108. Bank Building Is Leased; Purchase Option Is Given. *The Coos Bay Times.* September 1, 1937: 6.

109. Dr. Walton Haydon, 78, Long-Time Resident of Coos Bay, Succumbs. *The Coos Bay Times.* December 16, 1932: 1.

110. Appendix to the Eighteenth Volume of the Journals of the House of Commons Dominion of Canada. In. Ottawa, Canada: Maclean, Roger & Co.; 1884:58.

111. A Funny Little Pain. *The Eugene Guard.* December 20, 1932: 4.

112. Noted Coos Bay Physician and Man of Science Dead. *Oregonian.* December 18, 1932: 18.

113. T. H. Hermann. *The Coos Bay Times.* August 28, 1922: 6.

114. J. F. Schroeder one of Few Left. *The Coos Bay Times.* August 28, 1922: 6.

115. Hermannsville. *The World.* September 21, 1974: 41.

116. Project The Oregon History. The Baltimore Colony. Oregon History Society. https://oregonhistoryproject.org. Published 2018.

117. Dr. Henry Hermann house. *The Coos Bay Times.* December 16, 1924: 34.

118. Family reunion Held Sunday Descendants of Doctor and Mrs Henry Hermann Gather at Camas Valley. *The News-Review.* September 4, 1923: 1.

119. Dr. Henry Hermann. *The World.* April 23, 1977: 91.

120. Simpson Breaks Record. *The Coquille Herald.* July 25, 1916: 1.

121. Binger Hermann Will is Admitted. *The Eugene Guard.* April 22, 1926: 2.

122. Early Valley and Curry County Doctors. *The World.* November 27, 1968: 10.

123. Hodson. *Weekly Coastal Mail.* August 22, 1903: 8.

124. Peterson Emil R. Doctors Last Long In Coos Bay Area. *Oregonian.* November 7, 1948: 77.

125. Aged Couple Keep Golden Wedding. *The Bandon Recorder.* October 12, 1915.

126. Dr. William Horsfall. Find a Grave. https://www.findagrave.com. Published 2011.

127. Old Days Recalled as Kentuck School Closes Doors; Early Teachers, Pupils Meet for Reunion. *The Coos Bay Times.* June 3, 1949: 1.

128. Dr. William Horsfall. *The Coos Bay Times.* March 23, 1912: 43.

129. Death of a Pioneer. *Coos County record.* January 22, 1876: 3.

130. The Horsfall Hospital. *Bandon Recorder.* July 6,, 1905: 1.

131. Exploits of Pioneer Doctors Recalled; Coos Bay Enjoys rare Medical Protection. *The Coos Bay Times.* October 22, 1943: 1 & 6.

132. In the Night. *The Coos Bay Times.* June 30, 1951: 5.

133. Doctor Swims Bay In Race With Stork During The Course of Career That Spanned Era From Shanks Mare To Auto. *The World.* January 18, 1963: 7.

134. George Horsfall Breaks Crater Lake Swim Marks. *The Coos Bay Times.* July 27, 1928: 1.

135. Moving the Horsfall residence. *The Coos Bay Times.* May 2, 1947: 12.

136. Horsfall Named No. 1 Citizen for Bay Area. *The Coos Bay Times.* December 16, 1939: 1 & 2.

137. Letter about Dr. Horsfall. *The World.* January 20, 1958: 4.

138. Open Forum-Coos Bay Doffs its hat to Dr. Horsfall. *The Coos Bay Times.* December 20, 1939: 4.

139. Dr. Horsfall Honored by Eagles At Big Party for Long Service. *The Coos Bay Times.* March 27, 1947: 1.

140. Medical Society of Oregon To Honor Dr. Geo. E. Houck, State's Oldest Physician. *The News-Review.* October 1, 1952: 1.

141. Coos 'Grand Old Doctor' Dies in Sleep at Age 91. *Oregonian.* January 18, 1958: 9.

142. Twin Brother Here on Visit. *The Coos Bay Times.* August 12, 1910: 4.

143. Dr. A. L. Houseworth. *The Coos Bay Times.* March 23, 1912: 43.

144. Undergoes Operation. *The Coos Bay Times.* December 1, 1908: 3.

145. Coos County Gold. *The Coos Bay Times.* April 17, 1914: 5.

146. Coos and Curry Medics Praised. *The Coos Bay Times.* November 30, 1921: 3.

147. Lebanon Hospital Corps to get New Officer. *Albany Evening Herald.* August 4, 1921: 2.

148. Harper Franklin. *Who's Who on the Pacific Coast A Biographical Compilation of notable Living Contemporaries West of the Rocky Mountains.* Los Angeles, California: Harper Publishing Company; 1913.

149. Prescription Caused Grief. *The Coos Bay Times.* September 29, 1914: 2.

150. Will Move to Bay. *The Coos Bay Times.* November 27, 1915: 8.

151. McGee Jerry. Keizer, Oregon. https://www.keizer.org. Published 2020.

152. Oral History Project Thomas Dove Keizeer. In:2015.

153. M.D. Philip John Keizer. In: Lansing B, ed2020.

154. North to Alaska. North Bend, Coos, Oregon, USA. Published 2019.

155. Dr. Phil Keizer Dies in Portland After Operation. *The Coos Bay Times.* October 15, 1929.

156. Captain Keizer Killed. *The Sunday Oregonian.* September 8, 1918: 16.

157. Northwest Medicine. *Northwest Medicine.* 1918;XVII:303.

158. Walk 34 Miles Through Storm. *The Coos Bay times.* January 8, 1923: 1.

159. Community Honors Mrs. Betty Keizer for 50-years Nursing Career in North Bend. *The World.* October 28, 1969: 14.

160. Keizer Hospital. *The Coos Bay Times.* July 31, 1928: 57.

161. Brooks Howard C. Quicksilver in Oregon. In. Vol Bulletin No. 551963.

162. Dr. Ennis Keizer. *The World.* December 30, 1998: 5.

163. Lifetime of Service Recognized. *The World.* July 13, 1988: 9.

164. Dr. John Phil Keizer. *The World.* June 14, 2008: 5.

165. Article Mentions Dr. John Keizer. *The Coos Bay Times.* April 13, 1954: 3.

166. Russell J. Keizer. *The World.* July 13, 2019: S7.

167. Keizer 50th. *The World.* August 23, 2008: 21.

168. Bear Attacked Dr. Leep. *The Coos Bay Times.* September 6, 1924: 8.

169. Bandon Man is Victim of Gun Shot Wound on Reef. *The Coos Bay Times.* July 1, 1929: 1.

170. Miscellaneous. *The Oregon Daily Journal.* February 16, 1921: 7.

171. Funeral of Mrs. Leneve Will be Held Sunday. *The Coos Bay Times.* July 31, 1920: 5.

172. An Old Soldier's Recommendation. *Coquille City Herald.* January 28, 1896.

173. *Coquille City Herald.* July 14, 1896.

174. Sore Throat. *Coquille City herald.* November 26, 1895: 3.

175. Dr. George Leslie, Marshfield Demo, Postmaster, Dies. *The Coos Bay Times.* December 23, 1936: 1.

176. Dr. G. W. Leslie in New Offices. *The Coos Bay Times.* November 6, 1924: 8.

177. Definition of Osteopathy by Dr. George W. Leslie. *The Coos Bay Times.* July 4, 1906: 3.

178. Dr. Donald Long John Peacock, Simpkin Offices. *The Coos Bay Times.* May 4, 1936: 3.

179. Dr. Donald M. Long. *The Coos Bay Times.* May 17, 1994: 5.

180. Coosonians are Organized. *Coquille Herald.* September 16, 1916: 1.

181. De. Low Sells Coos Maple on Trip East. *The Coos Bay times.* September 15, 1926: 3.

182. Dr. Earl Low Visits Site of Muskrat Farm. *The Coos Bay Times.* July 23, 1927: 6.

183. Escape In Air Crash 'Mystery". *The Coos Bay Times.* May 21, 1929: 1.

184. Dr. Low to Enter Business in Mexico. *The Coos Bay Times.* September 3, 1930: 5.

185. A patriotic Young Hardware Man. In:1917:87.

186. Shindler Bo. Dr. Lucas. In:2019.

187. Webb Wendell. Mussels To Be Eyed As Death Cause. *The Coos Bay Times.* September 30, 1933: 1 & 2.

188. Ellsworth Lucas. *The World.* June 16, 1970: 2.

189. Reuben, H. Mast. http://genealogytrails.com. Published 2019.

190. *The Coos Bay Times.* July 26, 1926: 1.

191. Tonsil Clinic at Powers. *The Coos Bay Times.* November 1, 1932: 2.

192. Dr. J. T. McCormac. *The Coos Bay times.* March 23, 1912: 43.

193. Marshfield's Handsome New High School Formally Opened to Public Last Evening. *The Coos Bay, Times.* February 27, 1909: 1 & 6.

194. Dr. J. T. McCormac Died Early Today At Berkeley, Cal. *The Coos Bay, Times.* July 25, 1925: 1.

195. Consolidate Cities. *The Coos Bay Times.* April 4, 1908: 1.

196. Asks Place on Ticket. *Oregonian.* July 30, 1909: 6.

197. Bennett Addison. Marshfield Appreciates Citizens Who Do things. *The Oregon Daily Journal.* March 19, 1909: 10.

198. Cedar Point Boom Site Changes Hands. *Coquille City Herald.* January 14, 1902: 1.

199. Marshfield's Handsome New High School Formally Opened to Public Last Evening. *Coos Bay Times.* February 27, 1909: 1.

200. Myrtle Mill Wanted. *Oregonian.* July 2, 1916: 1.

201. Bennett Addison. Tells of Voyage up the Coos River. *The Oregon Daily Journal.* March 22, 1909: 6.

202. Dr. J. T. McCormac Dies. *Oregonian.* July 26, 1925: 38.

203. Honors McKeown. *The World.* March 11, 1991: 2.

204. Coos Physician Defense Witnesses. *The Coos Bay Times.* January 28, 1950: 7.

205. Hearings before the Subcommittee on Health of the Committee on Labor and Public Welfare United States Senate June 25 and 26, 1974. In. Vol Part 5. Washington, DC: U. S. Government; 1975.

206. Nelson Sharlene. Patient Rapport vital, retired physician says. *Oregonian*. October 24, 1976: 52.

207. Dr. McKeown Named To State Medical Group's Committee. *The Coos Bay Times*. November 28, 1939: 8.

208. Dr. McKeown Begins Examining Men Put in Draft Class 1-A. *The Coos Bay Times*. December 2, 1940: 5.

209. Committee on Coos Head Unit Named for 1938. *The Coos Bay Times*. February 12, 1938: 1.

210. On Yale Committee. *The Coos Bay Times*. December 30, 1939: 3.

211. Dr. McKeown honored by Surgeons College. *The Coos Bay Times*. August 1, 1938: 5.

212. McKeown Spikes rumor He Will Accept Toga As Marshfield Mayor. *The Coos Bay Times*. September 20, 1938: 1.

213. AMA Elects Coos Physician. *Oregonian*. June 5, 1957: 61.

214. Littlefield Jon. *Dr. Everett J. Mingus (1867-1937) and Mingus Park*. Coos Bay, Oregon January 2019.

215. Life in a Company Town. http://www.cooshistory.com. Published 2006.

216. Coos County. *The Morning Oregonian*. January 1, 1901: 15.

217. Three Jump Quarantine. *The Coos Bay Times*. June 28, 1909: 1.

218. City Council Adopts Fly Ordinance to Eliminate Them. *The Coos Bay Times*. September 7, 1910: 1.

219. Contaminated water. *The Coos Bay Times*. April 25, 1911: 1.

220. Briquettes of Low-Grade Coal and Charcoal Prove Quite Successful. In. Vol 12. Portland, Oregon: George W. Cornwall; 1911:52.

221. Latest Process For Utilization of Mill Waste. In. Chicago, Illinois1911:66.

222. Pacific Coal-Briquette Company of Marshfield, Oregon. In. Vol XXIII. Pittsburgh, Pennsylvania1910.

223. Mingus Park THE FORUM. *The Coos Bay Times*. July 29, 1937: 4.

224. Jensen Andie E. *Images of America Coos Bay*. Charleston, South Carolina: Arcadia Publishing; 2012.

225. Mingus Everett. An Interview With Paul Bunyan. In: *Paul Bunyan in Coos county*. Marshfield, Oregon1930.

226. Dr. Everett Mingus. *The Coos Bay Times*. April 24, 1937: 4.

227. Dr. Peacock is New Fellow in Surgery College. *The Coos Bay Times*. November 18, 1942: 3.

228. Rigid Quarantine Imposed On All Coos Bay Homes. *The Coos Bay Times*. November 14, 1927, 1927: 1.

229. Obituaries Dr. A. B. Peacock. *The World*. December 12, 1966: 2.

230. Peacock Service Here Fits Him For Game Post. *The Coos Bay Times*. April 25, 1939: 7.

231. Obituary of Dr. A. B. Peacock. *The World*. December 12, 1966: 1 & 2.

232. Rankin Takes Leep Practice. *The Coos Bay times*. September 28, 1929: 8.

233. Barton Ben. The Coquille Valley Ancestor Review Wagon Wheels to Wireless Dr. John Rankin, Wife and Daughter. In. Vol The Coquille Valley Ancestor Review Wagon Wheels to Wireless. Volume II ed. Coquille, Oregon:634-636.

234. Move to Bay From Bandon. *The Coos Bay Times*. August 18, 1932: 1.

235. Dr, Gregson Will Move To Bandon. *The Coos Bay Times*. August 26, 1932: 2.

236. Hospital Deal Made. *The Coos Bay, Times*. June 17, 1940: 6.

237. Hospital Closes in Coquille; No Help Available. *The Coos Bay Times*. June 27, 1942: 2.

238. Coquille Hospital Building Is Sold. *The Coos Bay Times*. January 10, 1944: 3.

239. 23 Vets Sign For Homes at Coquille. *The Coos Bay Times*. February 27, 1946: 6.

240. Dr. Rankin To Head Doctors. *The Coos Bay Times*. October 15, 1951: 3.

241. *Northwest Medicine*. Vol 52. Seattle, Washington, Portland, Oregon and Boise, Idaho: Northwest Medical Publishing Association; 1953.

242. Coos County Civil Defense Problems Eyed. *The World*. August 31, 1961: 12.

243. Alumni Directory The University of Chicago. In. Chicago, Illinois: The University of Chicago Press; 1919:530.

244. Young Simpkin Seriously Hurt; Volts Rip Body. *The Coos Bay Times*. October 6, 1936: 1.

245. Dr. John Simpkin obituary. *The World*. January 17, 1962: 2.

246. Mayor E. E. Straw. *The Coos Bay Times*. March 23, 1912: 30.

247. Dr. E. E. Straw Dies Suddenly at Keizer Hospital. *The Coos Bay Times*. October 14, 1929: 1.

248. Young Mayor Looks at City. *The Coos Bay Times*. October 27, 1906: 1.

249. Marshfield Mayor Weds Miss Lakeman. *The Coos Bay Times*. April 23, 1907: 1.

250. D. E. E. Straw Presented With Residence. *The Coos Bay Times*. April 10, 1915: 23.

251. Lockley Fred. Spirit That Prompted Deportation of Leach Still Runs High in Marshfield. *Oregon Journal*. July 27, 1913: 1 and 7.

252. Bradlely W. C. Trout Raising New Industry. *The Coos Bay Times*. December 16, 1924: 64.

253. First Volunteer. *The Coos Bay Times*. June 19, 1916: 1.

254. *The Coos Bay Times*. November 13, 1917: 4.

255. Locates Here. *The Coos Bay Times*. August 28, 1911: 5.

256. Dr. C. C. Taggart Dies Suddenly. *The Coos Bay Times*. September 11, 1915: 1.

257. Differ About Paving Work. *The Coos Bay Times*. June 17, 1913: 6.

258. Hard Paving on Broadway. *The Coos Bay Times*. June 24, 1913: 6.

259. Dr. C. W. Tower. *The Coos Bay Times*. March 23, 1912: 43.

260. Tower Charlemagne. *Tower Genealogy An Account of the Descendants of John Tower of Hingham, Mass.*: John Wilson and Son University Press; 1891.

261. Dr. C. W. Tower Has Passed Away. *The Coos Bay Times*. February, 26, 1920: 1.

262. Shewey John. Classic Steelhead Flies. In: Headwater Books and Stackpole Books; 2015.

263. The Guide Newspaper. *The Coos Bay Times*. December 26, 1926: 2.

264. Clay Steve. Major Morton Tower House. In: National Park Service Historic places; 1985.

265. Major Morton F. Tower. https://www.findagrave.com. Published 2011.

266. Fire at Marshfield. *Coquille City Herald*. February 15, 1898: 3.

267. Jewels Giver Past Officers. *The Coos Bay Times*. May 28, 1912: 3.

268. A Pioneer Passes 5-years ago. *The Coos Bay Times*. February 27, 1920: 4.

269. Edward Watson, M.D. http://genealogytrails.com. Published 2019.

270. Dr. E. Watson, North Bend, is Taken by Death. *The Coos Bay Times*. January 14, 1937: 8.

271. Porter Andy. This Woman's city for a lifetime. *The World*. February 7, 2000: 6.

272. Historic Curio is Lost After 50 Years. *The Coos Bay Times*. July 8, 1930: 8.

273. Howell Edgar H. Dr. James D. Wetmore. *The Pacific Coast Journal of Homeopathy*. 1915;XXVI:254.

274. Dr. J. D. Wetmore Passes Away. *Lincoln County Leader*. December 25, 1914: 1.

275. Funeral of Physician Held Here Friday. *The Oregon Daily Journal*. December 20, 1914: 15.

276. Dies on Sunday; Ill Short Time. *The Coos Bay Times*. May 10, 1937: 1.

277. Wikipedia. Catherine McAuley. https://en.wikipedia.org. Published 2019.

278. Mary Catherine McAuley. Library Ireland. https://www.libraryireland.com Published 2018.

279. McAuley, Catherine (1778-1841). https://www.encyclopedia.com. Published 2019.

280. Mercy Hospital. *The Coos Bay times-Golden Jubilee Annual*. July 31, 1928: 78.

281. Mercy Hospital What is Accomplished by the Sisters of Mercy In Charge- A Modern Institution. *The Coos Bay times*. July 7, 1907: 5 and 8.

282. New Hospital Late 40's beginning. *The World*. September 21, 1974: 25.

283. Keizer Hospital Sale. *The Coos Bay Times*. October 28, 1954: 1 and 5.

284. Keizer Memorial: 42 Years. *The World*. May 11, 1965: 6.

285. From 1923 to Hospital Week...1965. *The World*. May 11, 1965: 6.

286. Toll Peter. Keizer Hospital Passes Its Half Century Mark. *The World*. February 3, 1973: 1 and 2.

287. Has Done Good Work. *The Coos Bay Times*. February 13, 1907: 5.

288. Marshfield General Hospital. *The Coos Bay Times*. August 25, 1907: 4.

289. Open Hospital. *The Coos Bay Times*. March 1, 1915: 3.

290. Marshfield Hospital *The Coos Bay Times*. April 15, 1920: 4.

291. Opens Maternity Hospital. *The Coos Bay Times*. March 9, 1915: 5.

292. Littlefield Jon. Between Two Worlds: Chinese of Marshfield, Oregon. In: Lansing B, ed2020.

293. Hospital Asks Old Cemetery. *The Coos Bay Times*. June 17, 1924: 2.

294. Chinese Will Ship Bodies. *The Coos Bay Times*. June 6, 1913: 1.

295. New $125,000 Wesley Hospital. *The Coos Bay Times*. December 16, 1924: 65.

296. Wesley Hospital Articles Filed. *The Coos Bay Times*. March 1, 1924: 1.

297. Wesley Hospital Formally Opens. *The Coos Bay times*. July 11, 1925: 4.

298. Hospital Hopes to be Approved by U. S. Group. *The Coos Bay Times*. July 21, 1939: 5.

299. Wesley Hospital to be Operated by Catholic Sisters After August 1. *The Coos Bay Times*. July 3, 1939: 1.

300. Sisters to Take Hospital Here Friday Morning. *The Coos Bay Times*. July 20, 1939: 1.

301. Hospital Sale To Sisters Is Now Completed. *The Coos Bay Times*. April 23, 1941: 4.

302. Novotny Tim. Fighting the good fight. *The World*2016.

303. Dr. Wetmore. *Coquille Herald*. July 4, 1906: 2.

304. Taylor Dorothy. Did you know this? *the Coquille Valley Sentinel*. February 11, 2009: 2.

305. Dunn Bert, Andie E. Jensen, Yvonne-Cher Skye and the Coquille Valley Museum. *Images of America COQUILLE*. Charleston, South Carolina: Arcadia Publishing; 2018.

306. Coquille Hospital. *Coos Bay times*. November 11, 1911: 3.

307. Close Coquille Hospital. *The Coos Bay Times*. January 6, 1914: 4.

308. Coover Walt. Belle Knife Recalls Pioneer Days. *The World*. January 17, 1974: 7.

309. Knife Hospital Will Remain In Operation. *The Coos Bay Times*. February 14, 1947: 1.

310. Rollin Falk. *The World*. March 3, 1964: 2.

311. MP Hospital Closes Down on Sunday. *The World*. January 30, 1970: 1 & 6.

312. Beckham Curt. *Myrtle Point Beginnings*. self; 1986.

313. Mast Hospital In MP Purchased by Bandon Man, His Son-In-Law. *The World*. March 6, 1970: 2.

314. Formal Opening Held. *The Coos Bay Times*. April 26, 1926: 4.

315. The Dentist. *The Coos Bay Times*. July 2, 1914: 3.

316. Feueerstein Paul. Dental Technology Over 150 Years: Evolution and Revolution. https://mydigimag.rrd.com. Published 2019.

317. The Oregon Encyclopedia. https://oregonencyclopedia.org Published 2019.

319. Honors for Dr. O. E. Smith. *The Eugene Guard*. April 15, 1903: 4.

320. Dr. W. A. Toye Died Here Early Today. *The Coos Bay Times*. August 15, 1923: 1.

321. A Private Dentist. *The Coos Bay Times*. November 9, 1907: 4.

322. E. D. McArthur Buys Sengstacken Pharmacy. *The Coos Bay Times*. September 20, 1907: 1.

323. Buys North Bend Store. *The Coos Bay Times*. December 28, 1916: 3.

324. Drug Stores Not To Handle Liquor. *The Coos Bay Times*. January 4, 1915, 1915: 3.

325. Kao Audie, M.D., PhD. Medical Quackery: the Pseudo-Science of Health and Well-Being. Virtual Mentor. https://journalofethics.ama-assn.org. Published 2002.

326. Patent Medicine & Popular Medicine Show. Legends of America. https://www.legendsofamerica.com. Published 2020.

327. Bahnemann Barabara. Made in Minnesota: Patent Medicine on the Prairie. Minnesota Digital Library. https://mndigital.org. Published 2020.

328. Doctors will War on Quacks. *The Coos Bay Times*. June 16, 1913: 1.

329. Holland Brynn. 7 of the Most Outrageous Medical Treatments in History. https://www.history.com. Published 2017.

330. Medical cures That Did More Harm Than Good.
https://www.sciencefriday.com. Published 2020.

331. Simple Medicines. *The Coos Bay Times.* November 25, 1906: 5.

332. Medicinal/Chemical/Druggist Bottles. https://sha.org.
Published 2020.

333. *Nostrums and Quackery Articles on the Nostrum Evil and
Quackery Reprinted, with Additions and Modifications, from
the Journal of the American Medical Association.* Vol second
Edition. Chicago, Illinois: American Medical Association
Press; 1912.

INDEX

S

T

U

W

Z